Using MPI

Scientific and Engineering Computation
Janusz Kowalik, editor

Data-Parallel Programming on MIMD Computers
by Philip J. Hatcher and Michael J. Quinn, 1991

Unstructured Scientific Computation on Scalable Multiprocessors
edited by Piyush Mehrotra, Joel Saltz, and Robert Voigt, 1992

Parallel Computational Fluid Dynamics: Implementations and Results
edited by Horst D. Simon, 1992

Enterprise Integration Modeling: Proceedings of the First International Conference
edited by Charles J. Petrie, Jr., 1992

The High Performance Fortran Handbook
by Charles H. Koelbel, David B. Loveman, Robert S. Schreiber, Guy L. Steele Jr.,
and Mary E. Zosel, 1994

PVM: Parallel Virtual Machine–A Users' Guide and Tutorial for Networked Parallel Computing
by Al Geist, Adam Beguelin, Jack Dongarra, Weicheng Jiang, Robert Manchek,
and Vaidy Sunderam, 1994

Using MPI: Portable Parallel Programming with the Message-Passing Interface
by William Gropp, Ewing Lusk, and Anthony Skjellum, 1994

Using MPI

Portable Parallel Programming with the
Message-Passing Interface

William Gropp
Ewing Lusk
Anthony Skjellum

The MIT Press
Cambridge, Massachusetts
London, England

Third printing, 1996

This book was set in LaTeX by the authors and was printed and bound in the United States of America.

Library of Congress Cataloging-in-Publication Data

Gropp, William.
    Using MPI : portable parallel programming with the message-passing interface / William Gropp, Ewing Lusk, Anthony Skjellum.
        p.   cm. — (Scientific and engineering computation)
    Includes bibliographical references and index.
    ISBN 0-262-57104-8
    1. Parallel programming (Computer science) 2. Parallel computers—Programming.
I. Lusk, Ewing.   II. Skjellum, Anthony.   III. Title.   IV Series.
QA76.642G76   1994
005.2—dc20   94-22946
                                                                                  CIP

To Patty, Brigid, and Jennifer

Contents

Series Foreword

The world of modern computing potentially offers many helpful methods and tools to scientists and engineers, but the fast pace of change in computer hardware, software, and algorithms often makes practical use of the newest computing technology difficult. The Scientific and Engineering Computation series focuses on rapid advances in computing technologies and attempts to facilitate transferring these technologies to applications in science and engineering. It will include books on theories, methods, and original applications in such areas as parallelism, large-scale simulations, time-critical computing, computer-aided design and engineering, use of computers in manufacturing, visualization of scientific data, and human-machine interface technology.

The series will help scientists and engineers to understand the current world of advanced computation and to anticipate future developments that will impact their computing environments and open up new capabilities and modes of computation.

This book in the series describes how to use the Message-Passing Interface (MPI), a communication library for both parallel computers and workstation networks. MPI has been developed as a proposed standard for message passing and related operations. Its adoption by both users and implementors will provide the parallel programming community with the portability and features needed to develop application programs and parallel libraries that will tap the power of today's (and tomorrow's) high-performance computers.

Janusz S. Kowalik

Preface

About This Book

During 1993, a broadly based group of parallel computer vendors, software writers, and application scientists collaborated on the development of a standard portable message-passing library definition called MPI, for Message-Passing Interface. MPI is a specification for a library of routines to be called from C and Fortran programs. As of mid-1994, a number of implementations are in progress, and applications are already being ported.

Using MPI: Portable Parallel Programming with the Message-Passing Interface is designed to accelerate the development of parallel application programs and libraries by demonstrating how to use the new standard. It fills the gap among introductory texts on parallel computing, advanced texts on parallel algorithms for scientific computing, and user manuals of various parallel programming languages and systems. Each topic begins with simple examples and concludes with real applications running on today's most powerful parallel computers. We use both Fortran (Fortran 77) and C. We discuss timing and performance evaluation from the outset, using a library of useful tools developed specifically for this presentation. Thus this book is not only a tutorial on the use of MPI as a language for expressing parallel algorithms, but also a handbook for those seeking to understand and improve the performance of large-scale applications and libraries.

Without a standard such as MPI, getting specific about parallel programming has necessarily limited one's audience to users of some specific system that might not be available or appropriate for other users' computing environments. MPI provides the portability necessary for a concrete discussion of parallel programming to have wide applicability. At the same time, MPI is a powerful and complete specification, and using this power means that the expression of many parallel algorithms can now be done more easily and more naturally than ever before, without giving up efficiency.

Of course, parallel programming takes place in an environment that extends beyond MPI. We therefore introduce here a small suite of tools that computational scientists will find useful in measuring, understanding, and improving the performance of their parallel programs. These tools include timing routines, a library to produce an event log for post-mortem program visualization, and a simple real-time graphics library for run-time visualization. Also included are a number of utilities that enhance the usefulness of the MPI routines themselves. We call the union of these libraries MPE, for MultiProcessing Environment. All the example programs and tools are freely available, as is a model portable implementation of MPI itself developed by researchers at Argonne National Laboratory and Mississippi State University [22].

Our order of presentation is guided by the level of complexity in the parallel algorithms we study; thus it differs substantially from the order in more formal presentations of the standard.

We begin in Chapter 1 with a brief overview of the current situation in parallel computing environments, the message-passing model, and the process that produced MPI in response to this situation. Chapter 2 introduces the basic concepts that are new in MPI, how they differ from familiar message-passing concepts, and what MPI contains in the way of both familiar and advanced features.

In Chapter 3 we set the pattern for the remaining chapters. We present several examples and the small number of MPI functions that are required to express them. We describe how to execute the examples using the model MPI implementation and how to investigate the performance of these programs using a graphical performance-analysis tool. We conclude with an example of a large-scale application, a nuclear structure code from Argonne National Laboratory, written using only the MPI functions introduced in this chapter.

Chapter 4 rounds out the basic features of MPI by focusing on a particular application prototypical of a large family: solution of the Poisson problem. We introduce MPI's facilities for application-oriented process structures called virtual topologies. Using our performance analysis tools, we illustrate how to improve performance using some of the slightly more advanced MPI message-passing functions. We conclude with a discussion of a production code currently being used to investigate the phenomenon of high-temperature superconductivity.

Some of the more advanced features for message passing provided by MPI are covered in Chapter 5. We use the N-body problem as a setting for much of the discussion. We complete our discussion of derived datatypes and demonstrate the use of the MPE graphics library with a version of Mandelbrot set computation.

We believe that the majority of programmers of parallel computers will, in the long run, access parallelism through libraries. Indeed, enabling the construction of robust libraries is one of the primary motives behind the MPI effort, and perhaps its single most distinguishing feature when compared with other parallel programming environments. In Chapter 6 we address this issue with a series of examples.

MPI contains a variety of advanced features that will only have been touched on or presented in their simplest form at this point in the book. Some of these features are mixed-type derived data types, user-defined topologies, elaborate collective data-distribution and data-collection schemes, and facilities for implementing client-server applications. In Chapter 7 we fill out the description of these features using further examples taken from applications. We also discuss in detail MPI's environmental-inquiry functions and error-handling options.

In Chapter 8 we describe an approach to implementing MPI that has already been used in two implementations. It uses an "abstract device interface" that both simplifies the implementation task and allows individual vendors to take maximal advantage of their highly tuned, specific hardware for peak performance.

Chapter 9 is devoted to the porting of existing applications written for other message-passing systems (such as PVM, NX, CMMD, p4, EUI, or TCGMSG), to MPI. For the most part this is a relatively straightforward task, since MPI is at the same level as these other libraries and has been designed to include most of their features along with its own new ones. Here we give concrete details, advice, and examples.

We recognize that message passing, as a computational paradigm, is not the last word in parallel computing. We briefly explore the topics of active messages, threads, distributed shared memory, and other items in Chapter 10. We also attempt to predict what course the development and extension of MPI might take in the future.

The appendixes for the most part contain information on the software used in running and studying the examples in this book. Appendix A provides the language bindings for both the C and Fortran versions of all of the MPI routines. Appendix B describes how to obtain, build, and run the model portable implementation of MPI. Appendix C describes how to obtain and use the Multiprocessing Environment library along with the `upshot` program visualization program that we use in this book. Appendix D describes how to obtain supplementary material for this book, including complete source code for the examples, as well as related MPI materials that are available via anonymous `ftp` and the World Wide Web. Appendix E discusses some issues of C and Fortran that are are relevant to MPI and may be unfamiliar to some readers.

In addition to the normal subject index, there is an index for the definitions and usage examples for the MPI functions used in this book. A glossary of terms used in this book may be found before the appendices.

We try to be impartial in the use of Fortran and C for the book's examples; many examples are given in each language. The MPI standard has tried to keep the syntax of its calls similar in Fortran and C; for the most part they differ only in case (all capitals in Fortran, although most compilers will accept all lower case as well, while in C only the "MPI" and the next letter are capitalized), and in the handling of the return code (the last argument in Fortran and the returned value in C). When we need to refer to an MPI function name without specifying whether it is Fortran or C, we will use the C version, just because it is a little easier to read in running text.

This book is not a reference manual, in which MPI routines would be grouped according to functionality and completely defined. Instead we present MPI routines informally, in the context of example programs. Precise definitions are given in [24]. Nonetheless, to increase the usefulness of this book to someone working with MPI, we have provided for each MPI routine that we discuss a reminder of its calling sequence, in both Fortran and C. These listings can be found set off in boxes scattered throughout the book, located near the introduction of the routines they contain. In the boxes for C, we use ANSI C style declarations. Arguments that can be of several types (typically message buffers) are typed as `void*`. In the Fortran boxes the types of such arguments are marked as being of type `<type>`. This means that one of the appropriate Fortran data types should be used. To find the "binding box" for a given MPI routine, one should use the appropriate bold-face reference in the Function Index (**f77** for Fortran, **C** for C). Another place to find this information is in Appendix A, which lists all MPI functions in alphabetical order.

Acknowledgments

Our primary acknowledgment is to the Message Passing Interface Forum (MPIF), whose members devoted their best efforts over the course of a year and a half to producing MPI itself. The appearance of such a standard has enabled us to collect and coherently express our thoughts on how the process of developing application programs and libraries for parallel computing environments might be carried out. The aim of our book is to show how this process can now be undertaken with more ease, understanding, and probability of success than has been possible before the appearance of MPI.

The MPIF is producing both a final statement of the standard itself and an annotated reference manual to flesh out the standard with the discussion necessary for understanding the full flexibility and power of MPI. At the risk of duplicating acknowledgments to be found in those volumes, we thank here the following MPIF participants, with whom we collaborated on the MPI project. Special effort was exerted by those who served in various positions of responsibility: Lyndon Clarke, James Cownie, Jack Dongarra, Al Geist, Rolf Hempel, Steven Huss-Lederman, Bob Knighten, Richard Littlefield, Steve Otto, Mark Sears, Marc Snir, and David Walker. Other participants included Ed Anderson, Joe Baron, Eric Barszcz, Scott Berryman, Rob Bjornson, Anne Elster, Jim Feeney, Vince Fernando, Sam Fineberg, Jon Flower, Daniel Frye, Ian Glendinning, Adam Greenberg, Robert Harrison,

Leslie Hart, Tom Haupt, Don Heller, Tom Henderson, Alex Ho, C.T. Howard Ho, John Kapenga, Bob Leary, Arthur Maccabe, Peter Madams, Alan Mainwaring, Oliver McBryan, Phil McKinley, Charles Mosher, Dan Nessett, Peter Pacheco, Howard Palmer, Paul Pierce, Sanjay Ranka, Peter Rigsbee, Arch Robison, Erich Schikuta, Ambuj Singh, Alan Sussman, Robert Tomlinson, Robert G. Voigt, Dennis Weeks, Stephen Wheat, and Steven Zenith.

While everyone listed here made positive contributions, and many made major contributions, MPI would be far less important if it had not had the benefit of the particular energy and articulate intelligence of James Cownie of Meiko, Paul Pierce of Intel, and Marc Snir of IBM.

Support for the MPI meetings came in part from ARPA and NSF under grant ASC-9310330, NSF Science and Technology Center Cooperative Agreement No. CCR-8809615, and the Commission of the European Community through Esprit Project P6643. The University of Tennessee kept MPIF running financially while the organizers searched for steady funding.

The authors specifically thank their employers, Argonne National Laboratory and Mississippi State University, for the time and resources to explore the field of parallel computing and participate in the MPI process. The first two authors were supported by the U.S. Department of Energy under contract W-31-109-Eng-38. The third author was supported in part by the NSF Engineering Research Center for Computational Field Simulation at Mississippi State University.

The MPI Language Specification is copyrighted by the University of Tennessee and will appear as a special issue of *International Journal of Supercomputer Applications*, published by MIT Press. Both organizations have dedicated the language definition to the public domain.

We also thank Nathan Doss of Mississippi State University and Hubertus Franke of the IBM Corporation, who participated in the early implementation project that has allowed us to run all of the examples in this book. We thank Ed Karrels, a student visitor at Argonne, who did most of the work on the MPE library and the profiling interface examples. He was also completely responsible for the new version of the upshot program for examining logfiles.

We thank James Cownie of Meiko and Brian Grant of the University of Washington for reading the manuscript and making many clarifying suggestions. Gail Pieper vastly improved the prose. We also thank those who have allowed us to use their research projects as examples: Robert Harrison, Dave Levine, and Steven Pieper.

Finally we thank several Mississippi State University graduate students whose joint research with us (and each other) have contributed to several large-scale examples in the book. The members of the *Parallel Scientific Computing* class in the Department of Computer Science at MSU, spring 1994, helped debug and improve the model implementation and provided several projects included as examples in this book. We specifically thank Purushotham V. Bangalore, Ramesh Pankajakshan, Kishore Viswanathan, and John E. West for the examples (from the class and research) that they have provided for us to use in the text.

1 Background

In this chapter we survey the setting in which the MPI Standard has been developed, from the current situation in parallel computing and the prevalence of the message-passing model for parallel computation to the actual process by which MPI was developed.

1.1 Why Parallel Computing?

Fast computers have stimulated the rapid growth of a new way of doing science. The two broad classical branches of theoretical science and experimental science have been joined by *computational* science. Computational scientists simulate on supercomputers phenomena too complex to be reliably predicted by theory and too dangerous or expensive to be reproduced in the laboratory. Successes in computational science have caused demand for supercomputing resources to rise sharply over the past ten years.

During this time parallel computers have evolved from experimental contraptions in laboratories to become the everyday tools of computational scientists who need the ultimate in computer resources in order to solve their problems.

Several factors have stimulated this evolution. It is not only that the speed of light and the effectiveness of heat dissipation impose physical limits on the speed of a single computer. (To pull a bigger wagon, it is easier to add more oxen than to grow a gigantic ox.) It is also that the cost of advanced single-processor computers increases more rapidly than their power. (Large oxen are expensive.) And price/performance ratios become really favorable if the required computational resources can be found instead of purchased. This factor has caused many sites to use existing workstation networks, originally purchased to do modest computational chores, as "SCAN"s (SuperComputers At Night) by utilizing the workstation network as a parallel computer. This scheme has proven so successful, and the cost effectiveness of individual workstations has increased so rapidly, that networks of workstations have been purchased in order to be dedicated to parallel jobs that used to run on more expensive supercomputers.

Thus, considerations of both peak performance and price/performance are pushing large-scale computing in the direction of parallelism. So why hasn't parallel computing taken over? Why isn't everyone writing parallel programs?

1.2   Obstacles to Progress

Barriers to the widespread use of parallelism are in all three of the usual large subdivisions of computing: hardware, algorithms, and software.

In the hardware arena, we are still trying to build intercommunication networks (often called switches) that keep up with speeds of advanced single processors. Although not needed for every application (many successful parallel programs use Ethernet for their communication environment and some even use electronic mail), in general, faster computers require faster switches to keep up with them. Over the past five years much progress has been made in this area, and today's parallel supercomputers have a better balance between computation and communication than ever before. The next few years will see this balance extended into the networked-workstation domain as well, through the growth of higher-speed local (and even wide-area) networks.

Algorithmic research has contributed as much to the speed of modern parallel programs as has hardware engineering research. Parallelism in algorithms can be thought of as arising in three ways: from the physics (independence of physical processes), from the mathematics (independence of sets of mathematical operations), and from the programmer's imagination (independence of computational tasks). A bottleneck occurs, however, when these various forms of parallelism in algorithms must be *expressed* in a real program to be run on a real parallel computer. At this point, the problem becomes one of software.

The biggest obstacle to the spread of parallel computing and its benefits in economy and power is the problem of inadequate software. The author of a parallel algorithm for an important computational science problem may find the current software environment obstructing rather than smoothing the path to use of the very capable, cost-effective hardware available.

Part of the obstruction consists of what is not there. Compilers that automatically parallelize sequential algorithms remain limited in their applicability. Although much research has been done, and parallelizing compilers work well on some programs, the best performance is still obtained when the programmer himself supplies the parallel algorithm. If parallelism cannot be provided automatically by compilers, what about libraries? Here there has been some progress, but the barriers to writing libraries that work in multiple environments are very great. The requirements of libraries and how these requirements are addressed by MPI is the subject matter of Chapter 6.

Other parts of the obstruction consist of what *is* there. The ideal mechanism for communicating a parallel algorithm to a parallel computer should be expressive, efficient, and portable. Current mechanisms all represent compromises among these three goals. Vendor libraries are efficient but not portable, and in most cases minimal with regard to expressiveness. High-level languages emphasize portability over efficiency. And programmers are never satisfied with the expressivity of their programming language. (Turing completeness is necessary, but not sufficient.)

MPI is a compromise too, of course, but its design has been guided by a vivid awareness of these goals in the context of the next generation of parallel systems. It is portable. It has been designed to impose no semantic restrictions on efficiency; that is, nothing in the design (as opposed to a particular implementation) forces a loss of efficiency. Moreover, the deep involvement of vendors in MPI's definition has ensured that vendor-supplied MPI implementations will be efficient. As for expressivity, MPI is designed to be a convenient, complete definition of the message-passing model, the justification for which we discuss in the next section.

1.3   Why Message Passing?

To put our discussion of message passing in perspective, we briefly review informally the principal parallel computational models. Then we will focus on the advantages of the message-passing model.

1.3.1   Parallel Computational Models

A *computational model* is a conceptual view of what types of operations are available to the program. It does not include the specific syntax of a particular programming language or library, and it is (almost) independent of the underlying hardware that supports it. That is, any of the models we discuss can be implemented on any modern parallel computer, given a little help from the operating system. The effectiveness of such an implementation, however, depends on the gap between the model and the machine.

Parallel computational models form a complicated structure. They can be differentiated along multiple axes: whether memory is physically shared or distributed, how much communication is in hardware or software, exactly what the unit of execution is, and so forth. The picture is made confusing by the fact that software can provide an implementation of any computational model on any hardware. This section is thus not a taxonomy; rather we wish to define our terms in order to delimit clearly our discussion of the message-passing model, which is the focus of MPI.

Data parallelism. Although parallelism occurs in many places and at many levels in a modern computer, one of the first places it was made available to the programmer was in vector processors. Indeed, the vector machine began the current age of supercomputing. The vector machine's notion of operating on an array of similar data items in parallel during a single operation has been extended to include the operation of whole programs on collections of data structures, as in SIMD (single-instruction, multiple data) machines like the Thinking Machines CM-2. The parallelism need not necessarily proceed instruction by instruction in lock step for it to be classified as data parallel. Data parallelism is now more a programming style than a computer architecture.

At whatever level, the model remains the same: the parallelism comes entirely from the data; the program itself looks very much like a sequential program. The partitioning of data that underlies this model may be done by a compiler; the High Performance Fortran (HPF) standard [54] specifies a set of additions to Fortran that help a compiler with the data-partitioning process.

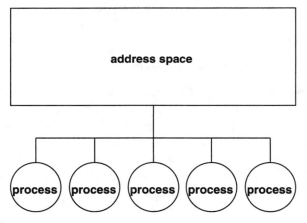

Figure 1.1
The shared-memory model

Shared memory. Parallelism that is not determined implicitly by data indepen- dence but is explicitly specified by the programmer is *control* parallelism. One simple model of control parallelism is the shared-memory model, in which each processor has access to all of a single, shared address space at the usual level of load and store operations. A schematic diagram of this arrangement is shown in Figure 1.1. Coordination of access to locations manipulated by multiple processes is done by some form of locking, although high-level languages may hide the explicit use of locks. Early examples of this model were the Denelcor HEP and Alliant family of shared-memory multiprocessors, as well as Sequent and Encore machines. The current Cray parallel vector machines are also of this same model.

It is difficult (and expensive) to make "true" shared-memory machines with more than a few tens of processors. To achieve the shared-memory model with large numbers of processors, one must allow some memory references to take longer than others. The BBN family (GP-1000, TC-2000) maintained the shared-memory model on hardware architectures that provided nonuniform memory access (NUMA). The current exponent of this idea is the Kendall Square family. For a discussion of a different version of this method of providing shared memory, see [43].

A variation on the shared-memory model occurs when processes have both a local memory (accessible only by one process) and also share a portion of memory (accessible by some or all of the other processes). The Linda programming model [14] is of this type.

Message passing. The message-passing model posits a set of processes that have only local memory but are able to communicate with other processes by sending and receiving messages. It is a defining feature of the message-passing model that data transfer from the local memory of one process to the local memory of another requires operations to be performed by both processes. Since MPI is a specific realization of the message-passing model, we discuss message passing in detail below.

In Figure 1.2 we don't show a specific communication network because it is not part of the computational *model*. The IPSC/860 has a hypercube topology, the Delta and Paragon from Intel are mesh-connected, and machines like the Meiko CS-2, Thinking Machines CM-5, and IBM SP1 have various forms of multi-level switches that go a long way toward making the precise connection topology irrelevant.

Remote memory operations. Halfway between the shared-memory model, where processes access memory without knowing whether they are triggering remote communication at the hardware level, and the message-passing model, where both the local and remote processes must participate, is the remote memory operation model. This model is typified by *put* and *get* operations on such current machines as the Cray T3D and the Meiko CS-2. In this case one process can access the memory of another without its participation, but it does so explicitly, not the the same way it accesses its local memory. A related type of operation is the "active message", [75] which causes execution of a (typically short) subroutine in

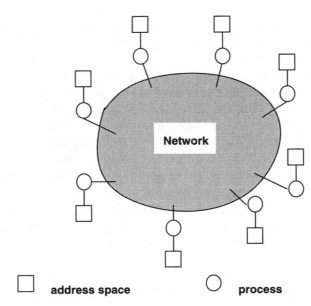

Figure 1.2
The message-passing model

the address space of the other process. Active messages are often used to facilitate *remote memory copying*, which can be thought of as part of the active-message model. Such remote memory copy operations are exactly the "one-sided" sends and receives unavailable in the message-passing model. The first machine to popularize this model is the TMC CM-5, which uses active messages both directly and as an implementation layer for the TMC message-passing library.

Threads. Early forms of the shared-memory model provided processes with separate address spaces, which could obtain shared memory through explicit memory operations, such as special forms of the C `malloc` operation. The more common version of the shared-memory model now specifies that all memory is shared. This allows the model to be applied to multi-threaded systems, in which a single process (address space) has associated with it several program counters and execution stacks. Since the model allows fast switching from one thread to another and requires no explicit memory operations, it can be used portably in Fortran programs. The difficulty imposed by the thread model is that any "state" of the program defined by the value of program variables is shared by all threads simultaneously.

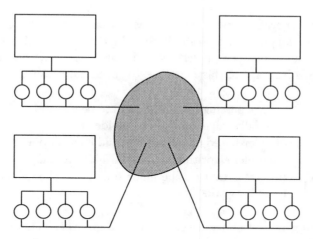

Figure 1.3
The cluster model

Combined models. Combinations of the above models are also possible, in which some clusters of processes share memory with one another but communicate with other clusters via message passing (Figure 1.3), or in which single processes may be multithreaded (so separate threads share memory) yet not share memory with one another. Such a model is not yet widely available but is appearing rapidly from two different directions:

• As processors become cheaper, it becomes feasible to add them to the nodes of existing distributed-memory machines.
• Workstation vendors, such as Sun, DEC, and SGI, are now offering shared-memory multiprocessor versions of their standard products. These machines on a high-speed network represent early platforms for the combined model.

1.3.2 Advantages of the Message-Passing Model

In this book we focus on the message-passing model of parallel computation, and in particular the MPI instantiation of that model. While we do not claim that the message-passing model is uniformly superior to the other models, we can say here why it has become widely used and why we can expect it to be around for a long time.

Universality. The message-passing model fits well on separate processors connected by a (fast or slow) communication network. Thus, it matches the hardware of most of today's parallel supercomputers, as well as the workstation networks that are beginning to compete with them. Where the machine supplies extra hardware to support a shared-memory model (as KSR machines do), the message-passing model can take advantage of this hardware to speed data transfer.

Expressivity. Message passing has been found to be a useful and complete model in which to express parallel algorithms. It provides the control missing from the data-parallel and compiler-based models. Some find its anthropomorphic flavor useful in formulating a parallel algorithm. It is well suited to adaptive, self-scheduling algorithms and to programs that can be made tolerant of the imbalance in process speeds found on shared networks.

Ease of debugging. Debugging of parallel programs remains a challenging research area. While debuggers for parallel programs are perhaps easier to write for the shared-memory model, it is arguable that the debugging process itself is easier in the message-passing paradigm. This is because one of the most common causes of error is unexpected overwriting of memory. The message-passing model, by controlling memory references more explicitly than any of the other models (only one process has direct access to any memory location), makes it easier to locate erroneous memory reads and writes.

Performance. The most compelling reason that message passing will remain a permanent part of the parallel computing environment is performance. As modern CPUs have become faster, management of their caches and the memory hierarchy in general has become the key to getting the most out of them. Message passing provides a way for the programmer to explicitly associate specific data with processes and thus allow the compiler and cache-management hardware to function fully. Indeed, one advantage distributed-memory computers have over even the largest single-processor machines is that they typically provide more memory and more cache. Memory-bound applications can exhibit superlinear speedups when ported to such machines. And even on shared-memory computers, use of the message-passing model can improve performance by providing more programmer control of data locality in the memory hierarchy.

This analysis explains why message passing has emerged as one of the more widely used paradigms for expressing parallel algorithms. Although it has shortcomings, message passing comes closer than any other paradigm to being a standard approach for the implementation of parallel applications.

1.4   Current Message-Passing Systems

Message passing does not, however, come close to being a standard in *portability*, either syntactically or semantically. Several factors have contributed to this situation.

Vendors of parallel computing systems, while embracing standard sequential languages, have offered different, proprietary message-passing libraries. There have been two (good) reasons for this situation:

• No standard has emerged, and—until now—no coherent effort has been made to create one. This situation reflects the fact that parallel computing is a new science, and experimentation has been needed to identify the most useful concepts.

• Without a standard, vendors have quite rightly treated the excellence of their proprietary libraries as a competitive advantage and have focused on making their advantages unique (thus nonportable).

To deal with the portability problem, the research community has contributed a number of libraries to the collection of alternatives. The better known of these are PICL [31], PVM [5], PARMACS [7], p4 [8, 11], Chameleon [41], Zipcode [72], and TCGMSG [44]; these libraries have been publicly available and are widely used. Many other experimental systems, of varying degrees of portability, have been developed at universities. In addition, commercial portable message-passing libraries have been developed, such as Express [16], with considerable added functionality. These portability libraries, from the user's point of view, also compete with one another, and some users have been driven to then write their own meta-portable libraries to hide the differences among them. Unfortunately, the more portable the code thus produced, the less functionality in the libraries the code can exploit, because it must be a least common denominator of the underlying systems. Thus, to achieve portable syntax, one must restrict oneself to deficient semantics, and many of the performance advantages of the nonportable systems are lost.

1.5   The MPI Forum

The plethora of solutions being offered to the user by both commercial software makers and researchers eager to give away their advanced ideas for free has necessitated unwelcome choices for the user among portability, performance, and features.

The user community, which quite definitely includes the software suppliers themselves, recently determined to address this problem. In April 1992, the Center for

Research in Parallel Computation sponsored a one-day workshop on Standards for Message Passing in a Distributed-Memory Environment [76]. The result of that workshop, which featured presentations of many systems, was a realization both that a great diversity of good ideas existed among message-passing systems and that people were eager to cooperate on the definition of a standard.

At the Supercomputing '92 conference in November, a committee was formed to define a message-passing standard. At the time of creation, few knew what the outcome might look like, but the effort was begun with the following goals:

• Define a portable standard for message passing. It would not be an official, ANSI-like standard, but it would attract both implementors and users.
• Operate in a completely open way. Anyone would be free to join the discussions, either by attending meetings in person or by monitoring e-mail discussions.
• Be finished in one year.

The MPI effort has been a lively one, as a result of the tensions among these three goals. The MPI Forum decided to follow the format used by the High Performance Fortran Forum, which had been well received by its community. (We even decided to meet in the same hotel in Dallas.)

The MPI effort will be successful in attracting a wide class of vendors and users because the MPI Forum itself was so broadly based. The parallel computer vendors were represented by Convex, Cray, IBM, Intel, Meiko, nCUBE, NEC, and Thinking Machines. Members of the groups associated with the portable software libraries were also present: PVM, p4, Zipcode, Chameleon, PARMACS, TCGMSG, and Express were all represented. In addition, a number of parallel application specialists were on hand. In addition to meetings every six weeks for more than a year, there were continuous discussions via electronic mail, in which many persons from the worldwide parallel computing community participated. Equally important, an early commitment to producing a model implementation [40] helped demonstrate that an implementation of MPI was feasible.

The MPI Standard [24] is just being completed (May 1994). This book is a companion to the standard itself, showing how MPI is *used*, and how its advanced features are exploited, in a wide range of situations.

2 What's New about MPI?

In this chapter we introduce MPI, focusing particularly on its similarity to and differences from existing message-passing systems.

2.1 A New Point of View

The primary goal of the MPI specification is to demonstrate that users need not compromise among efficiency, portability, and functionality. This means that one can write portable programs that can still take advantage of the specialized hardware and software offered by individual vendors. At the same time, advanced features, such as application-oriented process structures and dynamically managed process groups with an extensive set of collective operations, can be expected in every MPI implementation and can be used in every parallel application program where they might be useful. One of the most critical families of users is the parallel library writers, for whom efficient, portable, and highly functional code is most important. MPI is the first specification that allows them to write truly portable libraries. The goal of MPI is ambitious, but if the collective effort of collaborative design and competitive implementation is successful, it will remove the need for alternatives to MPI as means of specifying message-passing algorithms to be executed on any computer platform that implements the message-passing model.

This tripartite goal—portability, efficiency, functionality—forces many of the design decisions that make up the MPI specification. We describe in the following sections just how these decisions have affected both the fundamental *send* and *receive* operations of the message-passing model and the set of advanced message-passing operations included in MPI.

2.2 What's Not New?

MPI is not a revolutionary new way of programming parallel computers. Rather, it is an attempt to collect the best features of many existing message-passing systems, improve them where appropriate, and standardize them. So, we begin by summarizing the familiar side of MPI.

• MPI is a library, not a language. It specifies the names, calling sequences, and results of subroutines to be called from Fortran 77 programs and functions to be called from C programs. The programs that users write in Fortran 77 and C are compiled with ordinary compilers and linked with the MPI library.[1]

• MPI addresses the message-passing model. Although it is far more than a minimal system, its features do not extend beyond the fundamental computational model described in Chapter 1. A computation remains a collection of *processes* communicating with *messages*.

The familiar structure of MPI makes it straightforward to port existing codes and to write new ones without learning a new set of fundamental concepts. Nevertheless, the attempts to remove the shortcomings of existing systems have made even the basic operations a little different. We explain these differences in the next section.

2.3 Basic MPI Concepts

Perhaps the best way to introduce the concepts in MPI that might initially appear unfamiliar is to show how they have arisen as necessary extensions of quite familiar concepts. Let us consider what is perhaps the most elementary operation in a message-passing library, the basic *send* operation. In most of the current message-passing systems, it looks very much like this:

```
send(address, length, destination, tag )
```

where

• `address` is a memory location signifying the beginning of the buffer containing the data to be sent,
• `length` is the length in bytes of the message,
• `destination` is the process identifier of the process to which this message is sent (usually an integer), and
• `tag` is an arbitrary nonnegative integer to restrict receipt of the message (sometimes also called *type*).

This particular set of parameters is frequently chosen because it is a good compromise between what the programmer needs and what the hardware can do efficiently (transfer a contiguous area of memory from one processor to another). In particular, the system software is expected to supply queuing capabilities so that a receive operation

---

[1]Since Fortran 90 is a superset of Fortran 77, MPI can be used by Fortran 90 programmers as well. A binding of MPI to Fortran 90 would offer some advantages but is not yet available. Similar comments hold for C++.

```
recv(address, maxlen, source, tag, actlen )
```

will complete successfully only if a message is received with the correct tag. Other messages are queued until a matching receive is executed. In most current systems `source` is an output argument indicating where the message came from, although in some systems it can also be used to restrict matching and to cause message queuing. On a receive, `address` and `maxlen` together describe the buffer into which the received data is to be put; `actlen` is the number of bytes received.

Message-passing systems with this sort of syntax and semantics have proven extremely useful, yet have imposed restrictions that are now recognized as undesirable by a large user community. The MPI Forum has sought to lift these restrictions by providing more flexible versions of each of these parameters, while retaining the familiar underlying meanings of the basic *send* and *receive* operations. Let us examine these parameters one by one, in each case discussing first the current restrictions and then the MPI version.

Describing Message Buffers. The `(address, length)` specification of the message to be sent was a good match for early hardware but is no longer adequate for two different reasons:

- In many situations, the message to be sent is *not contiguous*. In the simplest case, it may be a row of a matrix that is stored columnwise. In general, it may consist of an irregularly dispersed collection of structures of different sizes. In the past, programmers (or libraries) have provided code to pack this data into contiguous buffers before sending it and to unpack it at the receiving end. However, as communications processors appear that can deal directly with strided or even more generally distributed data, it becomes more critical for performance that the packing be done "on the fly" by the communication processor in order to avoid the extra data movement. This cannot be done unless we describe the data in its original (distributed) form to the communication library.

- The past few years have seen a rise in the popularity of *heterogeneous computing* [10]. The popularity comes from two sources. The first is the distribution of various parts of a complex calculation among different semi-specialized computers (e.g., SIMD, vector, graphics). The second is the use of workstation networks as parallel computers. Workstation networks, consisting of machines acquired over time, are frequently made up of a variety of machine types. In both of these situations, messages must be exchanged between machines of different architectures, where `(address,length)` is no longer an adequate specification of the semantic content of the message. For example, with a vector of floating-point numbers, not only might the floating-point formats be different, but even the length may be different. This situation is true for integers as well. The communication library can do the necessary conversion *if* it is told precisely what is being transmitted.

The MPI solution, for both of these problems, is to specify messages at a higher level and in a more flexible way than (`address`, `length`) to reflect the fact that the content of a message contains much more structure than just a string of bits. Instead, an MPI message buffer is defined by a triple (`address`, `count`, `datatype`), describing `count` occurrences of the data type `datatype` starting at `address`. The power of this mechanism comes from the flexibility in the values of datatype.

To begin with, datatype can take on the values of elementary data types in the host language. Thus (`A,300,MPI_REAL`) describes a vector `A` of 300 real numbers in Fortran, regardless of the length or format of a floating point number. An MPI implementation for heterogeneous networks guarantees that the same 300 reals will be received, even if the receiving machine has a very different floating-point format.

The real power of data types, however, comes from the fact that users can construct their own data types using MPI routines and that these data types can describe noncontiguous data. Details of how to construct these "derived" data types can be found in Chapter 5.

Separating Families of Messages.   Nearly all message-passing systems provide a `tag` argument for the *send* and *receive* operations. This argument allows the programmer to deal with the arrival of messages in an orderly way, even if the arrival of messages is not in the order desired. The message-passing system queues messages that arrive "of the wrong tag" until the program(mer) is ready for them. Usually a facility exists for specifying wild-card tags that match any tag.

This mechanism has proven necessary but insufficient, because the arbitrariness of the tag choices means that the entire program must use tags in a predefined, coherent way. Particular difficulties arise in the case of libraries, written far from the application programmer in time and space, whose messages must not be accidentally received by the application program.

MPI's solution is to extend the notion of tag with a new concept: the *context*. Contexts are allocated at run time by the system in response to user (and library) requests and are used for matching messages. They differ from tags in that they are allocated by the system instead of the user and no wild-card matching is permitted.

The usual notion of message tag, with wild-card matching, is retained in MPI.

Naming Processes.   Processes belong to *groups*. If a group contains n processes, then its processes are identified within the group by *ranks*, which are integers from 0 to $n-1$. There is an initial group to which all processes in an MPI implementation belong. Within this group, then, processes are numbered similarly to the way in which they are numbered in many existing message-passing systems, from 0 up to 1 less than the total number of processes.

Communicators.   The notions of context and group are combined in a single object called a *communicator*, which becomes an argument to most point-to-point and collective operations. Thus the `destination` or `source` specified in a send or receive operation always refers to the rank of the process in the group identified with the given communicator.

That is, in MPI the basic (blocking) *send* operation has become

```
MPI_Send(buf, count, datatype, dest, tag, comm)
```

where

- `(buf, count, datatype)` describes `count` occurrences of items of the form `datatype` starting at `buf`,
- `dest` is the rank of the destination in the group associated with the communicator `comm`,
- `tag` is as usual, and
- `comm` identifies a group of processes and a communication context.

The *receive* has become

```
MPI_Recv(buf, count, datatype, source, tag, comm, status)
```

The source, tag, and count of the message actually received can be retrieved from `status`.

Several other message-passing systems return the "status" parameters by separate calls that implicitly reference the most recent message received. MPI's method is one aspect of its effort to be reliable in the situation where multiple threads are receiving messages on behalf of a process.

2.4   Other Interesting Features of MPI

Our focus so far has been on the basic *send* and *receive* operations, since one may well regard as the most fundamental new feature in MPI the small but important way in which each of the arguments of the "traditional" send/receive has been modified. Nevertheless, MPI is a large specification and does offer many other advanced features, including the following:

Collective Communications. Another proven concept from existing message-passing libraries is the notion of *collective operation*, performed by all the processes in a computation. Collective operations are of two kinds:

- *Data movement* operations are used to rearrange data among the processes. The simplest of these is a broadcast, but many elaborate scattering and gathering operations can be defined (and are supported in MPI).
- *Collective computation* operations (minimum, maximum, sum, logical OR, etc., as well as user-defined operations).

In both cases, a message-passing library can take advantage of its knowledge of the structure of the machine to optimize and increase the parallelism in these operations.

MPI has a large set of collective communication operations, and a mechanism by which users can provide their own. In addition, MPI provides operations for creating and managing groups in a scalable way. Such groups can be used to control the scope of collective operations.

MPI has an extremely flexible mechanism for describing data movement routines. These are particularly powerful when used in conjunction with the derived datatypes.

Virtual topologies. One can conceptualize processes in an application-oriented topology, for convenience in programming. Both general graphs and grids of processes are supported. Topologies provide a high-level method for managing process groups without dealing with them directly. Since topologies are a standard part of MPI, we do not treat them as an exotic, advanced feature. We use them early in the book (Chapter 4) and freely from then on.

Debugging and Profiling. Rather than specify any particular interface, MPI requires the availability of "hooks" that allow users to intercept MPI calls and thus define their own debugging and profiling mechanisms. In Chapter 7 we will give an example of how to write such hooks for visualizing program behavior.

Communication modes. MPI has both the blocking send and receive operations described above and nonblocking versions whose completion can be tested for and waited for explicitly. It is possible to test and wait on multiple operations simultaneously. MPI also has multiple communication *modes*. The *standard* mode corresponds to current common practice in message-passing systems. The *synchronous* mode requires sends to block until the corresponding receive has occurred (as opposed to the standard mode blocking send which blocks only until the buffer can be reused). The *ready* mode (for sends) is a way for the programmer to notify the system that the receive has been posted, so that the underlying system can use a faster protocol if it is available.

Support for libraries. The structuring of all communication through communicators provides to library writers for the first time the capabilities they need to write parallel libraries that are completely independent of user code and inter-operable with other libraries. Libraries can maintain arbitrary data, called *attributes*, associated with the communicators they allocate, and can specify their own error handlers. The tools for creating MPI parallel libraries that take advantage of these features are described in Chapter 6.

Support for heterogeneous networks. MPI programs can run on networks of machines that have different lengths and formats for various fundamental datatypes, since each communication operation specifies a (possibly very simple) structure and all the component datatypes, so that the implementation always has enough information to do data format conversions if they are necessary. MPI does not specify how this is done, however, thus allowing a variety of optimizations. We discuss heterogeneity specifically in Chapter 7.

2.5 Is MPI Large or Small?

Perhaps the most fundamental decision for the MPI Forum was whether MPI would be "small and exclusive," incorporating the minimal *intersection* of existing libraries, or "large and inclusive," incorporating the *union* of the functionality of existing systems.

In the end, although some ideas were left out, an attempt was made to include a relatively large number of features that had proven useful in various libraries and applications. The debate over whether "MPI is too complex" recurred in various contexts. We believe that MPI is large but *not* complex, and discuss why in this section.

2.5.1   MPI Is Large (125 Functions)

The many features described in the last section mean that the MPI standard has many functions in it (about 125). Does this mean that MPI is impossibly complex? Is it the PL/1, the Ada, of message passing?

The answer is no for two reasons. First, the number of functions in MPI comes from combining a small number of orthogonal concepts. The number of *ideas* in MPI is small. Second, many of the routines represent added functionality that can be ignored until needed.

2.5.2   MPI Is Small (6 Functions)

By way of demonstrating just how little one needs to learn to write MPI programs, we present here a list of the indispensable functions, the ones that the programmer really cannot do without. There are six. With only these functions a vast number of useful and efficient programs can be written. The other functions all add flexibility (datatypes), robustness (nonblocking send/receive), efficiency ("ready" mode), modularity (groups, communicators), or convenience (collective operations, topologies). Nonetheless, one can forego all of these concepts and use only the routines from MPI shown in Table 2.1. One can write complete message passing programs with just these six functions.

MPI_INIT	Initialize MPI
MPI_COMM_SIZE	Find out how many processes there are
MPI_COMM_RANK	Find out which process I am
MPI_SEND	Send a message
MPI_RECV	Receive a message
MPI_FINALIZE	Terminate MPI

Table 2.1
The six-function version of MPI

2.5.3   MPI Is Whatever Size You Like

The designers of MPI attempted to make the features of MPI consistent and orthogonal. This means that users can incrementally add sets of functions to their repertoire as needed without learning everything at once. For example, for collective communication, one can accomplish a lot with just `MPI_BCAST` and `MPI_REDUCE`, as we show in Chapter 3. The unfolding of topics in this book will be driven by examples, which will motivate the introduction of MPI routines a little at a time.

2.6 Decisions Left to the Implementor

The MPI Standard does not specify *every* aspect of a parallel program. Some aspects of parallel programming that are left to the specific implementation are as follows:

- Process startup is left to the implementation. This strategy allows considerable flexibility in how an MPI program is executed, at some cost in portability of the parallel programming environment.
- Although MPI specifies a number of error codes, the implementation is allowed to return a richer set of error codes than is specified in the standard.
- The amount of system buffering provided for messages is implementation dependent, although the user can exert some control if he chooses. We describe what we mean by buffering and techniques for dealing with the buffering problem in Chapter 4.

The net result of this discussion is that the complete presentation of examples, particularly the way they are run by the programmer, must refer to some specific implementation. Here we use the freely available model implementation whose design is outlined in Chapter 8 and described more fully in [22]. Instructions for getting both the model implementation of MPI and the examples in this book are presented in Appendix D.

3 Using MPI in Simple Programs

In this chapter we introduce the most basic MPI calls and use them to write some simple parallel programs. Simplicity of a parallel algorithm does not limit its usefulness, however: even a small number of basic routines are enough to implement a major application. We also demonstrate in this chapter a few of the tools that we use throughout this book to study the behavior of parallel programs.

3.1 A First MPI Program

For our first parallel program, we choose a "perfect" parallel program: it can be expressed with a minimum of communication, load balancing is automatic, and we can verify the answer. Specifically, we compute the value of π by numerical integration. Since

$$\int_0^1 \frac{1}{1+x^2}\, dx = \arctan(x)|_0^1 = \arctan(1) - \arctan(0) = \arctan(1) = \frac{\pi}{4},$$

we will integrate the function $f(x) = 4/(1+x^2)$. To do this integration numerically, we divide the interval from 0 to 1 into some number n of subintervals and add up the areas of the rectangles as shown in Figure 3.1 for $n = 5$. Larger values of the parameter n will give us more accurate approximations of π. This is not, in fact, a very good way to compute π, but it makes a good example.

To see the relationship between n and the error in the approximation, we write an interactive program in which the user supplies n and the program first computes an approximation (the parallel part of the program) and then compares it with a known, highly accurate approximation to π.

The parallel part of the algorithm occurs as each process computes and adds up the areas for a different subset of the rectangles. At the end of the computation, all of the local sums are combined into a global sum representing the value of π. Communication requirements are consequently simple. One of the processes (we'll call it the master) is responsible for communication with the user. It obtains a value for n from the user and broadcasts it to all of the other processes. Each process is able to compute which rectangles it is responsible for from n, the total number of processes, and its own rank. After reporting a value for π and the error in the approximation, the program asks the user for a new value for n.

The complete program is shown in Figure 3.2. In most of this book we will show only the "interesting" parts of programs and refer the reader to other sources for the complete, runnable version of the code. For our first few programs, however, we include the entire code and describe it more or less line by line. In the directory

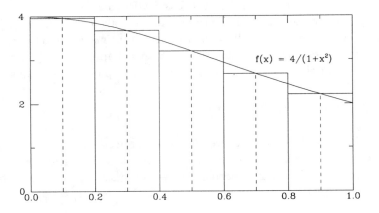

Figure 3.1
Integrating to find the value of π

of programs that accompanies this book, the **pi** program is available as
'**simplempi/pi.f**'. See Appendix D for details of how to obtain this code, other
examples, and a model implementation of MPI. Instructions for running the model
implementation of MPI are given in Appendix B.

Our program starts like any other, with the **program main** statement. The

```
include "mpif.h"
```

is necessary in every MPI Fortran program and subprogram to define various constants and variables. For Fortran compilers that do not support the **include** di-
rective, the contents of this file must be inserted by hand into each function and
subroutine that uses MPI calls.

After a few lines of variable definitions, we get to three lines that will probably
be found near the beginning of every Fortran MPI program:

```
call MPI_INIT( ierr )
call MPI_COMM_RANK( MPI_COMM_WORLD, myid, ierr )
call MPI_COMM_SIZE( MPI_COMM_WORLD, numprocs, ierr )
```

```fortran
          program main
          include "mpif.h"
          double precision  PI25DT
          parameter         (PI25DT = 3.141592653589793238462643d0)
          double precision  mypi, pi, h, sum, x, f, a
          integer n, myid, numprocs, i, ierr
c                                    function to integrate
          f(a) = 4.d0 / (1.d0 + a*a)

          call MPI_INIT(ierr)
          call MPI_COMM_RANK(MPI_COMM_WORLD, myid, ierr)
          call MPI_COMM_SIZE(MPI_COMM_WORLD, numprocs, ierr)

 10       if ( myid .eq. 0 ) then
              print *, 'Enter the number of intervals: (0 quits) '
              read(*,*) n
          endif
c                                    broadcast n
          call MPI_BCAST(n,1,MPI_INTEGER,0,MPI_COMM_WORLD,ierr)
c                                    check for quit signal
          if ( n .le. 0 ) goto 30
c                                    calculate the interval size
          h = 1.0d0/n
          sum  = 0.0d0
          do 20 i = myid+1, n, numprocs
             x = h * (dble(i) - 0.5d0)
             sum = sum + f(x)
 20       continue
          mypi = h * sum
c                                    collect all the partial sums
          call MPI_REDUCE(mypi,pi,1,MPI_DOUBLE_PRECISION,MPI_SUM,0,
     $        MPI_COMM_WORLD,ierr)
c                                    node 0 prints the answer.
          if (myid .eq. 0) then
             print *, 'pi is ', pi, ' Error is', abs(pi - PI25DT)
          endif
          goto 10
 30       call MPI_FINALIZE(ierr)
          stop
          end
```

Figure 3.2
Fortran program for calculating π

The call to `MPI_INIT` is required in every MPI program and must be the first MPI call.[1] It establishes the MPI "environment." Only one invocation of `MPI_INIT` can occur in each program execution. Its only argument is an error code. Every Fortran MPI subroutine returns an error code in its last argument, which is either `MPI_SUCCESS` or an implementation-defined error code. In this example (and in many of our examples) we will be sloppy and not test the return codes from our MPI routines, assuming that they will always be `MPI_SUCCESS`. This approach will improve readability of the code at the expense of possible debugging time. We will discuss later (in Section 7.7) how to check, handle, and report errors.

As described in Chapter 2, all MPI communication is associated with a *communicator* that describes the communication context and an associated group of processes. In this program we will be using only the default communicator, predefined and named `MPI_COMM_WORLD`, that defines one context and the set of all processes. `MPI_COMM_WORLD` is one of the items defined in 'mpif.h'.

The call `MPI_COMM_SIZE` returns (in `numprocs`) the number of processes that the user has started for this program. Precisely how the user caused these processes to be started depends on the implementation, but any program can find out this number with this call. The value `numprocs` is actually the size of the group associated with the default communicator `MPI_COMM_WORLD`. We think of the processes in any group as being numbered with consecutive integers beginning with 0, called *ranks*. Each process finds out its rank in the group associated with a communicator by calling `MPI_COMM_RANK`. Thus although each process in this program will get the same number in `numprocs`, each will have a different number for `myid`.

Next, the master process (which can identify itself by using `myid`) gets a value for n, the number of rectangles, from the user. The line

```
call MPI_BCAST(n,1,MPI_INTEGER,0,MPI_COMM_WORLD,ierr)
```

sends the value of n to all other processes. The `MPI_BCAST` results in every process (in the groups associated with the communicator given in the fifth argument) ending up with a copy of n. The data to be communicated is described by the address (n), the datatype (`MPI_INTEGER`), and the number of items (1). The process with the original copy is specified by the fourth argument (0 in this case, the master process, which just reads it from the user). (MPI assigns a type to every data item. MPI datatypes are described in full in Section 5.1.)

Thus, after the call to `MPI_BCAST`, all processes have n and their own identifiers, which is enough information for each one to compute its contribution, `mypi`. Each

---

[1] An exception is the `MPI_Initialized` routine, which a library can call to determine whether `MPI_Init` has been called or not. See Section 7.8.2.

process computes the area of every `numprocs`'th rectangle, starting with `myid+1`. Next, all of the values of `mypi` held by the individual processes need to be added up. MPI provides a rich set of such operations, using the `MPI_REDUCE` routine, with an argument specifying which arithmetic or logical operation is being requested. In our case the call is

```
     call MPI_REDUCE(mypi,pi,1,MPI_DOUBLE_PRECISION,MPI_SUM,0,
   $       MPI_COMM_WORLD,ierr)
```

The first two arguments identify the source and result addresses, respectively. The data being collected consists of 1 (third argument) item of type `MPI_DOUBLE_PRECISION` (fourth argument). The operation is addition (`MPI_SUM`, the next argument), and the result of the operation is to be placed in `pi` on the process with rank 0 (fifth argument). The last two arguments are the communicator and error return code, as usual. The first two arguments of `MPI_Reduce` must not overlap (i.e., must be different variables or sections of an array). A full list of the operations is presented in Section 7.3.2; user-defined operations are discussed in Section 7.3.3.

All processes then return to the top of the loop (the master prints the answer first). The `MPI_BCAST` causes all the processes except the master to wait for the next value of n.

When the user types a zero in response to the request for a number of rectangles, the loop terminates and all processes execute

```
     call MPI_FINALIZE(ierr)
```

This call must be made by every process in an MPI computation. It terminates the MPI "environment"; no MPI calls may be made by a process after its call to `MPI_FINALIZE`. (`MPI_INIT` cannot be called again.)

The Fortran bindings for the MPI routines used in this section are summarized in Table 3.1. In the tables of Fortran bindings, the expression `<type>` stands for any Fortran datatype, such as `INTEGER` or `DOUBLE PRECISION`.

3.2   Running Your First MPI Program

The way in which MPI programs are "launched" on a particular machine or network is not itself part of the MPI standard. Therefore it may vary from one machine to another. On (most of) the supported machines, one would use

```
     mpirun -np 4 pi
```

MPI_INIT(ierror)
          integer ierror

MPI_COMM_SIZE(comm, size, ierror)
          integer comm, size, ierror

MPI_COMM_RANK(comm, rank, ierror)
          integer comm, rank, ierror

MPI_BCAST(buffer, count, datatype, root, comm, ierror)
          <type> buffer(*)
          integer count, datatype, root, comm, ierror

MPI_REDUCE(sendbuf, recvbuf, count, datatype, op, root, comm, ierror)
          <type> sendbuf(*), recvbuf(*)
          integer count, datatype, op, root, comm, ierror

MPI_FINALIZE(ierror)
          integer ierror

Table 3.1
Fortran bindings for routines used in the pi program

to run the program with four processes when using the portable, model implementation of MPI described in Appendix B.

3.3   A First MPI Program in C

In this section we repeat the program for computing the value of π in C rather than Fortran. In general, every effort has been made to keep the Fortran and C bindings similar. The primary difference is that error codes are returned as the value of C functions instead of in a separate argument. In addition, the arguments to most functions are more strongly typed than they are in Fortran, having specific C types such as `MPI_Comm` and `MPI_Datatype` where Fortran has integers. The included file is, of course, different: 'mpi.h' instead of 'mpif.h'. Finally, the arguments to `MPI_Init` are different, so that a C program can take advantage of command-line arguments. An MPI implementation is expected to remove from the **argv** array any command-line arguments that should be processed by the implementation before returning control to the user program and to decrement **argc** accordingly. Note that the arguments to `MPI_Init` in C are the *addresses* of the usual `main` arguments `argc` and `argv`.

The program is shown in Figure 3.3, and definitions of the C versions of the MPI routines used in this program are given in Table 3.2.

---

int **MPI_Init**(int *argc, char ***argv)

int **MPI_Comm_size**(MPI_Comm comm, int *size)

int **MPI_Comm_rank**(MPI_Comm comm, int *rank)

int **MPI_Bcast**(void *buf, int count, MPI_Datatype datatype, int root,
                  MPI_Comm comm)

int **MPI_Reduce**(void *sendbuf, void *recvbuf, int count, MPI_Datatype datatype,
                  MPI_Op op, int root, MPI_Comm comm)

int **MPI_Finalize**(void)

Table 3.2
C bindings for routines used in the `pi` program

3.4   Timing MPI Programs

Sequential algorithms are tested for correctness by seeing whether they give the right answer. For parallel programs, the right answer is not enough: one wishes to decrease the execution time. Therefore, measuring speed of execution is part of testing the program to see whether it performs as intended.

Many operating systems and libraries provide timing mechanisms, but so far all of those that are both portable and provide access to high resolution clocks are cumbersome to use. Therefore MPI provides a simple routine that can be used to time programs or sections of programs.

`MPI_Wtime()` returns a double-precision floating-point number of seconds since some arbitrary point of time in the past. The point is guaranteed not to change during the lifetime of a process. Thus, a time interval can be measured by calling this routine at the beginning and end of a program segment and subtracting the values returned. Making this a floating-point value allows the use of high-resolution timers if they are supported by the underlying hardware, although no particular resolution is specified. MPI provides a function to find out what the resolution

```
#include "mpi.h"
#include <math.h>
int main(argc,argv)
int argc;
char *argv[];
{
    int n, myid, numprocs, i, rc;
    double PI25DT = 3.141592653589793238462643;
    double mypi, pi, h, sum, x, a;
    MPI_Init(&argc,&argv);
    MPI_Comm_size(MPI_COMM_WORLD,&numprocs);
    MPI_Comm_rank(MPI_COMM_WORLD,&myid);
    while (1) {
        if (myid == 0) {
            printf("Enter the number of intervals: (0 quits) ");
            scanf("%d",&n);
        }
        MPI_Bcast(&n, 1, MPI_INT, 0, MPI_COMM_WORLD);
        if (n == 0)
            break;
        else {
            h   = 1.0 / (double) n;
            sum = 0.0;
            for (i = myid + 1; i <= n; i += numprocs) {
                x = h * ((double)i - 0.5);
                sum += (4.0 / (1.0 + x*x));
            }
            mypi = h * sum;
            MPI_Reduce(&mypi, &pi, 1, MPI_DOUBLE, MPI_SUM, 0,
                        MPI_COMM_WORLD);
            if (myid == 0)
                printf("pi is approximately %.16f, Error is %.16f\n",
                        pi, fabs(pi - PI25DT));
        }
    }
    MPI_Finalize();
}
```

Figure 3.3
C program for calculating π

is. This function, called `MPI_Wtick`, has no arguments. It returns a floating-point number that is the time in seconds between successive ticks of the clock. The bindings are shown in Tables 3.3 and 3.4.

DOUBLE PRECISION **MPI_WTIME**()
DOUBLE PRECISION **MPI_WTICK**()

Table 3.3
Fortran binding for MPI timing routines

double **MPI_Wtime**(void)
double **MPI_Wtick**(void)

Table 3.4
C binding for MPI timing routines

Suppose we wished to measure the *speedup* obtained by our program for computing π. Since this program is written as an interactive program, we wish to time only the section that does internal communications and computation. We don't want to include time spent waiting for user input. Figure 3.4 shows how the central part of our π program is modified to provide timings. Then, by running it with varying numbers of processes, we can measure speedup. Speedup for p processors is normally defined as

$$\frac{\text{time for 1 process}}{\text{time for } p \text{ processes}}$$

Thus, a nearly perfect speedup would be a phrase like "speedup of 97.8 with 100 processors."

3.5   A Self-Scheduling Example: Matrix-Vector Multiplication

So far, we have been able to write a "message-passing" program without explicitly sending and receiving messages. The next example will illustrate such explicit, point-to-point communication, and at the same time illustrate one of the most common of parallel algorithm prototypes: the *self-scheduling*, or *master-worker*, algorithm. We will demonstrate the self-scheduling prototype first in the context of matrix-vector multiplication, for simplicity, but the same abstract algorithm has

```
      double precision starttime, endtime
      ...
      starttime = MPI_WTIME()
c                                         broadcast n
      call MPI_BCAST(n,1,MPI_INTEGER,0,MPI_COMM_WORLD,ierr)
c                                         check for quit signal
      if ( n .le. 0 ) goto 30
c                                         calculate the interval size
      h   = 1.0d0/n
      sum = 0.0d0
      do 20 i = myid+1, n, numprocs
         x   = h * (dble(i) - 0.5d0)
         sum = sum + f(x)
 20   continue
      mypi = h * sum
c                                         collect all the partial sums
      call MPI_REDUCE(mypi,pi,1,MPI_DOUBLE_PRECISION,MPI_SUM,0,
     $     MPI_COMM_WORLD,ierr)
c                                         node 0 prints the answer.
      endtime = MPI_WTIME()
      if (myid .eq. 0) then
          print *, 'pi is ', pi, 'Error is ', abs(pi - PI25DT)
          print *, 'time is ', endtime-starttime, ' seconds'
      endif
      go to 10
```

Figure 3.4
Timing the program for calculating π

been used in many other contexts. In fact, it is the type of algorithm used in this chapter's major application, described in Section 3.9.

This example was chosen not because it illustrates the best way to parallelize this particular numerical computation (it doesn't), but because it illustrates the basic MPI *send* and *receive* operations in the context of a fundamental type of parallel algorithm, applicable in many situations.

The idea is that one process, which we call the master process, is responsible for coordinating the work of the others. This mechanism is particularly appropriate when the other processes (the *worker* or *slave* processes) do not have to communicate with one another and when the amount of work that each slave must perform is difficult to predict. In the case of matrix-vector multiplication, the first criterion holds but not the second. We can, of course, take the view that we might be computing on a network of workstations with varying loads, and so even if equal amounts of work were assigned, the time it takes for each slave to complete its task might vary widely. In any event, the point of this example is the use of the MPI *send* and *receive* routines to express the master-worker parallel algorithm, rather than the matrix-vector multiplication itself.

In our example of multiplying a matrix by a vector, a unit of work to be given out will consist of the dot product of one row of the matrix **A** with the (column) vector **b**. The master begins by broadcasting **b** to each slave. It then sends one row of the matrix **A** to each slave. At this point the master begins a loop, terminated when it has received all of the entries in the product. The body of the loop consists of receiving one entry in the product vector from whichever slave sends one, then sending the next task to that slave. In other words, completion of one task by a slave is considered to be a request for the next task. Once all tasks have been handed out, termination messages are sent instead.

Each slave, after receiving the broadcast value of **b**, also enters a loop, terminated by the receipt of the termination message from the master. The body of the loop consists of receiving a row of **A**, forming the dot product with **b**, and sending the answer back to the master.

Although the master and slaves execute distinct algorithms, and in some environments it is possible to have them compiled into separate executable files, the more portable and convenient alternative is to combine them into a single program, with a test near the beginning to separate the master code from the slave code.

We present the code here in three chunks: the code executed by all processes, the code executed only by the master, and the code executed only by the slaves. The code that is executed by all processes is shown in Figure 3.5. It does not contain any MPI calls that we have not already seen.

Now we fill in the sections carried out by the master and slaves. The way in which the master obtains the matrix **A** and the vector **b** is irrelevant, so we don't show their initialization here. We have arbitrarily made **A** of size 100×100, just to be specific. The code for the master is shown in Figure 3.6 on page 34. The new MPI call is the *send* operation, which the master uses to send a row of **A** to a slave. In this first version we pack the data into a contiguous buffer before sending it. (Later, in Section 5.2, we will show how MPI can do this for us.) Then the message is sent with

```fortran
      program main
      include "mpif.h"
      integer MAX_ROWS, MAX_COLS, rows, cols
      parameter (MAX_ROWS = 1000, MAX_COLS = 1000)
      double precision a(MAX_ROWS,MAX_COLS), b(MAX_COLS), c(MAX_COLS)
      double precision buffer(MAX_COLS), ans

      integer myid, master, numprocs, ierr, stat(MPI_STATUS_SIZE)
      integer i, j, numsent, numrcvd, sender
      integer anstype, row

      call MPI_INIT( ierr )
      call MPI_COMM_RANK( MPI_COMM_WORLD, myid, ierr )
      call MPI_COMM_SIZE( MPI_COMM_WORLD, numprocs, ierr )
      master = 0
      rows   = 100
      cols   = 100

      if ( myid .eq. master ) then
c        master initializes and then dispatches
         ...
      else
c        slaves receive b, then compute dot products until done message
         ...
      endif

      call MPI_FINALIZE(ierr)
      stop
      end
```

Figure 3.5
Fortran program for matrix-vector multiplication: common part

```
     call MPI_SEND(buffer, cols, MPI_DOUBLE_PRECISION, i,
    $               i, MPI_COMM_WORLD, ierr)
```

The first three arguments, `buffer`, `cols`, and `MPI_DOUBLE_PRECISION` describe the message in the usual MPI way: address, count, and datatype. The next argument, `i`, is the destination, an integer specifying the rank of the destination process in the group associated with the communicator given by the argument `MPI_COMM_WORLD`. The next argument is an integer message type, or *tag*, in MPI terminology. We use the tag in this case to send a little extra information along with the row, namely, the row number. The slave will send this number back with the dot product it computes, so the master will know where to store the answer in the vector **b**. Of course, we are assuming that there are enough tag values to keep track of the rows of **A**. MPI guarantees that at least the values from 0 to 32767 are valid, which will suffice for small tests of this program. (More tag values might be available; see Section 7.8 for how to find out.) We reserve tag value 0 for the termination message. Finally, a communicator is specified (in this case the "default" communicator `MPI_COMM_WORLD`, whose group includes all processes), and a place (`ierr`) in which to return an error code. (We will consider error codes in more detail in Section 7.7.)

The responses from the slaves are received by the line

```
     call MPI_RECV(ans, 1, MPI_DOUBLE_PRECISION, MPI_ANY_SOURCE,
    $               MPI_ANY_TAG, MPI_COMM_WORLD, stat, ierr)
```

This is a *blocking* receive; that is, control is not returned to the user program until the message has been received. The first three arguments specify a place to put the message. Here it is a single double-precision number, the dot product of one row of **A** with **b**. The master process can also specify that it wants to wait for a message from a specific process. Here it does not wish to be so selective, so it uses the predefined value `MPI_ANY_SOURCE` to indicate that it will accept messages from any process associated with the `MPI_COMM_WORLD` communicator. The use of `MPI_ANY_TAG` indicates that any row is acceptable.

The argument `stat` is an output argument that provides information about the message that is received. In Fortran, it is an array of integers of size `MPI_STATUS_SIZE`. It is declared in the user's program. Here we have called it `stat`. The entry `stat(MPI_SOURCE)` is filled in with the rank of the process that sent the message. It is important here because we will send the next unit of work (the next row) to that slave. We also need to know the value of `stat(MPI_TAG)` in

```
c          master initializes and then dispatches
c          initialize a and b  (arbitrary)
           do 20 i = 1,cols
               b(i) = 1
               do 10 j = 1,rows
                   a(i,j) = i
  10           continue
  20       continue
           numsent = 0
           numrcvd = 0
c          send b to each slave process
           call MPI_BCAST(b, cols, MPI_DOUBLE_PRECISION, master,
      $         MPI_COMM_WORLD, ierr)
c          send a row to each slave process; tag with row number
           do 40 i = 1,numprocs-1
               do 30 j = 1,cols
                   buffer(j) = a(i,j)
  30           continue
               call MPI_SEND(buffer, cols, MPI_DOUBLE_PRECISION, i,
      $             i, MPI_COMM_WORLD, ierr)
               numsent = numsent+1
  40       continue
           do 70 i = 1,rows
               call MPI_RECV(ans, 1, MPI_DOUBLE_PRECISION, MPI_ANY_SOURCE,
      $             MPI_ANY_TAG, MPI_COMM_WORLD, stat, ierr)
               sender    = stat(MPI_SOURCE)
               anstype   = stat(MPI_TAG)
               c(anstype) = ans
               if (numsent .lt. rows) then
                   do 50 j = 1,cols
                       buffer(j) = a(numsent+1,j)
  50               continue
                   call MPI_SEND(buffer, cols, MPI_DOUBLE_PRECISION, sender,
      $                 numsent+1, MPI_COMM_WORLD, ierr)
                   numsent = numsent+1
               else
                   call MPI_SEND(1.0, 0, MPI_DOUBLE_PRECISION, sender,
      $                 0, MPI_COMM_WORLD, ierr)
               endif
  70       continue
```

Figure 3.6
Fortran program for matrix-vector multiplication: master part

order to know where to store the answer in the vector **b**. In C, `stat` is a structure of type `MPI_Status`; the element `stat.MPI_SOURCE` is the source, and the element `stat.MPI_TAG` is the tag value. In C programs, the status is usually passed by reference (that is, `&stat`). Other entries in `stat` are used to determine the number of items that were actually received with the routine `MPI_Get_count`, which we will discuss in Section 7.1.3.

After all rows have been sent, the master sends a message of type 0 to the slaves to tell them they are finished. The content of this message is irrelevant; all the information is carried by the tag. In fact, since the content of the message is irrelevant, we send a message of zero length by setting the count field to 0.

The slave code is given in Figure 3.7. It is a simple loop in which a message is received from the master and then is acted upon. Whether the message is a row to work on or a termination message is determined by its tag, which is available in `stat(MPI_TAG)`.

```fortran
c         slaves receive b, then compute dot products until
c         done message received
          call MPI_BCAST(b, cols, MPI_DOUBLE_PRECISION, master,
     $          MPI_COMM_WORLD, ierr)
 90       call MPI_RECV(buffer, cols, MPI_DOUBLE_PRECISION, master,
     $          MPI_ANY_TAG, MPI_COMM_WORLD, stat, ierr)
          if (stat(MPI_TAG) .eq. 0) then
            go to 200
          else
            row = stat(MPI_TAG)
            ans = 0.0
            do 100 i = 1,cols
              ans = ans+buffer(i)*b(i)
 100        continue
            call MPI_SEND(ans, 1, MPI_DOUBLE_PRECISION, master, row,
     $            MPI_COMM_WORLD, ierr)
            go to 90
          endif
 200      continue
```

Figure 3.7
Fortran program for matrix-vector multiplication: slave part

If the message is a row (the tag is nonzero), then the dot product with **b** is computed and sent back to the master, and the slave waits for another task with

`MPI_RECV`. Otherwise the slave branches to the `MPI_FINALIZE` in the code shared by master and slave.

The new routines used in in this example are the basic *send* and *receive* routines. Their Fortran and C bindings are given in Tables 3.5 and 3.6, respectively.

MPI_SEND(buf, count, datatype, dest, tag, comm, ierror)
                        <type> buf(*)
                        integer count, datatype, dest, tag, comm, ierror

MPI_RECV(buf, count, datatype, source, tag, comm, status, ierror)
                        <type> buf(*)
                        integer count, datatype, source, tag, comm,
                        status(MPI_STATUS_SIZE), ierror

Table 3.5
Fortran bindings for send and receive routines

---

int **MPI_Send**(void *buf, int count, MPI_Datatype datatype, int dest, int tag,
                MPI_Comm comm)

int **MPI_Recv**(void *buf, int count, MPI_Datatype datatype, int source, int tag,
                MPI_Comm comm, MPI_Status *status)

Table 3.6
C bindings for send and receive routines

Now that we have discussed `MPI_Send` and `MPI_Recv`, we have covered all of the six functions listed in Chapter 2 as the minimal subset of MPI.

3.6 Studying Parallel Performance

In this section we take a first look at studying the behavior of parallel programs in more depth than just by timing them as we did in Section 3.4. We will begin with a very simple example of *scalability analysis*, applied to matrix-vector and matrix-matrix multiplication. This is an interesting and deep topic in its own right (see, for example, [25] or [55]). We can convey the flavor of an analysis by looking at the program we have just written. We will then switch from an analytical approach to an experimental one, and show how to instrument a program so that it produces a log that we can study with graphical tools. The tools we describe here are in the MPE library.

3.6.1   Elementary Scalability Calculations

Scalability analysis is the estimation of the computation and communication requirements of a particular problem and the mathematical study of how these requirements change as the problem size and/or the number of processes changes. As an elementary example, let us look at the matrix-vector multiplication algorithm that we have just presented. The amount of computation is easy to estimate. Let us suppose, for simplicity, that the matrix $\mathbf{A}$ is square, of size $n \times n$. Then for each element of the product $\mathbf{c}$ of $\mathbf{A}$ and $\mathbf{b}$, we have to perform n multiplications, and $n - 1$ additions. There are n elements of $\mathbf{c}$, so the total number of floating-point operations is

$$n \times (n + (n - 1)) = 2n^2 - n.$$

For simplicity, we assume that additions and multiplications take the same amount of time, which we call T_{calc}. We assume further that the total computation time is dominated by the floating-point operations. Thus our rough estimate for computation time is $(2n^2 - n) \times T_{calc}$.

Now let us estimate the communication costs. Let us not count the cost of sending $\mathbf{b}$ to each slave process, assuming that it arrived there some other way (perhaps it is computed there). Then the number of floating-point numbers that have to be communicated is n (to send a row of $\mathbf{A}$), $+ 1$ (to send the answer back) for each element of $\mathbf{c}$, for a grand total of

$$n \times (n + 1) = n^2 + n.$$

If we assume that the time it takes to communicate a floating-point number is T_{comm}, the total communication time is roughly $(n^2 + n) \times T_{comm}$.

Therefore the ratio of communication to computation is

$$\left(\frac{n^2 + n}{2n^2 - n} \right) \times \left(\frac{T_{comm}}{T_{calc}} \right).$$

Since the cost of a single floating-point operation is usually much less than the cost of communicating one floating-point number, we hope to make this ratio as small as possible. Often by making a problem larger, one can reduce to insignificance the communication overhead. Here the bad news is that it doesn't happen in this case. The ratio T_{comm}/T_{calc} is roughly independent of n. (For the purposes of this analysis, we will ignore the effects of message sizes on communication costs; more detail is presented in Section 4.6.) As n gets larger, the ratio $\frac{n^2+n}{2n^2-n}$ just gets closer to $\frac{1}{2}$. This means that communications overhead will always be a problem in this simplistic algorithm for matrix-vector multiply. (In Chapter 4, we will discuss the effect of message size on the communication cost.)

Better news is provided by a similar analysis of matrix-*matrix* multiplication. We can easily modify our matrix-vector algorithm to multiply two matrices instead. The vector **b** becomes a matrix **B**, we still distribute a copy of **B** to all the slave processes, and we collect back a whole row of the product matrix **C** from each process. The slave code is shown in Figure 3.8, and the master code is modified accordingly. (We save listing of the whole program until later, when we show the instrumented version.)

```
c        slaves receive B, then compute rows of C until done message
         do 85 i = 1,bcols
         call MPI_BCAST(b(1,i), brows, MPI_DOUBLE_PRECISION, master,
     $        MPI_COMM_WORLD, ierr)
85       continue
90       call MPI_RECV(buffer, acols, MPI_DOUBLE_PRECISION, master,
     $        MPI_ANY_TAG, MPI_COMM_WORLD, status, ierr)
         if (status(MPI_TAG) .eq. 0) then
           go to 200
         else
           row = status(MPI_TAG)
           do 100 i = 1,bcols
              ans(i) = 0.0
              do 95 j = 1,acols
                 ans(i) = ans(i) + buffer(j)*b(j,i)
95            continue
100        continue
           call MPI_SEND(ans, bcols, MPI_DOUBLE_PRECISION, master,
     $          row, MPI_COMM_WORLD, ierr)
           go to 90
         endif
200      continue
```

Figure 3.8
Matrix-matrix multiplication: slave part

Now let us do the scalability analysis for this (still not so very good) algorithm for matrix multiplication. For simplicity, let us again suppose that **A** is square and assume that **B** is square as well. Then the number of operations for each element of **C** is (as before) n multiplications and $n-1$ adds, but now there are n^2 elements of **C** to be computed, as opposed to n. Therefore the number of floating-point operations is

$$n^2 \times (2n - 1) = 2n^3 - n^2.$$

The number of floating-point numbers communicated for each row is n (to send the row of **A**, plus n to send the row of **C** back), and there are n rows, so

$$n \times 2n$$

is the answer. Now the ratio of communication to computation is

$$\left(\frac{2n^2}{2n^3 - n^2} \right) \times \left(\frac{T_{comm}}{T_{calc}} \right),$$

which approaches $1/n$ as n becomes large. Therefore for this problem we should expect communication overhead to play a smaller role than in large problems.

3.6.2 Gathering Data on Program Execution

Timing results provide some insight into the performance of our program, and our programs so far have not been difficult to understand. But suppose that we need to see in detail just exactly what the sequence of events was, just what amounts of time were spent on each phase of the computation, and just how long each individual communication operation took. The easiest way to understand this data at a glance would be through a graphical tool of some kind.

Several projects have been developed to create files of events with associated time stamps and then examine them in post-mortem fashion by interpreting them graphically on a workstation. Such files are called *logfiles*. The ability to generate logfiles automatically was an important component of one of the early portable programming libraries, PICL (for Portable *Instrumented* Communication Library) [31, 32]. Its latest logfile format has been proposed as a standard [79], and its logfile presentation program ParaGraph [46, 47] is widely used.

In this book we will use some simple tools for creating logfiles and viewing them. We treat the library for creation of logfiles as separate from the message-passing library. Viewing the logfile is independent of its creation, and multiple tools can be used. In the next few sections we describe routines in the MPE library for explicit logging of programmer-chosen events under program control, and we use the matrix-matrix multiplication program as an example. These routines will be used in Chapter 7 to build a completely automatic logging mechanism based on the standard MPI profiling interface.

The logfile viewing program we use is called `upshot`; it is a simple graphical display of parallel time lines and state durations, based on an earlier program of the same name [49]. `Upshot` is distributed with the model implementation of MPI and is a Tcl/Tk script [60], so it is easy to customize and extend. Further description of `upshot` is given in Appendix C.4.[2]

3.6.3   Instrumenting a Parallel Program with MPE Logging

Although there are advantages to having logfile creation and logfile examination be parts of a single integrated system, we separate them so that they can undergo separate development. We present in this section the MPE library for logfile creation. It is designed to coexist with any MPI implementation and is being distributed along with the model version of MPI. It is also used in the automatic instrumentation techniques for MPI programs discussed in Chapter 7. Reference bindings for MPE are given in Appendix C. Here we describe the routines needed to instrument a programs with explicit, programmer-controlled events. In Chapter 7 we show how automatic logging can be done, with a decrease in programmer involvement but a corresponding decrease in flexibility.

Generally speaking, we need only to call the `MPE_Log_event` routine when we wish to record a log. The time-stamp and process identifier are collected automatically; the user specifies an event type and optionally can also supply one integer data item and one (short) character string. In addition, each process must call `MPE_Init_log` to prepare for logging, and `MPE_Finish_log` to merge the files being stored locally at each process into a single logfile which is written out. `MPE_Stop_log` can be used to suspend logging, although the timer continues to run. `MPE_Start_log` causes logging to resume again.

3.6.4   Events and States

The programmer chooses whatever non-negative integers are desired for event types; the system attaches no particular meaning to event types. Events are considered to have no duration. To measure duration of program states, pairs of events are specified as the beginnings and endings of *states*. A state is defined by the `MPE_Describe_state` routine, which specifies the starting and ending event types. For the benefit of a logfile display program, whatever it might be,

---

[2]The strange name "Upshot" has arisen historically. Once there was a program called "Gist" that was written at BBN for the Butterfly software environment. It inspired a program written at Argonne, and the thesaurus suggested "Upshot" as related to "Gist."

`MPE_Describe_state` also adds a state name and a color (and a bitmap pattern for use by monochrome displays) for the state. The corresponding `MPE_Describe_event` provides an event description for an event type. Note that this differs from the approach taken in [79], for example, where every "event" has duration. We treat events as atomic and define states, whether long or short, in terms of events.

3.6.5 Instrumenting the Matrix-Matrix Multiply Program

Now let us instrument the matrix-matrix multiply program using these routines. The first decision to make is which events to log. In this example it is easier first to decide on the states to be visualized and then to provide starting and ending events for each state. We could get a reasonably complete picture of the matrix-matrix multiply by measuring in the master program

- broadcast of **B**,
- sending each row of **A**,
- receiving each row of **C**,

and in the slave program

- receipt of **B** (by broadcast),
- receipt of each row of **A**,
- computation of the row of **C**,
- sending each row of **C** back to the master.

The overall framework of the instrumented version of our matrix-matrix multiplication program is shown in Figure 3.9. This is much the same as Figure 3.5, except for some changes to the program variables to reflect the fact that this is matrix-matrix instead of matrix-vector multiplication. The logging setup section just before the main `if` that separates master and slave does the `MPE_INIT_LOG` and then defines four states, for broadcasting, computing, sending and receiving. For example, the line

```
call MPE_DESCRIBE_STATE(1, 2, "Bcast", "red:vlines3", ierror)
```

defines the "Bcast" state as the time between events of type 1 and events of type 2. We will use those event types to bracket the `MPI_BCAST` call in the program. The name of the state will be used in the logfile display program (whatever it may be) to label data associated with this state. The last argument is a hint to the display program about how we wish this state displayed. Here we are requesting

```
c       matmat.f - matrix - matrix multiply,
c       simple self-scheduling version
        program main
        include "mpif.h"
        integer MAX_AROWS, MAX_ACOLS, MAX_BCOLS
        parameter (MAX_AROWS = 20, MAX_ACOLS = 1000, MAX_BCOLS = 20)
        double precision a(MAX_AROWS,MAX_ACOLS), b(MAX_ACOLS,MAX_BCOLS)
        double precision c(MAX_AROWS,MAX_BCOLS)
        double precision buffer(MAX_ACOLS), ans(MAX_ACOLS)
        double precision starttime, stoptime
        integer myid, master, numprocs, ierr, stat(MPI_STATUS_SIZE)
        integer i, j, numsent, numrcvd, sender
        integer anstype, row, arows, acols, brows, bcols, crows, ccols
        call MPI_INIT( ierr )
        call MPI_COMM_RANK( MPI_COMM_WORLD, myid, ierr )
        call MPI_COMM_SIZE( MPI_COMM_WORLD, numprocs, ierr )
        arows = 10
        acols = 20
        brows = 20
        bcols = 10
        crows = arows
        ccols = bcols
        call MPE_INITLOG()
        if ( myid .eq. 0 ) then
           call MPE_DESCRIBE_STATE(1, 2, "Bcast",   "red:vlines3")
           call MPE_DESCRIBE_STATE(3, 4, "Compute","blue:gray3")
           call MPE_DESCRIBE_STATE(5, 6, "Send",    "green:light_gray")
           call MPE_DESCRIBE_STATE(7, 8, "Recv",    "yellow:gray")
        endif
        if ( myid .eq. 0 ) then
c          master initializes and then dispatches ...
        else
c          slaves receive b, then compute rows of c ...
        endif
        call MPE_FINISHLOG("pmatmat.log")
        call MPI_FINALIZE(ierr)
        stop
        end
```

Figure 3.9
Matrix-matrix multiplication with logging: common part

"red" on a color display and the bitmap pattern "vlines3" on a black-white-display. The black-and-white (bitmap) versions are the ones used in this book. Calling the MPE_DESCRIBE_STATE routine just inserts a record into the logfile that the display program can use if it wishes to do so.

At the end of the computation, the call to MPE_FINISH_LOG gathers the log buffers from all the processes, merges them based on the time-stamps, and process 0 writes the logfile to the file named as the argument of MPE_FINISH_LOG.

Code specific to the master process is shown in Figure 3.10. We have just inserted calls to MPE_LOG_EVENT before and after each of the sections of code that we wish to be represented as a state, using the event types that we chose above. In addition, we have in some cases added additional data in the integer data field (the loop index in this case).

We log in the "receive" event the loop index we have reached, and in the "received" event the number of the row that was received. We have not really used the character data field here, since we have not varied it according to the individual event being logged; here it is merely echoing the event type.

Code specific to the slave process is shown in Figure 3.11. Again, the placement of calls to MPE_LOG_EVENT is routine.

3.6.6   Notes on Implementation of Logging

It is important for accuracy that logging of an event be a low-overhead operation. MPE_Log_event stores a small amount of information in memory, which is quite fast. During MPE_Finish_log, these buffers are merged in parallel, and the final buffer, sorted by time-stamp, is written out by process 0.

One subtle aspect of collecting logs with time-stamps is the necessity of relying on local clocks. On some parallel computers there are synchronized clocks, but on others the clocks are only approximately synchronized. On workstation networks, the situation is much worse, and clocks even drift with respect to each other as well.

To compensate for this situation, the time-stamps are postprocessed with respect to synchronizations at MPE_Init_log and MPE_Finish_log. Postprocessing, which includes aligning and stretching the time axes of each process so that the MPE_Init_log and MPE_Finish_log take place at the same time, is done as part of MPE_Finish_log. MPI itself is used to combine the logs, and the combining process is done in parallel, with the logfile itself written out by the process with rank 0 in MPI_COMM_WORLD.

```fortran
c          master initializes and then dispatches
           .... initialization of a and b, broadcast of b
           numsent = 0
           numrcvd = 0
c          send a row of a to each other process; tag with row number
           do 40 i = 1,numprocs-1
              do 30 j = 1,acols
30                buffer(j) = a(i,j)
              call MPE_LOG_EVENT(5, i, "send", ierr)
              call MPI_SEND(buffer, acols, MPI_DOUBLE_PRECISION, i,
     $            i, MPI_COMM_WORLD, ierr)
              call MPE_LOG_EVENT(6, i, "sent", ierr)
40            numsent = numsent+1
           do 70 i = 1,crows
              call MPE_LOG_EVENT(7, i, "recv", ierr)
              call MPI_RECV(ans, ccols, MPI_DOUBLE_PRECISION,
     $            MPI_ANY_SOURCE, MPI_ANY_TAG, MPI_COMM_WORLD, stat,
     $            ierr)
              sender    = stat(MPI_SOURCE)
              anstype   = stat(MPI_TAG)
              call MPE_LOG_EVENT(8, anstype, "recvd", ierr)
              do 45 j = 1,ccols
45                c(anstype,j) = ans(j)
              if (numsent .lt. arows) then
                 do 50 j = 1,acols
50                   buffer(j) = a(numsent+1,j)
                 call MPE_LOG_EVENT(5, i, "send", ierr)
                 call MPI_SEND(buffer, acols, MPI_DOUBLE_PRECISION,
     $               sender, numsent+1, MPI_COMM_WORLD, ierr)
                 call MPE_LOG_EVENT(6, i, "sent", ierr)
                 numsent = numsent+1
              else
                 call MPE_LOG_EVENT(5, 0, "send", ierr)
                 call MPI_SEND(1.0, 1, MPI_DOUBLE_PRECISION, sender,
     $               0, MPI_COMM_WORLD, ierr)
                 call MPE_LOG_EVENT(6, 0, "sent", ierr)
              endif
70         continue
```

Figure 3.10
Matrix-matrix multiplication with logging: master part

```
c           slaves receive b, then compute rows of c until done message
            call MPE_LOG_EVENT(1, 0, "bstart")
            do 85 i = 1,bcols
            call MPI_BCAST(b(1,i), brows, MPI_DOUBLE_PRECISION, master,
     $           MPI_COMM_WORLD, ierr)
 85         continue
            call MPE_LOG_EVENT(2, 0, "bend")
            call MPE_LOG_EVENT(7, i, "recv")
 90         call MPI_RECV(buffer, acols, MPI_DOUBLE_PRECISION, master,
     $           MPI_ANY_TAG, MPI_COMM_WORLD, stat, ierr)
            if (stat(MPI_TAG) .eq. 0) then
               go to 200
            else
               row = stat(MPI_TAG)
               call MPE_LOG_EVENT(8, row, "recvd")
               call MPE_LOG_EVENT(3, row, "compute")
               do 100 i = 1,bcols
                  ans(i) = 0.0
                  do 95 j = 1,acols
                     ans(i) = ans(i) + buffer(j)*b(j,i)
 95               continue
 100           continue
               call MPE_LOG_EVENT(4, row, "computed")
               call MPE_LOG_EVENT(5, row, "send")
               call MPI_SEND(ans, bcols, MPI_DOUBLE_PRECISION, master,
     $              row, MPI_COMM_WORLD, ierr)
               call MPE_LOG_EVENT(6, row, "sent")
               go to 90
            endif
 200        continue
```

Figure 3.11
Matrix-matrix multiplication: slave part

3.6.7 Examining Logfiles with Upshot

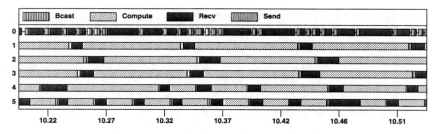

Figure 3.12
Upshot output

After an MPI program instrumented with the MPE logging routines has completed, the directory where it executed contains a file of events sorted by time, with time adjusted to correct for offset and drift. We can write many programs to extract useful data from this file. One that we describe here and use from time to time in the rest of this book is the graphical display program upshot. A sample of upshot output is shown in Figure 3.12, which displays a portion of the logfile collected while running the matrix-matrix multiplication program on six Suns on an Ethernet. One can tell which one was the Sparc-10; the others were Sparc-2's.

Upshot displays parallel time lines, with states indicated by colored bars on color displays and bitmaps on monochrome displays (like the page of this book). Time-stamp values, adjusted to start at 0, are shown along the bottom of the frame. A particular view is shown in Figure 3.12, but what is missing there is the upshot control window for horizontal and vertical zooming in and out and scrolling forward and backward in time. Such adjustment of the view is necessary in order to glean both fine detail and summary impressions from the same logfile. Details of upshot's control window, together with other features such as a state histogram display, can be found in Appendix C.4.

Of course, the information in logfiles can be displayed in simple summary form as well, without graphics. The model implementation contains, in addition to upshot, a short program called states. If we run states on the logfile that produced Figure 3.12, we get

```
State:    Time:
Bcast     0.146799
Compute   0.044800
Send      0.030711
Recv      0.098852
------------------
Total:    0.321162
```

Such summary information is a crude form of profiling; it tells us where the program is spending its time. Note that since the events and states may be described by the programmer and are not tied to the message-passing library, the MPE library can be useful in studying aspects of an algorithm that have nothing to do with interprocess communication.

3.7   Using Communicators

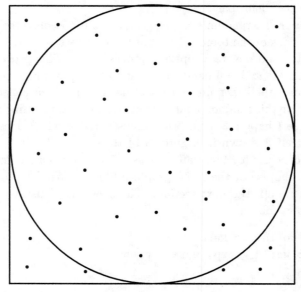

Figure 3.13
Monte Carlo computation of π

Up to this point, all of our examples have used `MPI_COMM_WORLD` as an argument to nearly every MPI call. What is it for, if it is always the same? In this section we describe *communicators*, which are perhaps the most pervasive and distinguishing feature of the MPI library specification. While a more comprehensive discussion of the purpose and use of communicators occurs in Chapter 6, we give here an extremely simple example that illustrates some of the MPI functions dealing with groups and communicators.

The example will illustrate the Monte Carlo method of integration. We will use it to find (again) the value of π. This will not be a particularly good way to find the value of π, but it will provide us with a simple example. To make it more interesting, we will introduce here some of the MPE real-time graphics operations, so that we can watch our program in action.

In Figure 3.13, if the radius of the circle is 1, then the area is π and the area of the square around it is 4. Therefore the ratio r of the area of the circle to that of the square is $\pi/4$. We will compute the ratio r by generating random points (x, y) in the square and counting how many of them turn out to be in the circle (by determining for each one whether $x^2 + y^2 < 1$. Then $\pi = 4r$. The testing of these points is highly parallelizable.

The issue of parallel random number generators is too deep for us here (see [1] or [9] for discussions of the topic). To avoid the issue, we will use only one random number generator and devote a separate process to it. This process will generate the random numbers and will hand them out to the other processes for evaluation and display. Since the other processes will need to perform collective operations that do not involve this random number "server," we need to define a communicator whose group (see Chapter 2 for a brief discussion of groups) does not include it. The program itself is shown in Figures 3.14 through 3.17. This example is in C and has two purposes: to illustrate the use of a nondefault communicator, and to demonstrate the use of the MPE graphics library. We delay discussion of the graphics routines until the next section. The code that illustrates communicator manipulation is as follows:

```
MPI_Comm world, workers;
MPI_Group world_group, worker_group;
int ranks[1];

MPI_Init(&argc,&argv);
world = MPI_COMM_WORLD;
MPI_Comm_size(world,&numprocs);
```

```
MPI_Comm_rank(world,&myid);
server = numprocs-1;                /* last proc is server */

MPI_Comm_group( world, &world_group );
ranks[0] = server;
MPI_Group_excl( world_group, 1, ranks, &worker_group );
MPI_Comm_create( world, worker_group, &workers );
MPI_Group_free(&worker_group);
MPI_Group_free(&world_group);
```

The new feature here is that we have *two* communicators, world and workers. The communicator workers will contain all the processes except the random number server. This code illustrates how to build a communicator that has all the processes except the server process in it. To do this, we deal explicitly with the *group* of processes associated with the default communicator MPI_COMM_WORLD. Let us go through this code line by line.

Two communicators, world and workers, are declared, along with two groups of processes, world_group and worker_group. In C, an MPI group is described by a MPI_Group type. After the required call to MPI_Init, MPI_COMM_WORLD is defined and is assigned to world. We find out how many processes there are with the call to MPI_Comm_size, and we assign to server the rank of the last process in the original group. The next few lines of code build the communicator that has as its group all of the processes except the random number server. First we extract from the MPI_COMM_WORLD communicator its group, which contains all processes. This is done with a call to MPI_Comm_Group. It returns in world_group the group of all processes. Next we build a new group. There are many ways that groups can be manipulated (see Chapter 7), but here the simplest approach is to use MPI_Group_excl, which takes a given group and forms a new group by excluding certain of the original group's members. The members to be excluded are specified with an array of ranks; here we exclude a single process. Then the call to MPI_Group_excl returns in worker_group the new group, containing all the processes except the random number server. We create the new communicator from MPI_COMM_WORLD by calling MPI_Comm_create with the old communicator and the new group, getting back the new communicator in workers. This is the communicator we will use when we wish to do collective operations that do not involve the random number server. At the end of the program, we release this communicator with a call to MPI_Comm_free. Finally, since we needed only the group

```
/* compute pi using Monte Carlo method */
#include <math.h>
#include "mpi.h"
#include "mpe.h"
#define CHUNKSIZE        1000
/* message tags */
#define REQUEST  1
#define REPLY    2
main(argc,argv)
int argc;
char *argv[];
{
    int iter;
    int in, out, i, iters, max, ix, iy, ranks[1], done, temp;
    double x, y, Pi, error, epsilon;
    int numprocs, myid, server, totalin, totalout, workerid;
    int rands[CHUNKSIZE], request;
    MPI_Comm world, workers;
    MPI_Group world_group, worker_group;
    MPI_Status stat;

    MPI_Init(&argc,&argv);
    world  = MPI_COMM_WORLD;
    MPI_Comm_size(world,&numprocs);
    MPI_Comm_rank(world,&myid);
    server = numprocs-1;            /* last proc is server */
    if (myid == 0)
        sscanf( argv[1], "%lf", &epsilon );
    MPI_Bcast( &epsilon, 1, MPI_DOUBLE, 0, MPI_COMM_WORLD );
    MPI_Comm_group( world, &world_group );
    ranks[0] = server;
    MPI_Group_excl( world_group, 1, ranks, &worker_group );
    MPI_Comm_create( world, worker_group, &workers );
    MPI_Group_free(&worker_group);
```

Figure 3.14
Monte Carlo computation of π: beginning

worker_group in order to create the workers communicator, we may now release
it by calling MPI_Group_free.

```
if (myid == server) {          /* I am the rand server */
    do {
        MPI_Recv(&request, 1, MPI_INT, MPI_ANY_SOURCE, REQUEST,
                world, &stat);
        if (request) {
            for (i = 0; i < CHUNKSIZE; i++)
                    rands[i] = random();
            MPI_Send(rands, CHUNKSIZE, MPI_INT, stat.MPI_SOURCE,
                    REPLY, world);
        }
    }
    while( request>0 );
}
```

Figure 3.15
Monte Carlo computation of π: server

The code that "tidies up" by freeing the group and communicator that we created
during the run merits further discussion, since it illustrates an important point.
Communicators contain internal references to groups. When we extract the group
explicitly, by a call to MPI_Comm_group, we create another *reference* to the group.
Later on, when we call MPI_Group_free with this reference, we are freeing the
reference, which becomes invalid, but we are not destroying the group itself, since
there is another reference inside the communicator. For this reason, we may actually
call

    MPI_Group_free(&worker_group);

and

    MPI_Comm_free(&workers);

in either order; the group does not cease to exist until both references to the group
have been freed. As an aid to safe programming, MPI sets the arguments to a free
call to a special null object; this makes it easier to detect the inadvertent use of
an (now) invalid object. These null objects have names (so that one can test for
them); they are MPI_GROUP_NULL and MPI_COMM_NULL. Others will be introduced
as they are needed.

```
        else {                              /* I am a worker process */
      request = 1;
      done = in = out = 0;
      max  = INT_MAX;            /* max int, for normalization */
      MPI_Send( &request, 1, MPI_INT, server, REQUEST, world );
      MPI_Comm_rank( workers, &workerid );
      iter = 0;
      while (!done) {
          iter++;
          request = 1;
          MPI_Recv( rands, CHUNKSIZE, MPI_INT, server, REPLY,
                  world, &stat );
          for (i=0; i<CHUNKSIZE; ) {
              x = (((double) rands[i++])/max) * 2 - 1;
              y = (((double) rands[i++])/max) * 2 - 1;
              if (x*x + y*y < 1.0)
                  in++;
              else
                  out++;
          }
          MPI_Allreduce(&in, &totalin, 1, MPI_INT, MPI_SUM,
                      workers);
          MPI_Allreduce(&out, &totalout, 1, MPI_INT, MPI_SUM,
                      workers);
          Pi = (4.0*totalin)/(totalin + totalout);
          error = fabs( Pi-3.141592653589793238462643);
          done = ((error < epsilon) || ((totalin+totalout)>1000000));
          request = (done) ? 0 : 1;
          if (myid == 0) {
              printf( "\rpi = %23.20lf", Pi );
              MPI_Send( &request, 1, MPI_INT, server, REQUEST,
                      world );
          }
          else {
              if (request)
                  MPI_Send( &request, 1, MPI_INT, server, REQUEST,
                          world );
          }
      }
  }
```

Figure 3.16
Monte Carlo computation of π: workers

The other new MPI library call introduced in this example is `MPI_Allreduce`. This differs from the `MPI_Reduce` that we have seen before in that the result of the reduction operation is available in all processes, not just in the one specified as root. Depending on implementation, `MPI_Allreduce` may be more efficient than the equivalent `MPI_Reduce` followed by an `MPI_Bcast`. Here we use it to test whether it is time to stop. We have provided an error value on the command line, and each process compares the current value of π with the precalculated value we have put into the program.

```
    if (myid == server) {          /* I am the rand server */
       ...
    } else {                       /* I am a worker process */
       ...
    }
    if (myid == 0) {
        printf( "\npoints: %d\nin: %d, out: %d, <ret> to exit\n",
                totalin+totalout, totalin, totalout );
        getchar();
    }
    MPI_Comm_free(&workers);
    MPI_Finalize();
}
```

Figure 3.17
Monte Carlo computation of π: ending

The specific bindings for the functions used in the Monte Carlo example are shown in Tables 3.7 and 3.8.

3.8   A Handy Graphics Library for Parallel Programs

A second reason for including this Monte Carlo example is that it allows us to introduce in its simplest possible form the MPE graphics library. In many programs, parallel or not, it would be convenient to provide some simple graphics output. The X Window System (X11) provides this capability, but it has a steep learning curve. We decided that in order to better represent some of the computations in the examples in this book, it would be useful to add to the model implementation a simple graphics interface. One unusual aspect of this library is that it allows shared access by parallel processes to a single X display. It is not the case that graphics

```
int MPI_Allreduce(void *sendbuf, void *recvbuf, int count,
            MPI_Datatype datatype, MPI_Op op, MPI_Comm comm)

int MPI_Comm_group(MPI_Comm comm, MPI_Group *group)

int MPI_Group_excl(MPI_Group group, int n, int *ranks, MPI_Group *newgroup)

int MPI_Group_free(MPI_Group *group)

int MPI_Comm_create(MPI_Comm comm, MPI_Group group,
            MPI_Comm *newcomm)

int MPI_Comm_free(MPI_Comm *comm)
```

Table 3.7
C bindings for new routines needed by Monte Carlo

```
MPI_ALLREDUCE(sendbuf, recvbuf, count, datatype, op, comm, ierror)
            <type> sendbuf(*), recvbuf(*)
            integer count, datatype, op, comm, ierror

MPI_COMM_GROUP(comm, group, ierror)
            integer comm, group, ierror

MPI_GROUP_EXCL(group, n, ranks, newgroup, ierror)
            integer group, n, ranks(*), newgroup, ierror

MPI_GROUP_FREE(group, ierror)
            integer group, ierror

MPI_COMM_CREATE(comm, group, newcomm, ierror)
            integer comm, group, newcomm, ierror

MPI_COMM_FREE(comm, ierror)
            integer comm, ierror
```

Table 3.8
Fortran bindings for new routines needed by Monte Carlo

output is explicitly sent via MPI to a single process that does the X graphics; rather, the processes may do parallel updates to a shared X display, which need not be associated with any of the processes in the MPI program. On the other hand, when they need to communicate, they use an MPI communicator for this purpose.

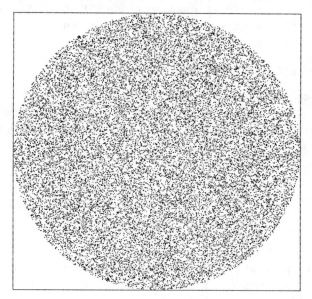

Figure 3.18
Monte Carlo computation of π: output

We can animate the Monte Carlo program with only four calls: to initialize shared access to an X display, to free it, to draw points, and to update the display with the points that have been drawn. All processes declare

```
MPE_XGraph graph;
```

which defines a "handle" to a graphics object that will be manipulated by the MPE graphics routines. The type `MPE_XGraph` is defined in the file 'mpe.h', which must be included. At the beginning of the program, all processes might do

```
MPE_Open_graphics( &graph, MPI_COMM_WORLD, (char *)0, -1, -1,
                   WINDOW_SIZE, WINDOW_SIZE, MPE_GRAPH_INDEPENT );
```

which initializes this handle. The arguments in this case specify that the communicator `MPI_COMM_WORLD` will be used for communication for this graphics object, that the default display from the user's environment should be used as the X display ((`char *`)0 as third argument instead of a display name), and that the user will be asked to place the window that is created. One could specify a location (x,y) by using nonnegative integers instead of (-1, -1). The rest of the arguments specify that the window will be square with side `WINDOW_SIZE` and that graphics operations will not be collective. For details, see Appendix C.

At the end of the program, each process does

```
MPE_Close_graphics( &graph );
```

to terminate access to the display. The only drawing command in this program is used to draw single points on the display. We will draw the points that lie within the circle of radius 1. Therefore, as more points are generated, we expect to see a rounder and rounder circle emerge. We can see this happening in Figure 3.18. The subroutine call that draws a point is

```
MPE_Draw_point( graph,
                (int)(WINDOW_SIZE/2 + x*WINDOW_SIZE/2),
                (int)(WINDOW_SIZE/2 - y*WINDOW_SIZE/2),
                MPE_BLACK );
```

which draws a point at the two coordinates given by its second and third arguments, in the color given by its last argument (of type `MPE_Color`). Finally, the line

```
MPE_Update( graph );
```

causes all of the drawing actions that may have been buffered up to this point to be flushed to the display. We can cut down on traffic to the X server by only calling this after a large number of calls to `MPE_Draw_point`. In our program, `MPE_Update` is called after each process has finished with one batch of points.

3.9   Application: Determination of Nuclear Structures

Although we have presented only a few MPI routines in this chapter, they are enough to express an application in theoretical physics. Researchers in Argonne's Physics Division, in collaboration with a colleague at the University of Illinois at Urbana-Champaign, are computing the properties of light (up to 40 neutrons and protons) nuclei using realistic two- and three-nucleon interactions. This research involves developing many-body methods for reliably computing the properties of a nucleus for complicated forces that are strongly dependent on the spins and charge states of the nucleons.

The methods used are described in [65] and [78]. New calculations being done on the IBM SP1 parallel computer at Argonne are using a new nuclear interaction and are obtaining much better (when compared with experiment) results for the binding energy and density profile of oxygen than had previously been obtained. In particular, physicists are now able to find parameters of the minimal energy solution for sixteen nucleons much more precisely than ever before. Before this computation, theory did not clearly predict that the nucleus of an oxygen atom would remain stable; the previous computational results would have allowed it to disintegrate into four helium atoms. Thus in some sense this research has proven that oxygen can exist! Work on calcium (forty nucleons), which could not be contemplated before, is now in progress.

The programs were originally developed for Cray computers and had been designed to use long vectors; significant modifications (required by the cache size and other considerations) were made to speed up the programs on the SP1. The effort involved in adapting the programs to parallel processors was much less than this single-processor tuning.

The algorithm is a master-slave algorithm, just like our matrix-vector multiplication example in Section 3.5. A reasonable run takes 5,000 to 10,000 Monte Carlo samples while searching for the best variational parameters; final runs can take about 50,000 samples. There is no requirement that the master receive the results in the order it sends positions to the slaves. Slaves that are busy with other work will automatically be used for fewer positions. There is no significant I/O; all of the I/O is done by the master node. Runs using all 128 nodes of the SP1 have demonstrated speedups of 122. Thus communication, synchronizing, etc, are using less than 5% of the time. Hence, any significant improvements in the speed must be obtained by further optimizing the subroutines on a single node.

This program is of nontrivial size (23,000 lines of Fortran), but as a message-passing program it is quite straightforward. In fact, it uses the same basic self-scheduling structure as the matrix-vector multiplication program shown in Figures 3.5, 3.6, and 3.7. It was originally written for the IBM SP1 using p4 and was ported to MPI in one afternoon. It drives the SP1 to a speed of nearly 6 gigaflops.

3.10   Summary of a Simple Subset of MPI

In this chapter we have introduced basic MPI routines through very simple example programs. In some ways we have already provided enough of the MPI library to write serious applications (like the nuclear structure example of the preceding section). In other ways we have barely scratched the surface; there is much more in MPI, as we will see in the upcoming chapters.

In particular, we have defined the six functions that make up the minimal MPI subset that we discussed in Chapter 2. We have added to those the two most common collective operations, the basic timing routine, and shown how to work with groups and communicators. We have also introduced a few useful tools: MPE logging, MPE graphics, and `upshot`. We will continue to make use of these tools as we look at more example programs in the chapters to come.

4 Intermediate MPI

In the preceding chapter we considered a number of straightforward parallel algorithms. We wrote parallel programs for the these algorithms using straightforward MPI subroutine calls, and we verified with timing and program visualization tools that our programs behaved as we expected.

In this chapter we introduce several important issues that require more subtlety in our analysis and more precision in our tools. The mathematical problem we will address here (the Poisson problem) will be only a little more complicated than the problems of the preceding chapter, but the parallel algorithm, particularly the communication pattern, will admit more options.

We introduce several new MPI routines. For example, our mathematical problem takes place on a finite-difference computational grid, and so we introduce the MPI notion of *virtual topology*, which makes the allocation of processes to particular parts of a grid convenient to manage. We also describe many of the variations on the basic *send* and *receive* operations supported by MPI; indeed, the communication patterns needed here by our parallel algorithm motivated some of the more esoteric MPI features.

Our first goal in this chapter is thus to show how MPI enables efficient programs to be written concisely. A secondary goal is to explain some of the issues that arise in analysis of communication patterns in grid-based problems.

We approach both of these goals by examining a number of programs for the 2-D and 3-D Poisson problem, a model partial differential equation. Because Fortran provides a much more convenient syntax for manipulating multidimensional arrays than does C, the bulk of the examples in this chapter are written in Fortran 77.

We also use the Poisson problem as a means to introduce the different mechanisms by which an MPI program can send data from one process to another, particularly with respect to both how data is buffered in the message passing system and how nonblocking communications can be used. By examining the different approaches in the context of a single application, we make clear the distinctions between these approaches. We begin by explaining the mathematical problem and an approach to solving it computationally. Then we describe MPI's virtual topology feature, which allows us to manage a grid of processes. As we progress, we introduce several new MPI functions while considering various ways of organizing the communications. Finally, to help in understanding the reasons for the different implementation choices, we will make another brief foray into scalability analysis.

This chapter may also be viewed as a discussion of the sparse matrix-vector product, because that is really the fundamental operation at work in these algorithms. While we will not discuss it in this book, the message-passing operations discussed in this chapter are the same as are used in implementing a parallel sparse matrix-vector product. The Jacobi method was chosen for its simplicity in the computational part of the program, allowing us to present a complete application.

4.1   The Poisson Problem

The Poisson problem is a simple partial differential equation (PDE) that is at the core of many applications. More elaborate problems and algorithms often have the same communication structure that we will use here to solve this problem. Thus, by studying how MPI can be used here, we are providing fundamentals on how communication patterns appear in more complex PDE problems. At the same time, we can demonstrate a wide variety of message-passing techniques and how MPI may be used to express them.

We emphasize that while the Poisson problem is a useful example for describing the features of MPI that can be used in solving partial differential equations and other problems that involve decomposition across many processes, the numerical techniques in this section are not the last word in solving PDEs and give poor performance relative to more recent and sophisticated methods. For information on more sophisticated, freely available parallel solvers for PDE's that use MPI, see [42]. For more details about the mathematical terminology used in this chapter, consult [56], among other sources.

The Poisson problem is expressed by the equations

$$\nabla^2 u \;=\; f(x,y) \text{ in the interior} \tag{4.1.1}$$
$$u(x,y) \;=\; g(x,y) \text{ on the boundary} \tag{4.1.2}$$

To simplify the discussion, we use the unit square as the domain.

To find an approximate solution to this problem, we define a square *mesh* (also called a *grid*) consisting of the points (x_i, y_j), given by

$$x_i \;=\; \frac{i}{n+1}, i = 0, \ldots, n+1,$$

$$y_j \;=\; \frac{j}{n+1}, j = 0, \ldots, n+1,$$

where there are $n+2$ points along each edge of the mesh (see Figure 4.1). We will find an approximation to $u(x,y)$ only at the points (x_i, y_j). We use the shorthand $u_{i,j}$ to refer to the approximation to u at (x_i, y_j). The value $1/(n+1)$ is used frequently; we will denote it by h (following common practice). We can approximate (4.1.1) at each of these points with the formula [56]

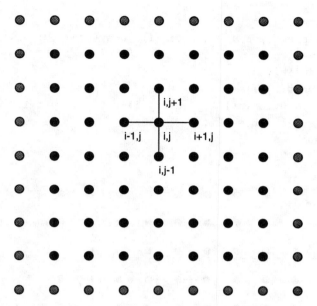

Figure 4.1
Five-point stencil approximation for 2-D Poisson problem, with $n = 7$. The boundaries of the domain are shown in gray.

$$\frac{u_{i-1,j} + u_{i,j+1} + u_{i,j-1} + u_{i+1,j} - 4u_{i,j}}{h^2} = f_{i,j}. \tag{4.1.3}$$

We wish to solve (4.1.3) for $u_{i,j}$ everywhere on the mesh. Since the formula involves u at five points, we must find some way to solve for u everywhere. One approach is to rewrite (4.1.3) as

$$u_{i,j} = \frac{1}{4}\left(u_{i-1,j} + u_{i,j+1} + u_{i,j-1} + u_{i+1,j} - h^2 f_{i,j}\right),$$

iterate by choosing values for all mesh points $u_{i,j}$, and then replace them by using[1]

$$u_{i,j}^{k+1} = \frac{1}{4}\left(u_{i-1,j}^k + u_{i,j+1}^k + u_{i,j-1}^k + u_{i+1,j}^k - h^2 f_{i,j}\right).$$

This process, known as *Jacobi iteration*, is repeated until the solution is reached. Fortran code for this is shown in Figure 4.2.

---

[1]The ways in which arrays and matrices correspond to one another and are laid out in memory by Fortran and C compilers are often a source of confusion. We discuss this topic in excruciating detail in Appendix E.1.

```
      integer i, j, n
      double precision u(0:n+1,0:n+1), unew(0:n+1,0:n+1)
      do 10 j=1, n
         do 10 i=1, n
            unew(i,j) =
     $          0.25*(u(i-1,j)+u(i,j+1)+u(i,j-1)+u(i+1,j)) -
     $          h * h * f(i,j)
10    continue
```

Figure 4.2
Jacobi iteration

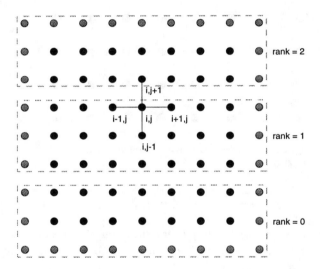

Figure 4.3
1-D decomposition of the domain

To parallelize this algorithm, we need to parallelize the loops in this code. To do this, we must distribute the data, in this case the arrays u, unew, and f, across the processes. Several approaches are possible.

One of the simplest decompositions is shown in Figure 4.3. In this decomposition, the physical domain is sliced into slabs, with the computations on each slab being handled by a different process.

It is easy to describe this decomposition in Fortran. On each process, the arrays are dimensioned as

```
      double precision u(0:n+1,s:e)
```

where s:e indicates the values of j that this process is responsible for. This way of declaring u changes the code for the algorithm to that shown in Figure 4.4.

```
      integer i, j, n
      double precision u(0:n+1,s:e), unew(0:n+1,s:e)
      do 10 j=s, e
         do 10 i=1, n
            unew(i,j) =
     $             0.25*(u(i-1,j)+u(i,j+1)+u(i,j-1)+u(i+1,j)) -
     $             h * h * f(i,j)
 10      continue
```

Figure 4.4
Jacobi iteration for a slice of the domain

Unfortunately, a problem arises. The loop will require elements such as u(i,s-1), that is, data from a different process. The rest of this chapter will discuss how to identify which process the data is from and how to get that data.

But first, let us fix our routine. Since the data is needed, we must expand our arrays to hold the data. In this case, a dimension of

```
      double precision u(0:n+1,s-1:e+1)
```

is sufficient (see Figure 4.5). The elements of the array that are used to hold data from other processes are called *ghost points*. We will show how to get the data for these ghost points in Section 4.3.

4.2 Topologies

Our next task is deciding how to assign processes to each part of the decomposed domain. An extensive literature on this subject (e.g., [33, 39, 59]) exists. Handling this assignment of processes to regions is one of the services that MPI provides to the programmer, exactly because the best (or even a good) choice of decomposition depends on the details of the underlying hardware.

The description of how the processes in a parallel computer are connected to one another is often called the *topology* of the computer (or more precisely, of the interconnection network). In most parallel programs, each process communicates with only a few other processes; the pattern of communication is called an *application topology*. The relationships between the topology of the parallel computer's

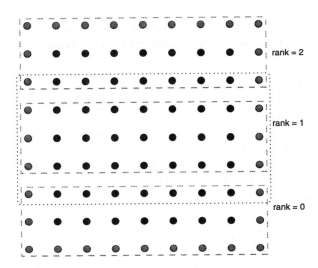

Figure 4.5
The computational domain, with ghost points, for one of the processes

hardware and the application can be made in many ways; some are better than others.

For example, it may seem that simply assigning processes in increasing rank from the bottom is the best approach. On some parallel computers, however, this ordering can lead to performance degradation (see [50, 53] for more details). It is hard for anyone but the vendor to know the best way for application topologies to be fitted onto the physical topology of the parallel machine. MPI allows the vendor to help optimize this aspect of the program through his implementation of the MPI topology functions.

MPI allows the user to define a particular application, or virtual topology. An important virtual topology is the *Cartesian* topology. This is simply a decomposition in the natural coordinate (e.g., x, y) directions. A two-dimensional Cartesian decomposition is shown in Figure 4.6. Each element of the decomposition (rectangles in the figure) is labeled by a coordinate tuple indicating the position of the element in each of the coordinate directions. For example, the second process from the left and the third from the bottom is labeled (1,2). (The indices start from zero, following the practice of C, rather than starting at one, which may be more natural for Fortran users.) MPI provides a collection of routines for defining, examining, and manipulating Cartesian topologies.

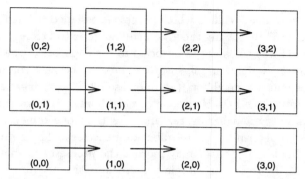

Figure 4.6
A two-dimensional Cartesian decomposition of a domain, also showing a shift by one in the first dimension. Tuples give the coordinates as would be returned by MPI_Get_coords.

The routine MPI_Cart_create creates a Cartesian decomposition of the processes, with the number of dimensions given by the ndim argument. The user can specify the number of processes in any direction by giving a positive value to the corresponding element of dims. For example, to form the decomposition shown in Figure 4.6, one can use the following code:

```
dims(1)    = 4
dims(2)    = 3
periods(1) = .false.
periods(2) = .false.
reorder    = .true.
ndim       = 2
call MPI_CART_CREATE( MPI_COMM_WORLD, ndim, dims, periods,
$                       reorder, comm2d, ierr )
```

This creates a new communicator in the sixth argument from the communicator in the first argument. The new communicator has the Cartesian topology defined by the second through fifth arguments. The periods argument indicates whether the processes at the "ends" are connected together (for example, is the right neighbor of the process at the right end the *leftmost* process in that row?). This is useful for "periodic" domains. For example, in simulating the weather on the Earth within the temperate latitudes using a three-dimensional grid with the dimensions referring to east-west, north-south, and up-down, the first of these is periodic and the other two are not.

Note that we have not specified which process is assigned to each of the elements of the decomposition. By setting the argument `reorder` to `.true.`, we have allowed MPI to find a good way to assign the process to the elements of the decomposition.

In one dimension, we can simply use the rank in the new communicator, plus or minus one, to find our neighbors (and not use `MPI_Cart_create`). Even in this case, this may not be the best choice, since neighbors defined in this way may not be neighbors in the actual hardware. In more than one dimension, however, it is more difficult to determine the neighboring processes. The `reorder` argument, when true, lets MPI know that it may reorder the processes for better perforance.

Fortunately, MPI provides a simple way to find the neighbors of a Cartesian mesh. The most direct way is to use the routine `MPI_Cart_get`. This routine returns both values of the `dims` and `periods` argument used in `Mpi_Cart_create` as well as an array `coords` that contains the Cartesian coordinates of the calling process. For example, the code

```
call MPI_CART_GET( comm1d, 2, dims, periods, coords, ierr )
print *, '(', coords(1), ',', coords(2), ')'
```

will print the coordinates of the calling process in the communicator `comm1d`. Another way is to use `MPI_Cart_coords`; this routine, given a rank in a communicator, returns the coordinates of the process with that rank. For example, to get the coordinates of the calling process, one can use

```
call MPI_COMM_RANK( comm1d, myrank, ierr )
call MPI_CART_COORDS( comm1d, myrank, 2, coords, ierr )
```

However, there is another way that is more closely related to what we are trying to accomplish. Each process needs to send and receive data from its neighbors. In the 1-D decomposition, these are the neighbors above and below. There are many ways to do this, but a simple one is illustrated in Figure 4.7. This represents a copy of the top row from one process to the bottom ghost-point row of the process above it, followed by a copy of the bottom row to the top ghost-point row of the process below. If we look at the first of these operations, we see that each process is both sending and receiving data. In fact, one way to look at this is that data is being shifted up from one process to another. This is a common operation, and MPI provides the routine `MPI_Cart_shift` that may be used to find the neighbors.

Figure 4.6 shows a (nonperiodic) shift by one in the first dimension in a two-dimensional Cartesian grid. `MPI_Cart_shift` may be used to find the destination and source of a shift for each process. For example, the process at Cartesian coordinates $(1, 1)$ has destination at $(2, 1)$ and source at $(0, 1)$. This gives the

```
MPI_CART_CREATE(commold, ndims, dims, periods, reorder, newcomm,ierror)
                integer commold, ndims, dims(*), newcomm, ierror
                logical periodic(*),reorder

MPI_CART_SHIFT(comm, direction, shift, src, dest, ierror )
                integer comm, direction, shift, src, dest, ierror

MPI_CART_GET(comm, maxdims, dims, periods, coords, ierror)
                integer comm, maxdims, dims(*), coords(*), ierror
                logical periods(*)

MPI_CART_COORDS(comm, rank, maxdims, coords, ierror)
                integer comm, rank, maxdims, coords(*), ierror
```

Table 4.1
Fortran bindings for topology routines

neighbors to the left (the rank of the process at coordinates $(0, 1)$) and to the right (the rank of the process at coordinates $(2, 1)$).

What happens for a right shift at the right edge? For example, what is the right neighbor of $(3, 0)$ in Figure 4.6? If the grid were periodic, the right neighbor would be $(0, 0)$. In our application, however, the grid is not periodic, and thus there is no neighbor. This is indicated by the value `MPI_PROC_NULL`. This value is a valid source and a valid destination for all the MPI send and receive routines. The behavior of an `MPI_Send` or `MPI_Recv` with `MPI_PROC_NULL` as a source or destination is identical to code of this form:

```
if (source .ne. MPI_PROC_NULL) then
    call MPI_SEND( ..., source, ... )
endif
```

We will exploit `MPI_PROC_NULL` when we write the code to move data between the processes.

The last routine that we need in defining the decomposition helps us determine the array limits (s and e in the sample code), given the Cartesian coordinate of the process and the size of the array (n in our sample). Because it is a common need, we have provided `MPE_Decomp1d`. To determine the values of s and e, we use

```
call MPE_DECOMP1D( n, size, rank, s, e )
```

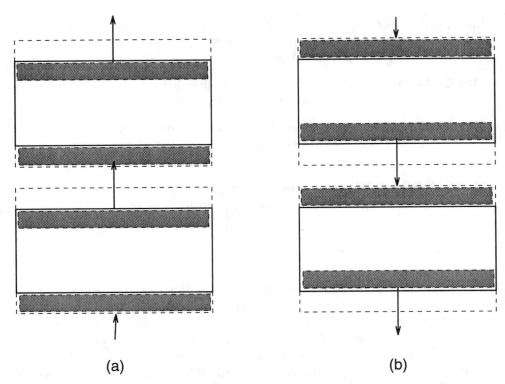

$$(a) \qquad\qquad (b)$$

Figure 4.7
Two-step process to transfer data. Ghost point areas are shown in dashed boxes; data to be
moved is shaded.

where `size` is the number of processes in the Cartesian coordinate, `rank` is the
Cartesian coordinate of the calling process, and `n` is the size of the array (assumed
to run from 1 to `n`). `MPE_Decomp1d` computes values for `s` and `e`. If `n` is evenly
divisible by `size`, this routine isn't really needed; in that case we have

$$s = 1 + rank * \text{floor}(n/size)$$
$$e = s + \text{floor}(n/size) - 1$$

By using this routine, we are ensured that if `size` does not evenly divide `n`, we
will still get correct decomposition of the data, with good load balancing. To see
why, consider using these formulas with `size=64` and `n=127`. Every process gets
$\text{floor}(n/size) = 1$ elements except for the last, which gets $n - 63*\text{floor}(n/size) = 64$.

MPI_SENDRECV(sendbuf, sendcount, sendtype, dest, sendtag, recvbuf,
                recvcount, recvtype, source, recvtag, comm, status, ierror)
                <type> sendbuf(*), recvbuf(*)
                integer sendcount, sendtype, dest, sendtag, recvcount, recvtype,
                source, recvtag, comm, status(MPI_STATUS_SIZE), ierror

MPI_ISEND(buf, count, datatype, dest, tag, comm, request, ierror)
                <type> buf(*)
                integer count, datatype, dest, tag, comm, request, ierror

MPI_IRECV(buf, count, datatype, source, tag, comm, request, ierror)
                <type> buf(*)
                integer count, datatype, source, tag, comm, request, ierror

MPI_WAIT(request, status, ierror)
                integer request, status(MPI_STATUS_SIZE), ierror

MPI_TEST(request, flag, status, ierror)
                logical flag
                integer request, status(MPI_STATUS_SIZE), ierror

MPI_WAITALL(count, array_of_requests, array_of_statuses, ierror)
                integer count, array_of_requests(*),
                array_of_statuses(MPI_STATUS_SIZE,*), ierror

MPI_WAITANY(count, array_of_requests, index, status, ierror)
                integer count, array_of_requests(*), index,
                status(MPI_STATUS_SIZE), ierror

Table 4.2
Fortran bindings for various data exchange routines

MPE_Decomp1d in this case gives processes 0 through 62 two elements and gives the last process a single element.

Now that we know how the data is decomposed among the processes, and how the processes are ranked in the decomposition, we can write the routine to get the data that we need. For each process, we must get the ghost-point data for the s-1 row from the process below and the data for the e+1 row from the process above. Many methods exist to do even this simple operation, and we will investigate several of them through the course of this chapter.

---

int **MPI_Cart_create**(MPI_Comm comm_old, int ndims, int *dims,int *periods,
                   int reorder, MPI_Comm *new_comm)

int **MPI_Cart_shift**(MPI_Comm comm, int direction, int displ,int *src, int *dest)

int **MPI_Cart_get**(MPI_Comm comm, int maxdims, int *dims, int *periods,
              int *coords)

int **MPI_Cart_coords**(MPI_Comm comm, int rank, int maxdims, int *coords)

Table 4.3
C bindings for topology routines

---

int **MPI_Sendrecv**(void *sendbuf, int sendcount, MPI_Datatype sendtype,int dest,
            int sendtag, void *recvbuf, int recvcount, MPI_Datatype recvtype,
            int source, MPI_Datatype recvtag, MPI_Comm comm,
            MPI_Status *status)

int **MPI_Isend**(void* buf, int count, MPI_Datatype datatype, int dest,int tag,
            MPI_Comm comm, MPI_Request *request)

int **MPI_Irecv**(void* buf, int count, MPI_Datatype datatype, int source,int tag,
            MPI_Comm comm, MPI_Request *request)

int **MPI_Wait**(MPI_Request *request, MPI_Status *status)

int **MPI_Test**(MPI_Request *request, int *flag, MPI_Status *status)

int **MPI_Waitall**(int count, MPI_Request *array_of_requests,
            MPI_Status *array_of_statuses)

int **MPI_Waitany**(int count, MPI_Request *array_of_requests,int *index,
            MPI_Status *status)

Table 4.4
C bindings for various data exchange routines

4.3   A Code for the Poisson Problem

In this section we will assemble the pieces of the code that we have defined, as well as the first version of the MPI routines needed to exchange the ghost points between the processes.

The only piece of this code that we have not yet described is the routine to exchange data between the processes. The rest of this chapter will be concerned with different ways to perform this communication operation, and it will pay particular attention to some subtle issues that are often ignored in discussions of message passing. With the warning that we are about to embark on a long journey, we start with perhaps the simplest approach, shown in Figure 4.8.

```
      subroutine exchng1( a, nx, s, e, comm1d, nbrbottom, nbrtop )
      include "mpif.h"
      integer nx, s, e
      double precision a(0:nx+1,s-1:e+1)
      integer comm1d, nbrbottom, nbrtop
      integer status(MPI_STATUS_SIZE), ierr
c
      call MPI_SEND( a(1,e), nx, MPI_DOUBLE_PRECISION,
     $               nbrtop, 0, comm1d, ierr )
      call MPI_RECV( a(1,s-1), nx, MPI_DOUBLE_PRECISION,
     $               nbrbottom, 0, comm1d, status, ierr )
      call MPI_SEND( a(1,s), nx, MPI_DOUBLE_PRECISION,
     $               nbrbottom, 1, comm1d, ierr )
      call MPI_RECV( a(1,e+1), nx, MPI_DOUBLE_PRECISION, \
     $               nbrtop, 1, comm1d, status, ierr )
      return
      end
```

Figure 4.8
Code to exchange data for ghost points using blocking sends and receives

In this routine, each process sends data to the process on top and then receives data from the process below it. The order is then reversed, and data is sent to the process below and received from the process above. We will see below that, while this strategy is simple, it is not necessarily the best way to implement the exchange of ghost points.

We now have all of the pieces needed to put together our first version of the Poisson solver program. This program uses MPI_Cart_create to create the decomposition of processes and the routine MPE_Decomp1d to determine the decomposition of the arrays. The routine onedinit simply initializes the elements of the arrays a, b, and f. The solution is computed alternately in the array a and then b; this is why there are two calls to exchng1 and sweep1d in the loop. The iteration is terminated when the difference between two successive approximations to the solution is less than 1×10^{-5}. The difference between the local parts of a and b is computed with the routine diff; the routine MPI_Allreduce is used to ensure that all processes compute the same value for the difference in all of the elements. The program prints both the progress of the iterations and the final iteration count. A do-loop with a maximum iteration count ensures that the program terminates even if the iteration is not converging. The computational part of the program is shown in Figure 4.9.

Let's run this program, using the MPI profiling interface and the graphical tools to understand the behavior. Using the "automatic" profiling method described in Chapter 7, we use the MPE profiling files mpe_proff.o and mpe_prof.o to generate a logfile of the communication. The 'Makefile' in 'intermediate' contains a target for 'oned'; this is the first version of our Poisson solver. To run it, we give the command

```
oned -np 8
```

(This assumes that we are using the model MPI implementation.)

Using the MPE logging tools described in Section 3.6.3, we can get a graphical display of the communication. One output from upshot is shown in Figure 4.10. Note that the communication is entirely sequential! What went wrong?

Although this is a frequently used communication pattern, it is not a safe one, particularly for large values of nx (long messages). The reason is that the amount of parallelism depends in a subtle way on the amount of buffering provided by the message passing system, which is not explicitly specified by MPI and may be difficult to determine. Let us suppose that we run this on a system with a small amount of system buffer space or with a large message size. Then we will get the behavior displayed in Figure 4.10.

Looking at the upshot output gives us a clue to what has happened. The sends do not complete until the matching receives are issued on the destination process. Since one process (the "top" process) does not send to anyone in the first step, it can receive from the process below it, thus allowing that process to receive from below it, etc. This produces a staircase pattern of sends and receives. We illustrate this in Figure 4.11.

```
c Get a new communicator for a decomposition of the domain
c and my position in it
      call MPI_CART_CREATE( MPI_COMM_WORLD, 1, numprocs, .false.,
     $      .true., comm1d, ierr )
      call MPI_COMM_RANK( comm1d, myid, ierr )
      call MPI_CART_SHIFT( comm1d, 0,  1, nbrbottom, nbrtop, ierr )
c Compute the actual decomposition
      call MPE_DECOMP1D( ny, numprocs, myid, s, e )
c Initialize the right-hand-side (f) and the initial solution guess (a)
      call ONEDINIT( a, b, f, nx, s, e )
c
c Actually do the computation.  Note the use of a collective operation to
c check for convergence, and a do-loop to bound the number of iterations.
c
      do 10 it=1, maxit
c              get ghost points
        call EXCHNG1( a, nx, s, e, comm1d, nbrbottom, nbrtop )
c              perform one Jacobi "sweep"
        call SWEEP1D( a, f, nx, s, e, b )
c              repeat to get a solution back into array a
        call EXCHNG1( b, nx, s, e, comm1d, nbrbottom, nbrtop )
        call SWEEP1D( b, f, nx, s, e, a )
c              check for convergence
        diffw = DIFF( a, b, nx, s, e )
        call MPI_ALLREDUCE( diffw, diffnorm, 1, MPI_DOUBLE_PRECISION,
     $                      MPI_SUM, comm1d, ierr )
        if (diffnorm .lt. 1.0e-5) goto 20
        if (myid .eq. 0) print *, 2*it, ' Difference is ', diffnorm
10      continue
      if (myid .eq. 0) print *, 'Failed to converge'
20      continue
      if (myid .eq. 0) then
          print *, 'Converged after ', 2*it, ' Iterations'
      endif
```

Figure 4.9
Implementation of the Jacobi iteration

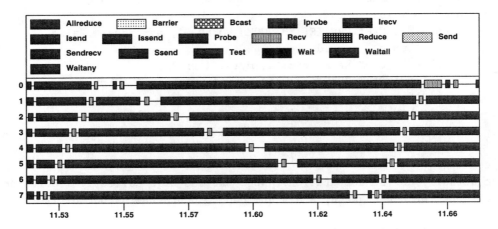

Figure 4.10
Communication in a single iteration for send followed by receive

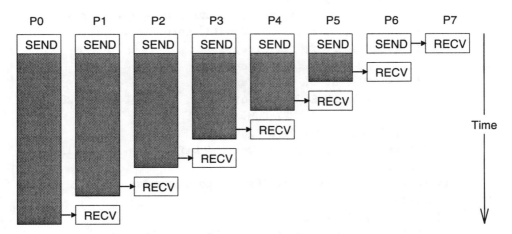

Figure 4.11
Sequentialization caused by sends blocking until the matching receive is posted. The shaded area indicates the time a process is idle, waiting for the send to be allowed to transfer data to the neighboring process

Before we go any further, we need to understand in more detail what happens when we ask MPI (or any message-passing system) to send a message.

Consider the following code:

```
if (rank .eq. 0) then
    call MPI_Send( sbuffer, ..., 1, ... )
else
    call MPI_Recv( rbuffer, ..., 0, ... )
endif
```

What happens on the process with rank zero?

The easy answer is that the message in `sbuffer` is sent to process one. But what if process one is not ready to receive it? Perhaps process one is still computing a previous result. What can process zero do? There are three possibilities: process zero can stop and wait until process one is ready to receive the message, it can copy the message out of `sbuffer` into some internal buffer (which may be located on process zero, process one, or somewhere else) and return from the `MPI_Send` call, or it can fail.

There are good arguments for the first two of these. The argument for the second case is the easiest: as long as there is space available to hold a copy of the message, the message-passing system should provide this service to the programmer rather than forcing the process to stop dead in its tracks until the matching receive is called.

The argument for the first case is, in part, a rebuttal to this. What if there isn't enough space available? We don't want the computation to fail just because the matching receive has not yet been made; perhaps that `MPI_Recv` is about to be called. Since we cannot guarantee that there will be enough space to store a copy of an arbitrary message, why not simply say that we will never copy the message into internal storage?

The MPIF had long and impassioned discussions about these choices; in the end, both of these interpretations were allowed. That is, an MPI implementation is permitted to copy the message to be sent into internal storage in order to permit the `MPI_Send` to return, but it is not required to do so. If the MPI implementation does copy the send buffer into internal storage, we say that it *buffers* the data. Different buffering strategies provide differing levels of convenience and performance.

The third case is also interesting because it allows for certain performance improvements. The use of this kind of send operation is described in Section 7.1.4.

For large applications that are already using a large amount of memory, even requiring the message-passing system to use all "available" memory may not provide enough memory to make this code work. For example, consider a value of nx in the above example that represents more memory space than is free on the process. There is no place to store this message on the sending process, and, until the receiver begins the matching receive, there is no place to store the message on the receiving process. For large applications that are already using large amounts of memory, the value of nx that triggers this situation may be quite small.

The performance problem shown here is even more dangerous. As we saw, the code runs (it does not deadlock) but it does not execute in parallel. All of these issues suggest that programmers should be aware of the pitfalls in assuming that the system will provide adequate buffering. In the next few sections, we will describe ways in which the MPI programmer can ensure that the correct parallel execution of a program does not depend on the amount of buffering, if any, provided by the message-passing system.

Ordered send and receive. One of the easiest ways to correct for a dependence on buffering is to order the sends and receives so that they are paired up. That is, the sends and receives are ordered so that if one process is sending to another, the destination will do a receive that matches that send before doing a send of its own. The code for this approach is shown in Figure 4.12. In this code, the even processes (in Cartesian coordinates) send first, and the odd processes receive first.

Figure 4.13 shows the communication pattern in a single iteration of the Jacobi code when using this approach.

Combined send and receive. The approach of pairing the sends and receives is effective but can be difficult to implement when the arrangement of processes is complex (for example, with an irregular grid). An alternative is to use the MPI routine MPI_Sendrecv. This routine allows you to send and receive data without worrying about deadlock from a lack of buffering. Each process then sends to the process below it and receives from the process above it. The code fragment for this sequence of operations is shown in Figure 4.14.

Buffered sends. Instead of requiring the programmer to determine a safe ordering of the send and receive operations, MPI allows the programmer to provide a buffer into which data can be placed until it is delivered (or at least left the buffer). The change to the exchange routine is simple; one just replaces the MPI_SEND calls with MPI_BSEND. The resulting routine is shown in Figure 4.15.

In addition to the change to the exchange routine, MPI requires that the programmer provide the storage into which the message may be placed with the routine MPI_BUFFER_ATTACH. This buffer should be large enough to hold all of the messages

```
      subroutine exchng1( a, nx, s, e, comm1d, nbrbottom, nbrtop )
      include "mpif.h"
      integer nx, s, e
      double precision a(0:nx+1,s-1:e+1)
      integer comm1d, nbrbottom, nbrtop, rank, coord
      integer status(MPI_STATUS_SIZE), ierr
c
      call MPI_COMM_RANK( comm1d, rank, ierr )
      call MPI_CART_COORDS( comm1d, rank, 1, coord, ierr )
      if (mod( coord, 2 ) .eq. 0) then
        call MPI_SEND( a(1,e), nx, MPI_DOUBLE_PRECISION,
     $                 nbrtop, 0, comm1d, ierr )
        call MPI_RECV( a(1,s-1), nx, MPI_DOUBLE_PRECISION,
     $                 nbrbottom, 0, comm1d, status, ierr )
        call MPI_SEND( a(1,s), nx, MPI_DOUBLE_PRECISION,
     $                 nbrbottom, 1, comm1d, ierr )
        call MPI_RECV( a(1,e+1), nx, MPI_DOUBLE_PRECISION,
     $                 nbrtop, 1, comm1d, status, ierr )
      else
        call MPI_RECV( a(1,s-1), nx, MPI_DOUBLE_PRECISION,
     $                 nbrbottom, 0, comm1d, status, ierr )
        call MPI_SEND( a(1,e), nx, MPI_DOUBLE_PRECISION,
     $                 nbrtop, 0, comm1d, ierr )
        call MPI_RECV( a(1,e+1), nx, MPI_DOUBLE_PRECISION,
     $                 nbrtop, 1, comm1d, status, ierr )
        call MPI_SEND( a(1,s), nx, MPI_DOUBLE_PRECISION,
     $                 nbrbottom, 1, comm1d, ierr )
      endif
      return
      end
```

Figure 4.12
Exchange routine with paired sends and receives

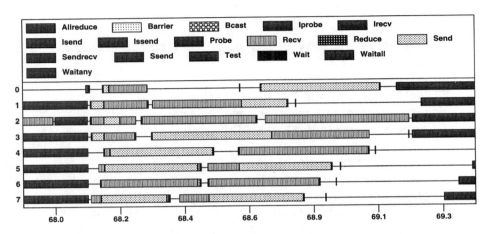

Figure 4.13
Communication in a single iteration with paired sends and receives

```
      subroutine exchng1( a, nx, s, e, comm1d, nbrbottom, nbrtop )
      include "mpif.h"
      integer nx, s, e
      double precision a(0:nx+1,s-1:e+1)
      integer comm1d, nbrbottom, nbrtop
      integer status(MPI_STATUS_SIZE), ierr
c
      call MPI_SENDRECV(
     $          a(1,e), nx, MPI_DOUBLE_PRECISION, nbrtop, 0,
     $          a(1,s-1), nx, MPI_DOUBLE_PRECISION, nbrbottom, 0,
     $          comm1d, status, ierr )
      call MPI_SENDRECV(
     $          a(1,s), nx, MPI_DOUBLE_PRECISION, nbrbottom, 1,
     $          a(1,e+1), nx, MPI_DOUBLE_PRECISION, nbrtop, 1,
     $          comm1d, status, ierr )
      return
      end
```

Figure 4.14
Exchange routine with send-receive

MPI_BSEND(buf, count, datatype, dest, tag, comm, ierror)
                        `<type> buf(*)`
                        `integer count, datatype, dest, tag, comm, ierror`

MPI_BUFFER_ATTACH(buffer, size, ierror)
                        `<type> buffer(*)`
                        `integer size, ierror`

MPI_BUFFER_DETACH(buffer, size, ierror)
                        `<type> buffer(*)`
                        `integer size, ierror`

Table 4.5
Fortran bindings for buffer operations

---

int **MPI_Bsend**(void* buf, int count, MPI_Datatype datatype, int dest, int tag,
                MPI_Comm comm)

int **MPI_Buffer_attach**(void* buffer, int size)

int **MPI_Buffer_detach**(void** buffer, int* size)

Table 4.6
C bindings for buffering routines

that must be sent before the matching receives are called. In our case, we need a buffer of 2*nx double precision values. We can provide this with code like this:

```
double precision buffer(2*MAXNX)
...
call MPI_BUFFER_ATTACH( buffer, 2*MAXNX*8, ierr )
```

The "8" here is the number of bytes in a double-precision value; this value could also be computed with `MPI_Type_extent` as described in Chapter 5.

Once a program no longer needs to use a buffer (or wishes to reclaim it for other use), the routine `MPI_BUFFER_DETACH` should be called. The bindings for these routines are shown in Tables 4.5 and 4.6. (The reason for the `buffer` and `size` arguments in `MPI_Buffer_detach` is that C programmers can use these to find out the location and size of an existing buffer.) It is important to remember that buffering may incur a performance penalty (extra effort copying data to and

```
      subroutine exchng1( a, nx, s, e, comm1d, nbrbottom, nbrtop )
      include "mpif.h"
      integer nx, s, e
      double precision a(0:nx+1,s-1:e+1)
      integer comm1d, nbrbottom, nbrtop
      integer status(MPI_STATUS_SIZE), ierr
c
      call MPI_BSEND( a(1,e), nx, MPI_DOUBLE_PRECISION, nbrtop, 0,
     $               comm1d, ierr )
      call MPI_RECV( a(1,s-1), nx, MPI_DOUBLE_PRECISION, nbrbottom, 0,
     $               comm1d, status, ierr )
      call MPI_BSEND( a(1,s), nx, MPI_DOUBLE_PRECISION, nbrbottom, 1,
     $               comm1d, ierr )
      call MPI_RECV( a(1,e+1), nx, MPI_DOUBLE_PRECISION, nbrtop, 1,
     $               comm1d, status, ierr )
      return
      end
```

Figure 4.15
Exchange routine with buffered sends

from the buffer), and may expose the program to failure if the amount of needed buffering is not calculated correctly.

Another approach involves using communications operations that do not block but permit the program to continue to execute instead of waiting for communications to complete. This also allows the program to compute while waiting for the communications to complete. However, the ability to overlap computation with communication is just one reason to consider the nonblocking operations in MPI; the ability to prevent one communication operation from preventing others from finishing is just as important.

4.4 Using Nonblocking Communications

On most parallel computers, moving data from one process to another takes more time than moving or manipulating data within a single process. For example, on one modern parallel computer, each process can compute up to 125 million floating-point results per second, but can move fewer than one million words per second between processes.[2] To keep a program from being slowed down (also described as "starved for data"), many parallel computers allow users to start sending (and receiving) several messages and to proceed with other operations. Programmers who have used "asynchronous I/O" will recognize this approach as a way of compensating for the relatively slow speed of access to external information (disks in the case of I/O, another process in the case of message passing). MPI supports this approach by providing *nonblocking* sends and receives.

The routine MPI_Isend begins the nonblocking send operation. The arguments are the same as for MPI_Send with the addition of a *handle* as the next to last argument (the last argument in C). The two routines also behave similarly except that, for MPI_Isend, the buffer containing the message to be sent must not be modified until the message has been delivered (more precisely, until the operation is complete, as indicated by one of the MPI_Wait or MPI_Test routines). In C, the type of this handle is MPI_Request.

The *handle* argument is used to determine whether a message has been delivered. The easiest way to test is with MPI_Test:

```
    call MPI_ISEND( buffer, count, datatype, dest, tag,
   $                comm, request, ierr )
     < do other work >
10  call MPI_TEST( request, flag, status, ierr )
    if (.not. flag) goto 10
```

Often, one wishes to wait until the send completes. Rather than writing the loop in the previous example, one can use MPI_Wait instead:

```
    call MPI_WAIT( request, status, ierr )
```

The routine MPI_Irecv begins the nonblocking receive operation. It has one additional argument, the handle, just as MPI_Isend does. It also has one *less* argument: the status argument, which is used to return information on the completed receive, is deleted from the argument list. Just as for MPI_Isend, MPI_Test may be used to test for the completion of a receive started with MPI_Irecv, and MPI_Wait may be used to wait for the completion of such a receive. The status arguments of these two routines return the information on the completed receive in the same form as MPI_Recv does for a blocking receive.

---

[2]This apparent mismatch of capabilities reflects underlying engineering and physical realities and is a major reason that the message-passing approach, which keeps the programmer reminded of the cost of accessing remote data, has been a successful way to program parallel computers.

In many cases, one wishes to test or wait for many nonblocking operations. Although one can simply loop through the operations, this approach is inefficient, since this forces the user's program to be constantly executing rather than waiting (possibly without consuming CPU time) for the "next" message. MPI provides a way to wait for all or any of a collection of nonblocking operations (with `MPI_Waitall` and `MPI_Waitany`) and to test all or any of a collection of nonblocking operations (with `MPI_Testall` and `MPI_Testany`). For example, to start two nonblocking receives and then wait on them, one can use

```
call MPI_IRECV( ..., requests(1), ierr )
call MPI_IRECV( ..., requests(2), ierr )
...
call MPI_WAITALL( 2, requests, status, ierr )
```

Here, `status` must be an array of two `MPI_status` objects; it can be declared with

```
integer status(MPI_STATUS_SIZE,2)
```

With these routines, we can rewrite the exchange routine `exchng1` using nonblocking operations, as shown in Figure 4.16. This approach allows for both sends and receives to take place at the same time. In principle, this approach can be almost twice as fast as the version in Figure 4.12, though few existing systems support this (don't forget that MPI was designed to support current and future message-passing systems). In the next section, we try them out and see what happens.

Note that in order to overlap communication and computation, we must make further changes to our program. In particular, we need to change the `sweep` program to allow us to do some of the work while we wait for data to arrive. We will come back to nonblocking operations in Section 4.9, where we discuss overlapping communication with computation.

4.5   Synchronous Sends and "Safe" Programs

What can we do to ensure that a program does not depend on buffering? In general, this is equivalent to the Turing halting-problem and is hence unanswerable, but in many special cases it is possible to show that if the program runs successfully with no buffering, it will run with any amount of buffering. MPI provides a way to send a message in such a way that the send does not return until the destination begins to receive the message. The routine is `MPI_Ssend`. The arguments to this

```
      subroutine exchng1( a, nx, s, e, comm1d,
$                         nbrbottom, nbrtop )
      include "mpif.h"
      integer nx, s, e
      double precision a(0:nx+1,s-1:e+1)
      integer comm1d, nbrbottom, nbrtop
      integer status_array(MPI_STATUS_SIZE,4), ierr, req(4)
c
      call MPI_IRECV (
$         a(1,s-1), nx, MPI_DOUBLE_PRECISION, nbrbottom, 0,
$         comm1d, req(1), ierr )
      call MPI_IRECV (
$         a(1,e+1), nx, MPI_DOUBLE_PRECISION, nbrtop, 1,
$         comm1d, req(2), ierr )
      call MPI_ISEND (
$         a(1,e), nx, MPI_DOUBLE_PRECISION, nbrtop, 0,
$         comm1d, req(3), ierr )
      call MPI_ISEND (
$         a(1,s), nx, MPI_DOUBLE_PRECISION, nbrbottom, 1,
$         comm1d, req(4), ierr )
c
      call MPI_WAITALL ( 4, req, status_array, ierr )
      return
      end
```

Figure 4.16
Row-exchange routine using nonblocking operations

send are identical to `MPI_Send`. Note that it is permissible for an MPI operation to implement `MPI_Send` with `MPI_Ssend`; thus, for maximum portability, one should ensure that any use of `MPI_Send` can be replaced with `MPI_Ssend`. Programs that do not require buffering (or, with `MPI_Bsend`, only the amount of buffering made available) for their correct operation are sometimes called *safe*.

4.6   More on Scalability

Because we have encapsulated the routines to exchange data between the processes, it is a simple matter to link the program with different methods and to compare

P	Blocking Send	Ordered Send	Sendrecv	Buffered Bsend	Noblock Isend
1	5.38	5.54	5.54	5.38	5.40
2	2.77	2.88	2.91	2.75	2.77
4	1.58	1.56	1.57	1.50	1.51
8	1.15	0.947	0.931	0.854	0.849
16	1.18	0.574	0.534	0.521	0.545
32	1.94	0.443	0.451	0.452	0.397
64	3.73	0.447	0.391	0.362	0.391

Table 4.7
Timings for variants of the 1-D decomposition of the Poisson problem

them. Table 4.7 shows the results for one particular parallel computer and MPI implementation.

Before going on, we note that each iteration of the loop calls `MPI_Allreduce`. This routine can take a significant amount of time; on networks of workstations, it can take many milliseconds. In many applications, the effective cost of the `MPI_Allreduce` is reduced by taking a number of iterations without computing the difference between successive iterates; this approach works because the Jacobi method converges very slowly.

A quick examination of Table 4.7 reveals a number of interesting features. First, with the exception of the blocking sends, the performance of the other methods is roughly the same. The blocking sends case shows the lack of parallelism in the communication; with thirtytwo processes, the computation actually takes longer than with four processes. More serious is the poor performance of the other methods. At 64 processes, the program is running only about fourteen times as fast as for a single process, for an efficiency of about 20%.

To understand the performance of these methods, we perform a simple scalability analysis similar to the one in Chapter 3. We will need a slightly more sophisticated model of communication cost than used in Chapter 3. There, we used T_{comm} as the time to send a word. We will replace this with $s + rn$ as the time to send n bytes; for n large, we have $T_{comm} \approx r * 8$. The term s is the latency or startup time; it can be thought of as the time to send a message containing no data beyond the message tag and source. The term r is the inverse rate; it is the time to send a single byte and is given by one over the bandwidth. For example, if the bandwidth of a connection is 10 MB/sec, $r = 1/(10\text{MB/sec}) = 10^{-7}$ sec/byte. Using this

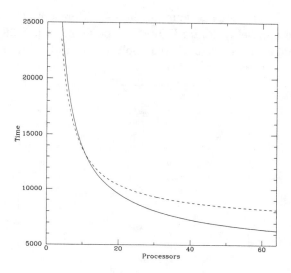

Figure 4.17
Predicted time for a 1-D (dashed) and 2-D (solid) decomposition of the 2-D Poisson problem

formula, we can easily see that the `exchng1d` routine in Figure 4.12 takes roughly $2(s + rn)$ time, where $n = 8$ `nx` (assuming 8-byte double-precision data).

In a two-dimensional decomposition, let there be p_x processes in the x direction and p_y processes in the y direction, with each process having the same number of mesh points. Then, with the exception of the processes on any edge of the domain, the amount of communication T_c is

$$T_c = 2 \left(s + r \frac{n}{p_x} \right) + 2 \left(s + r \frac{n}{p_y} \right).$$

If $p_x = p_y = \sqrt{p}$, this takes a particularly simple form:

$$T_c = 4 \left(s + r \frac{n}{\sqrt{p}} \right).$$

Figure 4.17 shows the expected performance for both 1-D and 2-D decompositions of the domain, based on these estimates. The situation is even more extreme in 3-D, as shown in Figure 4.18. Note that, for small numbers of processes, this model suggests that a 1-D decomposition is actually better than a 2-D decomposition. Care must be exercised here, as our analysis is good in the 2-D case only for $p \geq 9$, since for $p < 9$, no process has four neighbors. More details on analyzing the communication in parallel codes for PDEs may be found in [36, 38]; an example of using these techniques to analyze a large application can be found in [25].

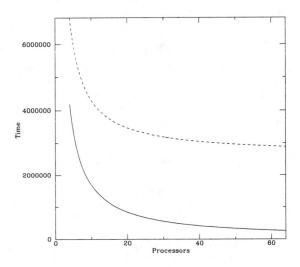

Figure 4.18
Predicted time for a 1-D (dashed) and 3-D (solid) decomposition of the 3-D Poisson problem

4.7   Jacobi with a 2-D Decomposition

Figures 4.17 and 4.18 and this scalability analysis suggest that we need to rewrite our program to use these higher-dimensional decompositions. Fortunately, MPI makes this task relatively easy. We will show how a few modifications to the program in Figure 4.9 changes it from a one-dimensional to two-dimensional decomposition.

First, we let MPI compute the decomposition of the domain for us with MPI_Cart_create:

```
      periods(1) = .false.
      periods(2) = .false.
      reorder    = .true.
      call MPI_CART_CREATE( MPI_COMM_WORLD, 2, dims, periods,
```

```
$                                     reorder, comm2d, ierr )
```

Compare this with the 1-D code in Section 4.2.

Next, we get left and right neighbors as well as the top and bottom neighbors:

```
call MPI_CART_SHIFT( comm2d, 0,  1, nbrleft, nbrright, ierr )
call MPI_CART_SHIFT( comm2d, 1,  1, nbrbottom, nbrtop, ierr )
```

We change the body of the sweep routine to

```
      integer i, j, n
      double precision u(sx-1:ex+1,sy-1:ey+1),
$                      unew(sx-1:ex+1,sy-1:ey+1),
      do 10 j=sy, ey
        do 10 i=sx, ex
          unew(i,j) =
$               0.25*(u(i-1,j)+u(i,j+1)+u(i,j-1)+u(i+1,j)) -
$               h * h * f(i,j)
 10   continue
```

The last routine that we need to change is the data exchange routine (exchng1d in the 1-D examples). This is a little more difficult because, while the data sent to the top and bottom processes is stored contiguously in memory, the data sent to the left and right processes is not.

4.8   An MPI Derived Datatype

One of MPI's novel features is its use of a datatype associated with every message. Specifying the length of a message as a given count of occurrences of a given datatype is more portable than using length in bytes, since lengths of given types may vary from one machine to another. It also allows MPI to provide translations between machine formats.

So far all of our messages have consisted of contiguous areas in memory, so the basic datatypes such as MPI_INTEGER and MPI_DOUBLE_PRECISION, accompanied by a count, have been sufficient to describe our messages. In this section we introduce MPI's *derived datatypes*, which allow us to specify *noncontiguous* areas in memory, such as a row of an array stored columnwise (or, in our case, a column of an array stored rowwise).

This is a common situation, and MPI provides a mechanism for describing this kind of data layout. We begin by defining a new datatype that describes a group of elements that are separated by a constant amount in memory (a constant *stride*). We do this with the `MPI_Type_vector`:

```
call MPI_TYPE_VECTOR( ey + 1 - (sy - 1), 1, ex + 1 - (sx - 1),
$                     MPI_DOUBLE_PRECISION, stridetype, ierr )
call MPI_TYPE_COMMIT( stridetype, ierr )
```

The arguments to `MPI_Type_vector` describe a *block*, which consists of a number of (contiguous) copies of the input datatype given by the second argument. The first argument is the number of blocks; the second is the number of elements of the old datatype in each block (this is often one). The old datatype is the fourth argument. The third argument is the *stride*; this is the distance in terms of the extent of the input datatype between successive elements. The fifth argument is the created derived datatype. In this example, there is one double precision item per block; the double-precision values are `ex + 1 - (sx - 1)` apart, and there are `ey + 1 - (sy - 1)` of them. Figure 4.19 illustrates an MPI vector datatype.

Note that after the new datatype is created with the `MPI_Type_vector` command, we *commit* it to the system with `MPI_Type_commit`. This routine takes the newly constructed datatype and gives the system the opportunity to perform any performance optimizations that it may wish to. All user-constructed data types must be committed before they can be used.

With this new datatype definition, the MPI code for sending a row differs from the code for sending a column only in the datatype argument. The final version of `exchng2d` is shown in Figure 4.20.

When a datatype is no longer needed, it should be freed with `MPI_Type_free`. The datatype variable (the first argument) is set to `MPI_TYPE_NULL` by `MPI_Type_free`. Bindings for these routines are shown in Tables 4.8 and 4.9.

An alternative definition of the strided type is described in Section 5.4 that allows the programmer to send any number of elements with the same datatype.

4.9   Overlapping Communication and Computation

Because of the time it can take to move data from one process to another, it is often advantageous to arrange the program so that some work can be done while the messages are "in transit." So far, we have used nonblocking operations to avoid deadlock in the communications. Here we describe some of the details in arranging a program so that computation and communication can take place simultaneously.

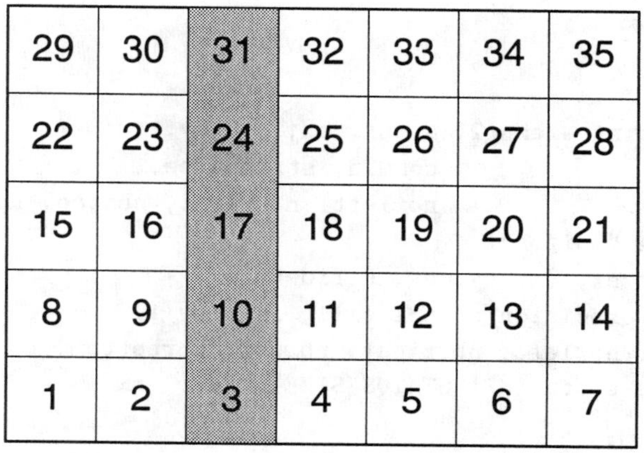

29	30	31	32	33	34	35
22	23	24	25	26	27	28
15	16	17	18	19	20	21
8	9	10	11	12	13	14
1	2	3	4	5	6	7

```
MPI_TYPE_VECTOR( 5, 1, 7, MPI_DOUBLE_PRECISION, newtype, ierr )
```

Figure 4.19
A strided data item (shaded) and its MPI definition. Numbers indicate consecutive memory locations.

MPI_TYPE_VECTOR(count, blocklength, stride, oldtype, newtype, ierror)
    integer count, blocklength, stride, oldtype, newtype, ierror

MPI_TYPE_COMMIT(datatype, ierror)
    integer datatype, ierror

MPI_TYPE_FREE(datatype, ierror)
    integer datatype, ierror

Table 4.8
Fortran bindings for elementary MPI datatype routines

---

int **MPI_Type_vector**(int count, int blocklength, int stride, MPI_Datatype oldtype,
    MPI_Datatype *newtype)

int **MPI_Type_commit**(MPI_Datatype *datatype)

int **MPI_Type_free**(MPI_Datatype *datatype)

Table 4.9
C bindings for MPI elementary datatype routines

```fortran
      subroutine exchng2( a, sx, ex, sy, ey,
     $                    comm2d, stridetype,
     $                    nbrleft, nbrright, nbrtop, nbrbottom  )
      include "mpif.h"
      integer sx, ex, sy, ey, stridetype
      double precision a(sx-1:ex+1, sy-1:ey+1)
      integer nbrleft, nbrright, nbrtop, nbrbottom, comm2d
      integer status(MPI_STATUS_SIZE), ierr, nx
c
      nx = ex - sx + 1
c  These are just like the 1-d versions, except for less data
      call MPI_SENDRECV( a(sx,ey),   nx, MPI_DOUBLE_PRECISION,
     $                          nbrtop, 0,
     $                   a(sx,sy-1), nx, MPI_DOUBLE_PRECISION,
     $                   nbrbottom, 0, comm2d, status, ierr )
      call MPI_SENDRECV( a(sx,sy),   nx, MPI_DOUBLE_PRECISION,
     $                   nbrbottom, 1,
     $                   a(sx,ey+1), nx, MPI_DOUBLE_PRECISION,
     $                   nbrtop, 1, comm2d, status, ierr )
c
c This uses the "strided" datatype
      call MPI_SENDRECV( a(ex,sy),   1, stridetype, nbrright, 0,
     $                   a(sx-1,sy), 1, stridetype, nbrleft, 0,
     $                   comm2d, status, ierr )
      call MPI_SENDRECV( a(sx,sy),   1, stridetype, nbrleft,    1,
     $                   a(ex+1,sy), 1, stridetype, nbrright, 1,
     $                   comm2d, status, ierr )
      return
      end
```

Figure 4.20
Two-dimensional exchange with sendrecv

In the Jacobi method, the values of unew at points of the mesh that are interior to the domain on each process may be computed without needing any data from any other process; this is shown in Figure 4.21.

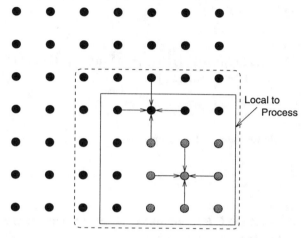

Figure 4.21
The shaded points show those mesh points whose computation does not depend on any data from other processes. The local domain is given by the solid outline; the domain with ghost points is given by the dashed box.

We can arrange our computational task as follows: (1), indicate where to receive data from other processes; (2), begin sending data to the other processes; (3), compute with the local data; and (4), receive data from the other processes and finish computing with it. Separating the code into these four steps does increase the amount of code, but all of it is easily derived from our existing code. For example, Step 3 is given by the code in Figure 4.22.

All that we have done here is to select the part of the domain that is one away from the edges of the local domain, ensuring that all of the data is available.

The communication routines change in similar ways; in addition, the calls are split into two sections of code, separated by the main computational section. The first part begins both the nonblocking sends and nonblocking receives:

```
call MPI_IRECV( ..., requests(1), ierr )
...
call MPI_ISEND( ..., requests(5), ierr )
```

```
      integer i, j, n
      double precision u(sx-1:ex+1,sy-1:ey+1),
     $                  unew(sx-1:ex+1,sy-1:ey+1)
      do 10 j=sy+1, ey-1
         do 10 i=sx+1, ex-1
            unew(i,j) =
     $              0.25*(u(i-1,j)+u(i,j+1)+u(i,j-1)+u(i+1,j)) -
     $                  h * h * f(i,j)
 10   continue
```

Figure 4.22
Code to compute a Jacobi iteration with only local data

These are followed by[3]

```
      do 100 i=1,8
          call MPI_WAITANY( 8, requests, idx, status, ierr )
c         Use tag to determine which edge
          goto (1,2,3,4,100,100,100,100), status(MPI_TAG,idx)
1         do 11 j=sy,ey
11            unew(si,j) = ...
          goto 100
2         do 21 j=sy,ey
21            unew(ei,j) = ...
          goto 100
3         do 31, i=sx,ex
31            unew(i,ej) = ...
          goto 100
4         do 41 i=sx,ex
41            unew(i,sj) = ...
          goto 100
100   continue
```

Here, requests(1) through requests(4) are receive handles, and requests(5) through requests(8) are send handles.

---

[3]For C programmers: the construction goto (...), variable is similar to the C switch (variable) except that the values are labels and the variable is in the range 1 to the number of labels.

```
MPI_BARRIER(comm,ierr)
                integer comm,ierr
```

Table 4.10
Fortran bindings for barrier routine

```
int MPI_Barrier( MPI_Comm comm )
```

Table 4.11
C bindings for barrier routine

4.10   More on Timing Programs

Our simple code can also be used to solve time-dependent PDEs. Many discretizations for time-dependent PDEs require only the data that our Jacobi iteration needs. The only difference is that the **sweep** routines change and there is no longer any need for the MPI_Allreduce to check for convergence. However, this does raise an issue when timing this program: how do we know that everyone is done when we call MPI_Wtime? We can use the MPI routine MPI_Barrier to ensure that everyone has completed the computation. A barrier is a special collective operation that does not let the process continue until all processes in the communicator have called MPI_Barrier.

```
call MPI_Barrier( MPI_COMM_WORLD, ierr )
t1 = MPI_Wtime()
<do work>
call MPI_Barrier( MPI_COMM_WORLD, ierr )
total_time = MPI_Wtime() - t1
```

The barriers ensure that all processes have reached the same point in the code and are ready to proceed. Many of the collective operations (e.g., MPI_Allreduce) have the same property; that is, no process can exit the operation until all processes have entered. Note that this is not true for operations like MPI_Reduce, where only the root process must wait for all other processes to enter the MPI_Reduce call. The bindings for MPI_Barrier are shown in Tables 4.10 and 4.11.

> **MPI_DIMS_CREATE**(nnodes,ndims,dims,ierr)
> integer nnodes, ndims, dims(*),ierr

Table 4.12
Fortran binding for `MPI_DIMS_CREATE`

> int **MPI_Dims_create**(int nnodes, int ndims, int *dims)

Table 4.13
C binding for `MPI_DIMS_CREATE`

4.11   Three Dimensions

So far, we have restricted ourselves to the 2-D problem. Now, we want to introduce the 3-D case, and also show the problem in a C implementation. Even a relatively small 3-D problem having 100 grid points on a side involves 10^6 grid points; it is common to encounter one or two orders of magnitude more grid points than this in 3-D simulations. These problems are consequently ideal candidates for parallel computing. The flexibility of MPI makes generalizing our previous 2-D problem solutions to 3-D straightforward.

One complication in developing a 3-D code is the decomposition of the domain among the processes. As we would expect from the scalability analysis in this chapter, we should use a 3-D virtual topology. MPI provides the routine `MPI_Dims_create` to help in generating a Cartesian virtual topology with any number of dimensions. This routine takes as input the total number of processes and the number of dimensions, and returns an array containing the Cartesian dimensions. The bindings are shown in Tables 4.12 and 4.13. Sample code for a 3-D problem is available in the directory 'intermediate/3d' and may be downloaded according to the directions in Appendix D.

4.12   Application: Simulating Vortex Evolution in Superconducting Materials

As an example of an application that uses the techniques described in this chapter, we briefly discuss a model of superconductivity.

The time-dependent Ginzburg-Landau (TDGL) equation can be used for the numerical simulation of vortex dynamics and phase transitions in type-II superconductors. The TDGL equation provides a phenomenological description of the macroscopic properties of high-temperature superconductors and has been remarkably successful in explaining experimental results on phase transitions. The TDGL equation is a partial differential equation for the complex-valued order parameter with stochastic coefficients. This model uses a field description of vortices as described by the time-dependent Ginzburg-Landau equation in three dimensions.

A group at Argonne National Laboratory [28] has parallelized a three-dimensional TDGL program by partitioning the superconductor data structure among the processes. Each processes' memory contains a "cubelet" of the original global data structure. Each process is then responsible for the time integration over its part of the superconductor. The time integration is done using the forward Euler technique. Finite differences are used to approximate the derivatives using a box (27-point) stencil.

Using this program, researchers have been able to answer several questions about the behavior of high-temperature superconductors. The computations require very high resolution.

The update step for each cell requires values from neighboring cells. Because of the array decomposition, neighbors of some of the cells that a process has require values from cells stored in other processes' memories. To communicate these values, routines similar to the exchange routines described for the Poisson problem are used.

5 Advanced Message Passing in MPI

This chapter discusses some of the more advanced features from the MPI Standard [24] that have not arisen in the discussion so far. It also provides a more complete discussion of some features already introduced briefly. We use the opportunity to introduce several interesting example programs.

5.1 MPI Datatypes

One of MPI's unusual features is the introduction of a datatype argument for all messages sent and received. In the early chapters of this book, we have relied primarily on elementary datatypes that correspond to the base datatypes in the host programming language—integers, floating-point numbers, etc., and arrays of these. In this section we discuss the complete set of datatypes and take the opportunity to describe the full power of MPI's derived datatype features. The examples we describe, the N-body problem and Mandelbrot computations, also allow us to exercise some more of the graphics part of the MPE library.

5.1.1 Basic Datatypes and Concepts

MPI starts by providing a rich set of predefined datatypes. These include all of the basic datatypes in C (Table 5.1) and Fortran (Table 5.2). Included in both lists are two datatypes specific to MPI: `MPI_BYTE` and `MPI_PACKED`. `MPI_BYTE` refers to a *byte* which is defined as eight binary digits. Many C and Fortran programmers may wonder why this is needed when they have `MPI_CHAR` and `MPI_CHARACTER`, respectively. There are two reasons. First, while many implementations represent `char` and `character` as bytes, this representation is not required. A version of C for Japanese could choose 16-bit `chars`, for example. The second reason is that in a heterogeneous environment, machines may have different character sets. For example, a system that uses ASCII uses different bits to represent the character A than does a system that uses EBCDIC. `MPI_PACKED` is described in Section 5.2.3.

As we have already seen in Section 4.8, it is often useful to define additional datatypes. MPI provides for arbitrary datatypes; the rest of this section concerns how MPI describes a general datatype.

In MPI, a datatype is an object that specifies a sequence of the basic datatypes (Tables 5.1 and 5.2) and displacements, in bytes, of each of these datatypes. These displacements are taken to be relative to the buffer that the datatype is describing (see Section 3.5). We will represent a datatype as a sequence of pairs of basic types and displacements as shown in (5.1.1); MPI calls this sequence the *typemap*.

MPI Datatype	C Datatype
`MPI_BYTE`	
`MPI_CHAR`	`signed char`
`MPI_DOUBLE`	`double`
`MPI_FLOAT`	`float`
`MPI_INT`	`int`
`MPI_LONG`	`long`
`MPI_LONG_DOUBLE`	`long double`
`MPI_PACKED`	
`MPI_SHORT`	`short`
`MPI_UNSIGNED_CHAR`	`unsigned char`
`MPI_UNSIGNED`	`unsigned int`
`MPI_UNSIGNED_LONG`	`unsigned long`
`MPI_UNSIGNED_SHORT`	`unsigned short`

Table 5.1
Basic (predefined) MPI datatypes for C

$$\text{Typemap} = \{(type_0, disp_0), \ldots, (type_{n-1}, disp_{n-1})\} \tag{5.1.1}$$

For example, the type `MPI_INT` can be represented as the typemap (`int,0`).

The *type signature* of a datatype is just a list of the basic datatypes in a datatype:

$$\text{Type signature} = \{type_0, \ldots, type_{n-1}\}$$

The type signature describes what basic types make up an MPI datatype; it is the type signature that controls how data items are interpreted when data is sent or received. In other words, it tell MPI how to interpret the bits in a data buffer. The displacements tell MPI where to find the bits.

To understand how MPI assembles user-defined datatypes, we need to introduce a few terms. Let an MPI datatype have typemap given by (5.1.1). We define

$$lb(\text{Typemap}) = \min_j(disp_j) \tag{5.1.2}$$

$$ub(\text{Typemap}) = \max_j(disp_j + \texttt{sizeof}(type_j)) \tag{5.1.3}$$

$$extent(\text{Typemap}) = ub(\text{Typemap}) - lb(\text{Typemap}) + pad \tag{5.1.4}$$

lb is the *lower bound* of the displacements of the components of the datatype; it can be considered the location of the first byte described by the datatype. *ub* is

MPI Datatype	Fortran Datatype
MPI_BYTE	
MPI_CHARACTER	CHARACTER
MPI_COMPLEX	COMPLEX
MPI_DOUBLE_PRECISION	DOUBLE PRECISION
MPI_INTEGER	INTEGER
MPI_LOGICAL	LOGICAL
MPI_PACKED	
MPI_REAL	REAL

Table 5.2
Basic (predefined) MPI datatypes for Fortran

the *upper bound* of the datatype; it can be considered the location of the last byte described by the datatype. The extent is the difference between these two, possibly increased to meet an alignment requirement. The `sizeof` operator in (5.1.3) is the size of the *basic* datatype in bytes.

To understand the role of the "pad," we need to discuss data *alignment*. Both C and Fortran require that the basic datatypes be properly aligned, that is, that the locations of, for example, an integer or a double-precision value occur only where allowed. Each implementation of these languages defines what is allowed (there are, of course, some restrictions). One of the most common requirements made by an implementation of these languages is that the address of an item in bytes be a multiple of the length of that item in bytes. For example, if an `int` takes four bytes, then the address of an `int` must be evenly divisible by four. This requirement is reflected in the definition of the extent of an MPI datatype. Consider the typemap

$$\{(int, 0), (char, 4)\} \tag{5.1.5}$$

on a computer that requires that `int`'s be aligned on 4-byte boundaries. This typemap has $lb = \min(0, 4) = 0$ and $ub = \max(0 + 4, 4 + 1) = 5$. But the next `int` can be placed with displacement eight from the `int` in the typemap. This makes the extent of this typemap *on the computer we are discussing* eight.

To find the extent of a datatype, MPI provides the routine `MPI_Type_extent`. The first argument is the MPI datatype; the extent is returned in the second argument. In C, the type of the second argument is `MPI_Aint`; this is an integer type that can hold an arbitrary address (on many but not all systems, this will be an `int`). The extent of the basic datatypes (those in Tables 5.1 and 5.2) are the same as the number of bytes in them.

The size of a datatype is the number of bytes that the data takes up. This is given by `MPI_Type_size`; the first argument is the datatype, and the size is returned in the second argument. The difference between the extent and size of a datatype is illustrated by the typemap in (5.1.5): the size is five bytes, but the extent (on a computer that requires `int`s be aligned on four-byte boundaries) is eight bytes. Rounding out the routines to get the properties of an MPI datatype are `MPI_Type_ub`, to get the upper bound, and `MPI_Type_lb`, to get the lower bound. Bindings for the datatype routines described here are given in Tables 5.3 and 5.4.

---

int **MPI_Type_contiguous**(int count, MPI_Datatype oldtype,
        MPI_Datatype *newtype)

int **MPI_Type_extent**(MPI_Datatype datatype, MPI_Aint *extent)

int **MPI_Type_size**(MPI_Datatype datatype, MPI_Aint *size)

int **MPI_Type_count**(MPI_Datatype datatype, int *count)

int **MPI_Type_lb**(MPI_Datatype datatype, MPI_Aint *displacement)

int **MPI_Type_ub**(MPI_Datatype datatype, MPI_Aint *displacement)

Table 5.3
C bindings for MPI datatype routines

5.1.2   Derived Datatypes

The typemap is a completely general way of describing an arbitrary datatype. However, it may not be convenient, particularly if the resulting typemap contains large numbers of entries. MPI provides a number of ways to create datatypes without explicitly constructing the typemap.

Contiguous: This is the simplest constructor. It produces a new datatype by making `count` copies of an existing one, with the displacements incremented by the extent of the `oldtype`.

Vector: This is a slight generalization of the contiguous type that allows for regular gaps in the displacements. Elements are separated by multiples of the extent of the input datatype. See Section 4.8.

MPI_TYPE_CONTIGUOUS(count, oldtype, newtype, ierror)
>   integer count, oldtype, newtype, ierror

MPI_TYPE_EXTENT(datatype, extent, ierror)
>   integer datatype, extent, ierror

MPI_TYPE_SIZE(datatype, size, ierror)
>   integer datatype, size, ierror

MPI_TYPE_COUNT(datatype, count, ierror)
>   integer datatype, count, ierror

MPI_TYPE_LB(datatype, displacement, ierror)
>   integer datatype, displacement, ierror

MPI_TYPE_UB(datatype, displacement, ierror)
>   integer datatype, displacement, ierror

Table 5.4
Fortran bindings for MPI datatype routines

Hvector: This is like vector, but elements are separated by a specified number of bytes.

Indexed: In this datatype, an array of displacements of the input datatype is provided; the displacements are measured in terms of the extent of the input datatype. See Section 5.2.3.

Hindexed: This is like indexed, but the displacements are measured in bytes. See Section 5.2.4.

Struct: This provides a fully general description. In fact, if the input arguments consist of the basic MPI datatypes, the input is just the typemap. See Section 5.3.

We will describe the MPI functions that create these datatypes as we encounter them. We will discuss the contiguous type here, because that datatype explains how the `count` argument in MPI routines applies to these derived datatypes.

The routine `MPI_Type_contiguous` produces a new datatype by making `count` copies of an existing one, with the displacements incremented by the extent of the `oldtype`. For example, if the original datatype (`oldtype`) has typemap $\{(int, 0), (double, 8)\}$, then

```
MPI_Type_contiguous( 2, oldtype, &newtype );
```

produces a datatype `newtype` with typemap

$\{(int, 0), (double, 8), (int, 16), (double, 24)\}$.

When a `count` argument is used in an MPI operation, it is the same as if a contiguous type of the that size had been constructed. That is,

```
MPI_Send( buffer, count, datatype, dest, tag, comm );
```

is the same as

```
MPI_Type_contiguous( count, datatype, &newtype );
MPI_Type_commit( &newtype );
MPI_Send( buffer, 1, newtype, dest, tag, comm );
MPI_Type_free( &newtype );
```

5.2 The N-Body Problem

Many simulations involve computing the interaction of a large number of particles or objects. If the force between the particles is completely described by adding the forces between all pairs of particles, and the force between each pair acts along the line between them, this is called an N-body central force problem (often just an N-body problem). Such a problem is a good choice for parallelization, since it can be described with N items (the particles) but requires $\mathcal{O}(N^2)$ computation (all the pairs of particles). This means that we can expect good speedups for large problems because the communication between processes will be small relative to the computation.

In this section, we will use the N-body problem to describe a number of MPI features, including some new collective operations, persistent communication requests, and some new derived datatypes.

In implementing an N-body code, we need first to decide how the particles are distributed among the processes. One simple way is to divide the particles evenly among the processes. For example, if there are 1000 particles and 10 processes, put the first 100 particles on process 0, the second 100 particles on process 1, and so forth. To compute the forces on the particles, it is necessary for each process to access all the particles on the other processes. (There is an important optimization that involves exploiting the fact that the forces are equal and opposite; this can reduce the computation by a factor of two. For simplicity, we do not make use of this property.)

To begin with, let us define a particle datatype. Let us assume that a particle is defined by the structure

```
typedef struct {
    double x, y, z;
    double mass;
    } Particle;
```

and that the particles are stored in an array:

```
Particle particles[MAX_PARTICLES];
```

To send this data, we could just always send four doubles for each particle, but it makes more sense in MPI to create a datatype for a particle consisting of four doubles:

```
MPI_Type_contiguous( 4, MPI_DOUBLE, &particletype );
MPI_Type_commit( &particletype );
```

(We should really use `MPI_Type_struct` to build this structure, but `MPI_Type_contiguous` will work on almost any system for this particular case. We will cover the use of `MPI_Type_struct` in Section 5.3.)

5.2.1 Gather

The simplest approach is for all processes to exchange all the particles and then compute with them. In this approach, all processes will have copies of all of the particles, computing only the forces on the particles held locally.[1] For example, each process could do

```
MPI_Comm_size( MPI_COMM_WORLD, &size );
for (i=0; i<size; i++) {
    MPI_Send( particles, count, particletype, i, 0,
            MPI_COMM_WORLD );
    }
for (i=0; i<size; i++) {
    MPI_Recv( particleloc[i], MAX_PARTICLES, particletype, i, 0,
            MPI_COMM_WORLD, &status );
    }
```

(For reasons that will soon be clear, we have deliberately left the sends and receives from a process to itself in this code.) This code has many problems: it does not scale (it takes time proportional to the number of processes), it may deadlock, and

---

[1]This approach is suitable only for relatively small number of particles; it may be used if the forces are particularly complicated or if long spans of time need to be computed.

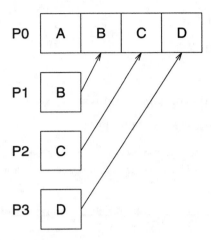

Figure 5.1
Data motion for a gather operation with p0 as root

it needs the locations `particleloc[i]` computed before this code can be used. We could use the techniques in Chapter 4 get around the deadlock (buffering) problem, but the others require more care. Fortunately, MPI provides routines to handle this common case. We will show how the routines `MPI_Allgather` and `MPI_Allgatherv` can be used to provide efficient ways to communicate data between processes.

First, let us handle the problem of determining how many particles each process has. Let each process have `count` contain the number of particles that it holds. We wish to fill an array `counts` such that `counts[i]` contains the number of particles on the ith process. One way to do this is to gather all the data to a single process and then use `MPI_BCAST` to send the data to all the processes. The routine that accomplishes this is `MPI_GATHER`.

```
MPI_Gather( &count, 1, MPI_INT, counts, 1, MPI_INT, 0,
            MPI_COMM_WORLD );
MPI_Comm_size( MPI_COMM_WORLD, &size );
MPI_Bcast( counts, size, MPI_INT, 0, MPI_COMM_WORLD );
```

The gather operation takes the data being sent by the ith process and places it in the ith location in the receive buffer on the root process. Only the process designated as the root receives the data.

Tables 5.5 and 5.6 show the bindings for the gather operations. The first three arguments describe the data to be sent; the fourth through sixth arguments describe

```
int MPI_Gather(void *sendbuf, int sendcount,MPI_Datatype sendtype,
               void *recvbuf, int recvcount,MPI_Datatype recvtype, int root,
               MPI_Comm comm)

int MPI_Allgather(void *sendbuf, int sendcount,MPI_Datatype sendtype,
               void *recvbuf, int recvcount,MPI_Datatype recvtype,
               MPI_Comm comm)

int MPI_Allgatherv(void *sendbuf, int sendcount,MPI_Datatype sendtype,
               void *recvbuf, int *recvcounts, int *displs,MPI_Datatype recvtype,
               MPI_Comm comm)
```

Table 5.5
C bindings for N-body code

the data to be received. For `MPI_Gather`, the seventh argument indicates which process will receive the data. `MPI_Gather` requires that all processes, including the root, send the same amount of data and that the type-signature of the `sendtype` match that of the `recvtype`. The value of `recvcount` is the number of data items sent by any *one* process; usually, `sendtype` = `recvtype` and `sendcount` = `recvcount`. Once all the data has been gathered to a single process, the data can be distributed to all processes with the broadcast routine `MPI_Bcast`. Note also that the `recvbuf` is longer than the `sendbuf` except for the trivial case where the `sendcount` is zero.

Just as the case of `MPI_Reduce` and `MPI_Allreduce`, it can be more convenient and efficient to combine the gather and broadcast operations into a single operation. `MPI_Allgather` does this; the code for collecting the counts onto all processes is shown here:

```
int counts[MAX_PROCESSES];
MPI_Allgather( &count, 1, MPI_INT, counts, 1, MPI_INT,
               MPI_COMM_WORLD );
```

If all processes had the same number of particles, then we could use `MPI_Allgather` to get the particles:

```
MPI_Allgather( myparticles, count, particletype,
               allparticles, counts, particletype, MPI_COMM_WORLD );
```

In most cases, however, there will be different numbers of particles on each process. In this case, we can use a variant of `MPI_Allgather` that permits differing sizes of

---

MPI_GATHER(sendbuf, sendcount, sendtype, recvbuf,recvcount, recvtype, root,
              comm, ierror)
              <type> sendbuf(*), recvbuf(*)
              integer sendcount, sendtype, recvcount, recvtype, root, comm,
              ierror

MPI_ALLGATHER(sendbuf, sendcount, sendtype, recvbuf,recvcount, recvtype,
              comm, ierror)
              <type> sendbuf(*), recvbuf(*)
              integer sendcount, sendtype, recvcount, recvtype, comm, ierror

MPI_ALLGATHERV(sendbuf, sendcount, sendtype,recvbuf, recvcounts, rdispls,
              recvtype, comm, ierror)
              <type> sendbuf(*), recvbuf(*)
              integer sendcount, sendtype,recvcounts(*), displs(*), recvtype,
              comm, ierror

Table 5.6
Fortran bindings for N-body code

data to be sent from each process. The routine `MPI_Allgatherv` takes the lengths
of each item to be received and the displacement relative to the receive buffer (in
units of the extent of the receive datatype) where the item will be stored. That
is, on the ith process, `recvcount[i]` items are received into the receive buffer
starting at location `recvbuf + displs[i]` (the value of `displs[i]` is relative to
the datatype of the receive buffer). In our case, we wish to receive the particles into
a single array `allparticles`. The displacement for the ith process is simply the
sum of counts for processes 0 through $i-1$. The code to gather all of the particles
is

```
displacements[0] = 0;
for (i=1; i<size; i++)
    displacements[i] = counts[i-1] + displacements[i-1];
MPI_Allgatherv( myparticles, count, particletype,
                allparticles, counts, displacements, particletype,
                MPI_COMM_WORLD );
```

The complete code for this version of the N-body code can be found in
'advmsg/nbodygthr.c'.

5.2.2   Nonblocking Pipeline

Another approach to the communications in the N-body problem can be used. When using `MPI_Allgatherv`, the computation and communication phases are distinct and nonoverlapping. A different approach is to use nonblocking communications, overlapping the communication with the computation. There are a number of ways to do this. One of the simplest is to create a *pipeline* where each process receives some data from left and sends data to the right. While the data is arriving, computations on data previously received are carried out. This approach is shown below:

```
while (not done) {
    MPI_Irecv( buf1, ..., source=left, ..., &handles[0] );
    MPI_Isend( buf2, ..., dest=right, ..., &handles[1] );
    <compute with buf2>
    MPI_Waitall( 2, handles, statuses );
    <swap buf1 and buf2>
    }
```

If enough data is being sent and the MPI implementation and computer hardware can effectively overlap computation and communication, this approach can be faster than using `MPI_Allgatherv`.

In many simulations, thousands to millions of these steps may be taken. As written above, each step requires the creation of a send and a receive request, with the same parameters being used in each cycle. In this situation, it is possible for a sophisticated MPI implementation to take advantage of the fact that the same operation is being performed many times. To express this, MPI provides routines to create "persistent" send and receive objects that can be used to perform the same operation multiple times. The form of the create call is very similar to a nonblocking send and receive; the only difference is that no communication takes place. Just as for the nonblocking operations `MPI_Isend` and `MPI_Irecv`, these routines return an `MPI_Request`. In order to begin communication with the request, the routine `MPI_Start` must first be called with the request. In order to complete the communication, one of the wait routines, such as `MPI_Wait`, must be called. Once a wait has succeeded with the request, `MPI_Start` may be called again. Multiple persistent communications may be initiated with `MPI_Startall`.

The code

```
MPI_Irecv( ..., &request );
```

```
int MPI_Send_init(void* buf, int count, MPI_Datatype datatype, int dest, int tag,
                  MPI_Comm comm, MPI_Request *request)

int MPI_Recv_init(void* buf, int count, MPI_Datatype datatype, int source,
                  int tag, MPI_Comm comm, MPI_Request *request)

int MPI_Start(MPI_Request *request)

int MPI_Startall(int count, MPI_Request *array_of_requests)

int MPI_Request_free(MPI_Request *request)
```

Table 5.7
C bindings for nonblocking pipeline

is equivalent to

```
    MPI_Recv_init( ..., &request );
    MPI_Start( request );
```

A MPI_Wait on an MPI_Irecv request is equivalent to

```
    MPI_Wait( &request );
    MPI_Request_free( &request );
```

In the N-body problem, the code is complicated by the fact that, if all processes do not have the same number of particles, then there must be a different MPI_Request created for each number of particles (or, for simplicity, for each process). The code is shown in Figure 5.2.[2]

Note that we call the communication routines only size-1 times; we do not need to send the particles back to their original processes. A complete N-body code using this approach is available in 'advmsg/nbodypipe.c'. Bindings for the MPI routines used here are shown in Tables 5.7 and 5.8.

5.2.3 Moving Particles between Processes

In many N-body problems, the force between the particles falls off rapidly with distance. At great enough distance, the influence of an individual particle becomes negligible. A number of algorithms have been devised to take advantage of this fact. They can reduce the order of the computation from $\mathcal{O}(N^2)$ to $\mathcal{O}(N \log N)$

---

[2]For Fortran programmers, the C expression a % b is roughly equivalent to the Fortran expression mod(a,b).

```
/* Setup */
for (i=0; i<size-1; i++) {
    MPI_Send_init( sendbuf, counts[(rank+i)%size],
                       particletype, right, i, MPI_COMM_WORLD,
                       &request[2*i] );
    MPI_Recv_init( recvbuf, counts[(rank+i-1+size)%size],
                       particletype, left, i, MPI_COMM_WORLD,
                       &request[2*i+1] );
    }
/* run pipeline */
while (!done)
    <copy local particles into sendbuf>
    for (i=0; i<size; i++) {
        MPI_Status statuses[2];
        if (i != size-1)
            MPI_Startall( 2, &request[2*i] );
        <compute using sendbuf>
        if (i != size-1)
            MPI_Waitall( 2, &request[2*i], statuses );
        <copy recvbuf into sendbuf>
         }
    <compute new particle postitions>
    }
/* Free requests */
for (i=0; i<2*(size-1); i++) {
    MPI_Request_free( &request[i] );
    }
```

Figure 5.2
Nonblocking pipeline implemented with MPI persistent communication objects

[2, 4, 51] or even to $\mathcal{O}(N)$ [35]. All of these algorithms organize the particles into groups based on their location. For example, the domain may be divided into cells and cells assigned to processes as shown in Figure 5.3. One important step in the implementation of these algorithms is that of transferring particles from one process to another as they move. We will discuss several ways in which this can be accomplished in MPI.

MPI_SEND_INIT(buf, count, datatype, dest, tag, comm, request, ierror)
                <type> buf(*)
                   integer request, count, datatype, dest, tag, comm, request, ierror

MPI_RECV_INIT(buf, count, datatype, source, tag, comm, request, ierror)
                <type> buf(*)
                   integer count, datatype, source, tag, comm, request, ierror

MPI_START(request, ierror)
                   integer request, ierror

MPI_STARTALL(count, array_of_requests, ierror)
                   integer count, array_of_requests(*), ierror

MPI_REQUEST_FREE(request, ierror)
                   integer request, ierror

Table 5.8
Fortran bindings for nonblocking pipeline

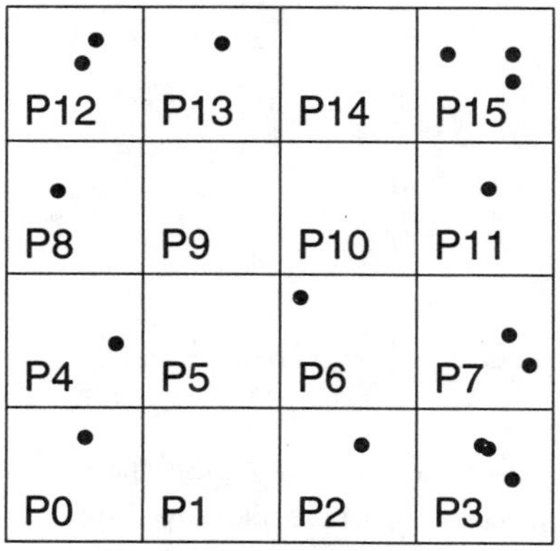

Figure 5.3
Sample of a decomposition of a domain into cells. The cells are labeled with process numbers and the dots are particles that belong to that process.

---

int **MPI_Type_indexed**(int count, int *array_of_blocklengths,
              int *array_of_displacements, MPI_Datatype oldtype,
              MPI_Datatype *newtype)

int **MPI_Get_count**(MPI_Status *status, MPI_Datatype datatype, int *count)

Table 5.9
C bindings used in moving particles

MPI_TYPE_INDEXED(count, array_of_blocklengths,array_of_displacements,
              oldtype, newtype, ierror)
              integer count,array_of_blocklengths(*), array_of_displacements(*),
              oldtype, newtype, ierror

MPI_GET_COUNT(status, datatype, count, ierror)
              integer status(*),datatype, count, ierror

Table 5.10
Fortran bindings used in moving particles

If the particles are all stored in a single array, say `myparticles[j]`, then the particles that need to be given to another process can be described by their indices into this array. MPI provides a way to describe the data to be moved directly in terms of these indices with `MPI_Type_indexed`. The input to this routine is the number of elements as the first argument, an array of block lengths (just as for `MPI_Type_vector`, these are often all ones) as the second argument, the array of index values as the third argument, and the type of the data to move as the fourth argument. The fifth argument is the new data type. Figure 5.4 shows how this routine can be used.

Note that this will work even if no particles leave the cell (`n_to_move=0`).

To receive, we can use

```
MPI_Recv( newparticles, MAX_PARTICLES, particletype,
          source, tag, comm, &status );
MPI_Get_count( &status, particletype, &number );
```

where `number` is the number of particles received. Here we use the routine `MPI_Get_count` to determine how many particles were delivered. `MPI_Get_count` uses the information in the `status` returned from an MPI receive, probe, wait, or test, and a datatype (in the second argument) to use in determining what the

```
n_to_move = 0;
for (i=0; i<count; i++) {
    if (...particle left cell...) {
        elmoffset[n_to_move] = i;
        elmsize[n_to_move]   = 1;
        n_to_move++;
    }
}
MPI_Type_indexed( n_to_move, elmsize, elmoffset,
                  particletype, &sendtype );
MPI_Type_commit( &sendtype );
MPI_Send( myparticles, 1, sendtype, dest, tag, comm );
MPI_Type_free( &sendtype );
```

Figure 5.4
Sketch of code to move particles from one process to another

output value is relative to. Bindings for these routines are given in Tables 5.9 and 5.10.

This approach requires us to preallocate enough space to receive any number of particles. This is not always possible. We can use MPI_Get_count along with MPI_Probe to determine the amount of space that we need before we use MPI_Recv to receive the message. Since MPI_Probe and MPI_Iprobe return a status, even when the message has not been received yet, they may be used to find out how big a pending message is and then allocate a buffer for it. This is one of the main situations where MPI_Probe is needed; MPI_Irecv will not do, since it requires pre-allocating the buffer into which the message is to be received. The code for this is:

```
MPI_Probe( source, tag, comm, &status );
MPI_Get_count( &status, particletype, &number );
MPI_Type_extent( particletype, &extent );
newparticles = malloc( number * extent );
MPI_Recv( newparticles, number, particletype,
          source, tag, comm, &status );
```

```
MPI_Aint elmoffset[MAX_PARTICLES];
n_to_move  = 0;
while (particle) {
    if (particle exited cell) {
        MPI_Address( particle, &elmoffset[n_to_move] );
        elmsize[n_to_move] = 1;
        n_to_move++;
        <make sure to unlink particle and de-allocate>
    }
    else {
        particle = particle->next;
    }
}
MPI_Type_hindexed( n_to_move, elmsize, elmoffset,
                   particletype, &particlemsg );
MPI_Type_commit( &particlemsg );
MPI_Send( MPI_BOTTOM, 1, particlemsg, dest, tag, comm );
MPI_Type_free( &particlemsg );
```

Figure 5.5
Sketch of code to move dynamically allocated particles to other processes

5.2.4 Sending Dynamically Allocated Data

In some implementations of N-body algorithms, the particles may be stored in
dynamically allocated storage. In this case, there isn't any single buffer that we
can use for the displacements to be relative to, as required by `MPI_Type_indexed`.
We can use instead a special location, `MPI_BOTTOM`, and the absolute addresses of
the items. Since we will be computing the displacements as addresses in bytes
rather than as indexes into an array, we use `MPI_Type_hindexed`. This routine
is identical to `MPI_Type_indexed` except that the third argument is measured in
bytes rather than in elements. For example, if the particles are stored in a linked
list whose elements are dynamically created, we can use the code in Figure 5.5.

The routine `MPI_Address` takes an item as the first argument and returns its
address, with type (in C) of `MPI_Aint` as the second argument. Fortran programmers will appreciate this function, but C programmers may be a bit puzzled by its
use, particularly in a C program. The reason is that in many C implementations, a
pointer to an item is identical to the address in memory of the item. However, this is

```
int MPI_Address(void* location, MPI_Aint *address)

int MPI_Type_hindexed(int count, int *array_of_blocklengths,
                      MPI_Aint *array_of_displacements, MPI_Datatype oldtype,
                      MPI_Datatype *newtype)
```

Table 5.11
C bindings for sending dynamically allocated data

```
MPI_Address(location, address)
            <type> location
            integer address

MPI_TYPE_HINDEXED(count, array_of_blocklengths, array_of_displacements,
            oldtype, newtype, ierror)
            integer count, array_of_blocklengths(*), array_of_displacements(*),
            oldtype, newtype, ierror
```

Table 5.12
Fortran bindings for sending dynamically allocated data

not required in C, and there are important machines (for example, supercomputers with word, not byte, addressability and practically every personal computer on the planet) for which pointers are *not* addresses. Using `MPI_Address` in C programs helps maintain portability. Bindings for these routines are shown in Tables 5.11 and 5.12.

5.2.5 User-Controlled Data Packing

In some cases, it is easier to assemble a contiguous buffer to be sent rather than to create a special datatype. MPI provides routines to pack and unpack data consisting of any MPI datatype into and out of a user-provided buffer. The routine `MPI_Pack` allows the programmer to incrementally add data to a user-provided buffer. Data that has been packed may be sent and received with the datatype `MPI_PACKED`. The input to `MPI_Pack` is the data to pack, the number and datatype of the items, output buffer and the size of the output buffer in bytes, the current `position`, and the communicator. The `position` is also an output argument; it is one of the few arguments in MPI that is both input and output. The `position` value must be set to zero before the first call to `MPI_Pack` each time a buffer is to be filled up with

```
Particle particles[MAX_PARTICLES];

nposition = 0;
MPI_Pack_size( MAX_SEND, particletype, comm, &bufsize );
buffer = malloc( (unsigned)bufsize );
while (particle) {
    if (particle exited cell) {
        MPI_Pack( particle, 1, particletype, buffer, bufsize,
            &position, comm );
        <make sure to unlink particle and de-allocate>
        }
    else {
        particle = particle->next;
        }
    }
MPI_Send( buffer, position, MPI_PACKED, dest, tag, comm );
```

Figure 5.6
Sketch of code to pack particles into an output buffer

data. MPI_Pack uses position to keep track of where in the output buffer it is; the exact meaning of position is implementation dependant.

One question that must be answered is, How big a buffer do I need to hold the data? The routine MPI_Pack_size answers this question. This routine takes the number of elements, the MPI datatype of those elements, and the communicator in which they will be communicated, and returns the maximum number of bytes that will be required by MPI_Pack to hold the data.

A version of the code in Section 5.2.4 that uses MPI_Pack is shown in Figure 5.6. Receiving the particles is managed with MPI_Unpack, as shown in Figure 5.7. Note the use of MPI_Get_count to get the length of the packed buffer and the test of position < length to determine when all of the particles have been unpacked. Bindings for these routines are given in Tables 5.13 and 5.14.

One can also receive a message assembled with MPI_Pack and sent with datatype MPI_PACKED with the appropriate datatype. In this case, we could use the particletype datatype:

```
MPI_Recv( buffer, maxcount, MPI_PACKED,
          source, tag, comm, &status );
MPI_Get_count( &status, MPI_PACKED, &length );
position = 0;
while (position < length) {
    MPI_Unpack( buffer, length, &position, &newparticle,
                1, particletype, comm );
    <add new particle to the list of particles>
    }
```

Figure 5.7
Sketch of code to unpack particles from a buffer

---

int **MPI_Pack**(void* inbuf, int incount, MPI_Datatype datatype, void *outbuf,
              int outsize, int *position, MPI_Comm comm)

int **MPI_Unpack**(void* inbuf, int insize, int *position, void *outbuf, int outcount,
              MPI_Datatype datatype, MPI_Comm comm)

int **MPI_Pack_size**(int incount, MPI_Datatype datatype, MPI_Comm comm,
              int *size)

Table 5.13
C bindings for buffer pack and unpack

```
MPI_Recv( buffer, maxparticle, particletype,
          source, tag, comm, &status );
MPI_Get_count( &status, particletype, &newparticles );
```

Multiple buffers can be maintained, of course. For example, in traversing the data, we would probably keep data for each neighboring process in a separate buffer, each with a separate position variable.

5.3   Visualizing the Mandelbrot Set

No book on parallel programming would be complete without an example of Mandelbrot computation. In this section we use it to illustrate the use of MPI's derived datatypes along with the MPE real-time graphics library. For our example we use

MPI_PACK(inbuf, incount, datatype, outbuf, outcount, position, comm, ierror)
       <type> inbuf(*), outbuf(*)
         integer incount, datatype, outcount, position, comm, ierror

MPI_UNPACK(inbuf, insize, position, outbuf, outcount, datatype, comm, ierror)
       <type> inbuf(*), outbuf(*)
         integer insize, position, outcount, datatype, comm, ierror

MPI_PACK_SIZE(incount, datatype, comm, size, ierror)
       integer incount, datatype, comm, size, ierror

Table 5.14
Fortran bindings for buffer pack and unpack

one of the many optimizations at the algorithm level that are possible for programs, parallel or not, that compute graphical representations of the Mandelbrot set.

The Mandelbrot set is a popular exercise for parallel computation because it is so obviously a parallel application, it introduces a load-balancing problem, and the results are fascinating to look at. To be at least a little original, we do it here with a slightly nonstandard algorithm. We would like to think we invented this trick, but we are not certain. Surely others have had the same idea.

Let z be a complex variable. That is, we think of z as a point (x, y) in the plane, with multiplication on points of the plane given by

$$(x_1, y_1) \cdot (x_2, y_2) = (x_1 x_2 - y_1 y_2, x_1 y_2 + x_2 y_1).$$

The *Mandelbrot set* $\mathcal{M}$ is defined in the following way. Given a complex number c, consider the function $f_c(z) = z^2 + c$. Then we can compute a series of points in the complex plane: $z_0 = 0$, $z_1 = f_c(0)$, $z_2 = f_c(z_1) = f_c^2(0)$, etc. This series either remains bounded, in which case c is in $\mathcal{M}$, or it gets farther and farther away from 0, in which case it is not. One can be prove that once a point in this sequence gets farther than a distance of 2 from the origin, the series becomes unbounded.

A "picture" of the Mandelbrot set can be made by plotting the points on the screen. Each pixel in the display corresponds to a point c in the complex plane and can be tested for membership in $\mathcal{M}$ by applying the function f_c repeatedly to 0. Either $|f_c^n(0)| > 2$ for some n, or some preset number of iterations has been reached, in which case we give up and declare that the point c is in $\mathcal{M}$ and color it, say, black. Details of the very complex boundary of $\mathcal{M}$ can be seen by "magnification," assigning the full area of the display to a small section of the complex plane. For more on the Mandelbrot set and related topics, see [58] or [64].

The region near the boundary of $\mathcal{M}$ is very interesting. Striking representations of this area can be made by assigning a color to the pixel representing point c according to the first value n for which $|f_c{}^n(0)| > 2$. As we explore the edge of $\mathcal{M}$ at greater and greater magnifications, we have a sense of exploring a huge universe of great variety. After a few random magnifications, we are likely to be looking at a part of the plane that no one has ever looked at before.

The calculation of each pixel's color value can be made independently of every other pixel's, so the program to compute such pictures is straightforwardly parallelizable, just by dividing up the screen into areas, one for each process. Unfortunately, this naive "prescheduled" approach works badly because of load imbalances. Some points escape the circle of radius 2 after only a few iterations, others take longer, and of course the points in $\mathcal{M}$ itself take the maximum number of iterations before we give up on them. As we magnify, we need more iterations to bring out detail, so some pixels may take thousands of times more iterations than others before we can assign them a color.

The most natural way to overcome this load-balancing problem is with self-scheduling. We divide up the screen into some moderately large number of squares and devote one process (the master) to sending them to the other processes (the slaves) for computation. Just as in the matrix-vector multiplication program in Chapter 3, completion of a task is a request for another assignment. Some tasks will take much longer than others (particularly the areas that are mostly black), but unless we have very bad luck, we will be able to keep all processes busy all the time.

We have included a parallel Mandelbrot program among the examples available with this book, in 'advmsg/mandel.c'. It is too long to present here, but it has three interesting aspects that we will expand on below.

- It illustrates the use of derived datatypes in MPI for sending scattered structures.
- It illustrates an interesting technique for accelerating the computation.
- It illustrates a few more functions from the MPE graphics library.

During the initialization phase of the computation, the master process broadcasts a highly miscellaneous collection of data to the slaves. We can think of it as a C structure, although not all the data is stored as a single C structure. We could broadcast each of these parameters separately, which would be wasteful of messages (and be expensive, because of the often high startup cost of sending a message), or we could rearrange them into arrays of ints, arrays of doubles, etc. The "MPI way" is to create a datatype that represents this structure and send it all at once.

MPI_TYPE_HVECTOR(count, blocklength, stride, oldtype, newtype, ierror)
    integer count, blocklength, stride, oldtype, newtype, ierror

MPI_TYPE_STRUCT(count, array_of_blocklengths, array_of_displacements,
    array_of_types, newtype, ierror)
    integer count, array_of_blocklengths(*), array_of_displacements(*),
    array_of_types(*), newtype, ierror

Table 5.15
Fortran bindings for MPI datatype routines

---

int **MPI_Type_hvector**(int count, int blocklength, MPI_Aint stride,
    MPI_Datatype oldtype, MPI_Datatype *newtype)

int **MPI_Type_struct**(int count, int *array_of_blocklengths,
    MPI_Aint *array_of_displacements, MPI_Datatype *array_of_types,
    MPI_Datatype *newtype)

Table 5.16
C bindings for MPI datatype routines

The algorithm we use is illustrated in Figures 5.8, 5.9, and 5.10. The example code implements a method for accelerating the computation. The trick is based on the fact that except at the very lowest magnification, if the border of any square is made up of pixels all of which have the same color, then all the pixels in the interior of the square must have that color too. This can speed things up a great deal, especially for large areas of $\mathcal{M}$ itself. In order to dynamically adapt the sizes of the squares, we do the following.

The queue of tasks to be done is managed by the master and consists of squares whose colors are to be computed. Initially there is just one task in the queue, the entire region selected for display. Given a square, we begin computing the colors of the pixels on its boundary. If we get all the way around the boundary without changing colors, then we color in the interior with the same color. If we come to a new color while computing the boundary, then we subdivide the square into four subsquares and send them back to the master as new tasks, while we carry on with the boundary. We carefully keep the squares nested tightly so that we never compute the color of any pixel more than once. There is a cutoff for subdivision so that when the squares get small enough, they are not subdivided further.

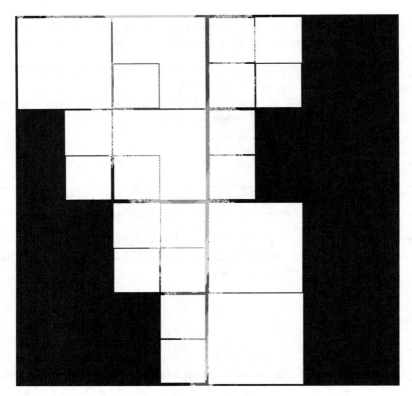

Figure 5.8
Box algorithm for Mandelbrot, starting

We watch the picture develop as the program runs by using the MPE graphics library to see whether the program is proceeding as we expect it to. In addition to drawing individual points as we did in Chapter 3, we draw line segments as we are computing the boundaries of squares. Even when the boundary is not all of the same color, there are stretches of boundary that are, and they are displayed with

```
MPE_Draw_line( handle, x1, y1, x2, y2, color );
```

where `handle` is a pointer to an `MPE_XGraph` structure initialized with `MPE_Open_graphics`; `x1,y1` and `x2,y2` are the endpoints of the line; and `color` is a color of type `MPE_Color`.

When we "win" and get to fill in a whole square, then we use

```
MPE_Fill_rectangle( handle, x, y, w, h, color );
```

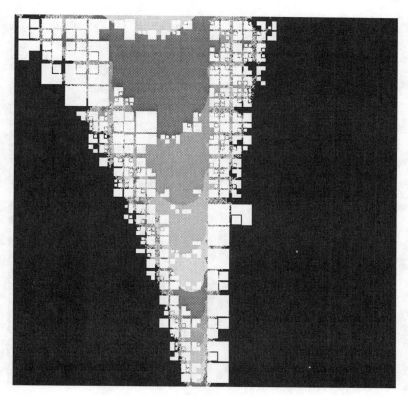

Figure 5.9
Box algorithm for Mandelbrot, a little later

where x,y is the position of the upper left corner of the rectangle, and w and h are the width and height of the rectangle, in pixels. On the occasions when we draw only one point at a time, we use

```
MPE_Draw_point( handle, x, y, color );
```

where where x and y are the coordinates of the point, in pixels.

Even these separate calls are "batched" in that we only call MPE_Update at the end of a task (an entire boundary, an entire square of the same color, or a small square of different colors). Figure 5.10 shows the completed picture.

We take this opportunity to introduce the most general of the MPI derived datatypes, which may be used for sending C structures or parts of them. The Mandelbrot program data structures contain a C structure that holds command

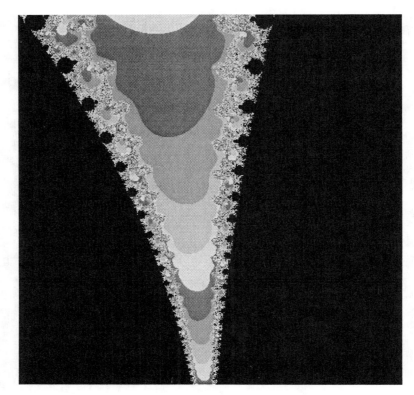

Figure 5.10
Mandelbrot, complete

line arguments, which specify a large number of options for the program. It is convenient to keep them in a structure so that they can easily be passed to various subroutines. MPI does not specify that all processes have access to the command line arguments through `MPI_Init`, so we broadcast them, assuming that at least the process with rank 0 in `MPI_COMM_WORLD` does get them when the program is started. After storing them in its copy of this structure, it broadcasts the structure to the other processes. The structure itself looks like

```
struct {
    char      display[50];    /* Name of display */
    int       maxiter;        /* max # of iterations */
    double    xmin, ymin;     /* lower left corner of rectangle */
    double    xmax, ymax;     /* upper right corner */
    int       width;          /* of display in pixels */
    int       height;         /* of display in pixels */
} cmdline;
```

We would like to broadcast this structure with a single `MPI_Bcast`, taking advantage of MPI's facilities for dealing with alignment, mixed types, and heterogeneous communication. We show here two ways to do so.

`MPI_Type_struct` is very general. It allows us to describe as a single datatype as a collection of data items of various elementary and derived types. It considers the data to be composed of a set of "blocks" of data, each of which has a count and datatype associated with it, and a location given as a displacement. The code to set up to broadcast the above structure would look like the following:

```
/* set up 4 blocks */
int           blockcounts[4] = {50,1,4,2};
MPI_Datatype types[4];
MPI_Aint      displs[4];
MPI_Datatype cmdtype;

/* initialize types and displs with addresses of items */
MPI_Address( &cmdline.display, &displs[0] );
MPI_Address( &cmdline.maxiter, &displs[1] );
MPI_Address( &cmdline.xmin,    &displs[2] );
MPI_Address( &cmdline.width,   &displs[3] );
types[0] = MPI_CHAR;
types[1] = MPI_INT;
types[2] = MPI_DOUBLE;
types[3] = MPI_INT;
```

Now we are ready to do the broadcast. First we adjust the displacement array so that the displacements are offsets from the beginning of the structure.

```
for (i = 3; i >= 0; i--)
    displs[i] -= displs[0];
```

Then we build the new type:

```
MPI_Type_struct( 4, blockcounts, displs, types, &cmdtype );
MPI_Type_commit( &cmdtype );
```

and broadcast it:

```
MPI_Bcast( cmdline, 1, cmdtype, 0, MPI_COMM_WORLD );
```

There is an alternative to the way the displacements are presented. The displacements need not be relative to the beginning of a particular structure; they can be "absolute" addresses as well. In this case, we treat them as relative to the starting address in memory, given by `MPI_BOTTOM`. Using this technique, we can omit the loop that adjusts the displacements, leaving them as originally given by calls to `MPI_Address`, and change the `MPI_Bcast` to

```
MPI_Bcast( MPI_BOTTOM, 1, cmdtype, 0, MPI_COMM_WORLD );
```

5.4 Gaps in Datatypes

In Section 4.8 we introduced the `MPI_Type_vector` routine and used it to create a datatype for prespecified number of elements. What can you do if you want to specify a variable number of elements?

We obviously wish to use the `count` argument of the send and receive routines, and so we need to describe a datatype that consists of the element followed by a "skip" to the next data element. We can define this by using `MPI_Type_struct` and a special MPI predefined datatype called `MPI_UB`. `MPI_UB` (for upper bound) is a datatype that has no size but serves as a way to change the extent of a datatype. By placing `MPI_UB` at a displacement that is the number of bytes between successive elements, we can skip over those bytes when using this datatype.

Figure 5.11 shows the code to create an MPI datatype for a double-precision array with `number_in_column` elements (assuming Fortran storage order for matrices).

This provides a good place to get a better understanding of the meaning of extent and MPI contiguous datatypes. Consider this attempt to define a datatype to access the rows of a matrix stored columnwise:

```
MPI_Type_vector( 1, 1, number_in_column, MPI_DOUBLE, &rowtype2 );
MPI_Type_commit( &rowtype2 );
```

The intent is to use the `count` argument in a send to send the desired number of elements, just as with the datatype `rowtype` constructed above. However, the

```
int blens[2], displs[2];
MPI_Datatype types[2], rowtype;
blens[0]  = 1;
blens[1]  = 1;
displs[0] = 0;
displs[1] = number_in_column * sizeof(double);
types[0]  = MPI_DOUBLE;
types[1]  = MPI_UB;
MPI_Type_struct( 2, blens, displs, types, &rowtype );
MPI_Type_commit( &rowtype );
```

Figure 5.11
Code to construct a general strided vector type

extent of `rowtype2` is the distance from the first to the last byte in the datatype; and since `rowtype2` contains only a single `double`, the extent is just the size of a `double`. Thus, a send or a receive using datatype `rowtype2` will use consecutive doubles, not doubles separated by `number_in_column` doubles.

The datatype `MPI_LB` is similar to `MPI_UB` except that it may be used to set the lower bound of a derived datatype.

6 Parallel Libraries

One of the primary motivations for MPI was to enable the development of parallel libraries. Libraries have been critical to the development of a software base for sequential computers. Lack of modularity in existing message-passing systems has hampered the comparable development of reliable parallel libraries, libraries that can be written independently of one another and of user code and still cooperate with one another in a single application.

We begin this chapter with a discussion of some of the issues that are raised by parallel libraries. We describe some of the shortcomings of existing message-passing systems when they are considered from the special point of view of the library writer, and we point out features of the MPI definition that have been introduced to overcome these shortcomings. We then give an example of a simple library; it contains only two functions but illustrates a number of MPI's features that support libraries. We devote a section to the interplay between linear algebra and partial differential equations as an example of an area where parallel libraries are likely to be heavily used. We briefly describe some aspects of the use of MPI in the solution of a dense system of linear equations. We conclude the chapter with a discussion of general strategies for building parallel libraries.

6.1 Motivation

In this section we outline the motivation for libraries and describe the special design features that help in building parallel libraries.

6.1.1 The Need for Parallel Libraries

Software libraries offer several advantages:

- they ensure consistency in program correctness,
- they help guarantee a high-quality implementation,
- they hide distracting details and complexities associated with state-of-the-art implementations, and
- they minimize repetitive effort or haphazard results.

Even in sequential libraries, library writers incorporate numerous heuristics and domain-specific "tricks." With the addition of parallelism based on message passing, the "detail work" of typical numerical methods grows significantly, strongly motivating the development of parallel libraries that encapsulate and hide this complexity from the user. MPI is the underlying system library that will help make scientific as well as application-oriented parallel libraries both reliable and commonplace.

6.1.2 Common Deficiencies of Message-Passing Systems

In the *sequential* Fortran and C environments, one can easily create libraries, because the stack-oriented procedural programming model has well-defined conditions about reasonable vs. erroneous programs. In the *distributed-memory, message-passing environment*, however, libraries are difficult to write with either vendor-supplied software or portability systems. The problem is one of modularity: a library needs a communication space isolated from the user's communication space precisely because it is a library. Its communication patterns are designed independently of the user code it is to be linked to.

The most obvious problem is that of having a message sent by the library accidentally received by user code, or vice versa. One might argue that tags could be used effectively to designate restrictions on message delivery. Such tags prove insufficient, however, for several reasons. First, more than one library (or invocation of the same library) could use the same tags. Second, wildcard receipt-selectivity on tags (e.g., `MPI_ANY_TAG`) destroys any promise of real protection that tags could otherwise afford. For this reason parallel libraries are often written in a style in which execution of user code and library code is alternated in a strict fashion, with care taken that no messages be in transit when control is passed from user to library and back (this is state often called quiescence). This type of design, inherited from the sequential case, introduces synchronization barriers that inhibit performance, and still leaves other problems unsolved.

Incorporated into MPI are various kinds of abstraction: process groups describe participants in collective operations and rank-naming in point-to-point communication, contexts separate unrelated message traffic, topologies let users describe process relationships as they prefer, and communicators encapsulate all this information in a useful object that also abstracts all these details for the typical user.

6.1.3 Review of MPI Features That Support Libraries

The requirements for effective libraries can be summarized as follows:

• A safe communication space guarantees that a library can send and receive point-to-point messages without interference from other point-to-point messages generated in the system.
• Collective operations take a process group (from a communicator) as the set of participants; processes that do not participate continue unimpeded.

- Abstract names for processes are based on virtual topologies, or at least rank-in-group names, thereby avoiding hardware dependencies, and ideally making application code more intuitive.

MPI offers several features that implement these important requirements.

Process Groups define a rank-naming for processes in point-to-point communication relative to the group. In addition, these groups define the scope of collective operations. (Note that the internal representations of process names are not revealed at the application level; that would spoil portability.) This scope makes it possible to make strong statements about the noninterference of sequential collective operations in the same communication context.

Contexts provide the ability to have separate safe "universes" (called contexts) of message passing in MPI. A context is conceptually implemented by a secondary or "hyper" tag that differentiates messages from one another. Unlike user-manipulated tags, these contexts provide totally separate communication space, each with a full complement of user-managed tags. Contexts are allocated by the system for safety; if users were to define contexts, two libraries might inadvertently define the same one. Users do not work directly with contexts; rather, they work with process groups and communicators.

Communicators encapsulate contexts, groups, and virtual topologies in an object that provides the appropriate scope for all communication operations in MPI. Communicators bind process groups and context information together to form a safe communication space within the group. The communicator also provides an object that can be used to maintain local (to the communicator) copies of data that the library needs to keep from one invocation to another. The MPI term for this is "attribute caching."

The use of separate communication contexts by distinct libraries (or distinct library invocations) insulates communication internal to the library execution from external communication (group safety). This approach allows one to invoke the library even if communications are pending. Moreover, it avoids the need to synchronize each entry into and exit from library code. Most such synchronizations are unnecessary, reduce performance, and can be avoided because of the context model.

6.2   A First MPI Library

In this section we describe a simple two-function library. It provides a feature that is not included in the MPI definition: a nonblocking broadcast. Recall that for all processes except the specified root, `MPI_Bcast` is a form of receive. Thus, it makes sense to post this "receive" and possibly others, then do whatever can be done, only waiting for completion when necessary. (This analogy with receive is not completely accurate, since intermediate processes in the broadcast tree must send as well as receive. However, the nonblocking broadcast may still be useful, particularly on multithreaded systems.) Use of this library is illustrated by the following sequence:

```
#include "ibcast.h"
Ibcast_handle *request;
...
Ibcast( buf, count, datatype, root, comm, &request );
...
Ibcast_wait( &request );
```

One important set of features in MPI that has not been introduced yet involves attaching user data to communicators. The MPI term for this is *caching* of *attributes*, and it is typically used to keep a pointer to a data structure used by the library to maintain information between calls. In Fortran, it is an integer. Attributes are identified by *key values*, which are system-allocated so that multiple libraries can attach attributes to the same communicator without knowledge of one another.

In this case the cached information includes a communicator to be used for `ibcast`'s internal communication and an ordering tag to be used to separate multiple `ibcasts` using the same communicator. Thus the header file for the nonblocking broadcast library is as shown in Figure 6.1.

The complete nonblocking broadcast library is supplied in the files 'libraries/ibcast.h' and 'libraries/ibcast.c'. It demonstrates how to use communicators and caching. The way that attributes are attached to communicators allows for their selective propagation when the call `MPI_Comm_dup` is used, as we define further in this example. The already-discussed call `MPI_Comm_create` never copies attributes to the newly created communicator. The nonblocking broadcast library requires the use of caching to store persistent information; it requires the use of a cached communicator to protect the user from communication actions of the library, and it illustrates the need to use the tag (within that cached communication context) as a further mechanism for safety in a nondeterministically ordered library of this form. The code for the main routine of `Ibcast` is shown in Figures 6.2 and 6.3.

```
#include "mpi.h"
/* handle for ibcast operations on a communicator */
typedef struct ibcast_syshandle
{
    MPI_Comm comm;
    int ordering_tag;
} Ibcast_syshandle;

/* handle for a particular ibcast operation */
typedef struct ibcast_handle
{
    MPI_Request        *req_array;
    MPI_Status         *stat_array;
    int                 num_sends;
    int                 num_recvs;
} Ibcast_handle;
```

Figure 6.1
The header file for Ibcast()

What's going on in this library? First, Ibcast checks to see whether it has ever been called before by this process, by seeing whether it has a valid value for the global integer ibcast_keyval. If not, Ibcast has to get an attribute *key value*, so that it can cache its information on this and all future communicators that may call Ibcast in this process; it does so with MPI_Keyval_create. Otherwise, ibcast_keyval is already the key value for use by this library.

Next, the code checks to see whether an Ibcast has ever been done on the current communicator, by looking up the attribute for the key value ibcast_keyval. If not, the system handle associated with this key value is created and attached to the communicator. The most notable call here is MPI_Comm_dup, which makes a complete duplicate of the input communicator, but with new contexts of communication. Any "other" attributes cached by the system will be selectively copied, according to the attribute-copying set up by the user when those attributes were attached. (See Table 6.1 for the bindings for attribute copying and deletion functions.) The next task for Ibcast is to determine all the specific data that needs to go in the user handle for this particular call, so that the work of transmitting data can begin, and so that the user can also legally call `Ibcast_wait`.

`Ibcast` builds a broadcast tree of sends and receives for the given root; for each such call, it assigns a new "ordering tag," to prevent any interference from previous, in-progress `Ibcast` calls. We call this type of interference "back-masking," in that a subsequent call to the `Ibcast` could potentially interpose its data in advance of the data of an earlier `Ibcast` call, yielding an erroneous result. The duplicated context (protects `Ibcast` from the user and other libraries), together with the incrementing tag strategy (protects one call to `Ibcast` from others), eliminates this possibility. Thus, `Ibcast` is isolated from all other collective and point-to-point communication of its communicator, because it uses a duplicated communicator. Furthermore, each call to `Ibcast` with a specific communicator is isolated from earlier ones because distinct tags are used for the sends and receives.[1]

Three general classes of process behavior arise with this library: the root, the leaves, and all other nodes of the broadcast tree. The root process only sends, the leaves only receive, and all other processes both send and receive. Specifics of the tree position of each process thus determine the number of persistent send and receive requests that `Ibcast` creates and stores in the "user handle." (The MPI calls `MPI_Send_init` and `MPI_Recv_init` generate the persistent operations, but do not start anything. They are used here not to allow the re-use of the `MPI_Requests` as in Section 5.2.2; rather, they give us an easy way to store the parameters for the `MPI_Isend` needed for processes that are neither the root or the leaves of the broadcast tree.) `Ibcast` then calls `Ibcast_work` to do the main body of the broadcast transmission,

The root, which has no receives, immediately starts all its send in `Ibcast_work`, using the MPI call `MPI_Startall`. All the other nodes of the broadcast tree start their receives using `MPI_Startall`. After these calls are started, `Ibcast_work` terminates, returning control to `Ibcast`. Finally, `Ibcast` has but one additional bit of bookkeeping: to increment the ordering tag used by the next call to `Ibcast`, which can legally come before the call to `Ibcast_wait`. It returns with the handle containing the persistent information, which will be passed by the user when he or she calls `Ibcast_wait`, when the broadcast must be finalized.

`Ibcast_wait` picks up where `Ibcast_work` left off. For the root, it waits on the sends; for the leaves, it waits on the receives. For the other nodes of the broadcast

---

[1] While the tag-incrementing strategy used here is probably overkill for `Ibcast`, which only has sends and receives without wild cards, and can consequently rely on *pairwise message ordering* (see the glossary) for correctness, the code illustrates an important general strategy for library design, which could also be used in libraries where wildcard receives are employed, where back-masking is a definite problem to be avoided.

tree, it waits on its receive, then starts its sends and waits on their completion. The calls `MPI_Startall` and `MPI_Waitall` figure in this process.

Communicators are frequently create by copying existing communicators (with `MPI_Comm_dup`) and are eventually freed, at which point one might wish to clean up storage associated with an attribute. In order to handle attached attributes during these operations, MPI specifies that when a key value is created, the user may supply functions to copy and delete the attribute value when the communicator is copied or freed.

---

int **MPI_Comm_dup**(MPI_Comm comm, MPI_Comm *newcomm)

int **MPI_Keyval_create**(MPI_Copy_function *copy_fn, MPI_Delete_function
        *delete_fn, int *keyval, void* extra_state)

int **MPI_Attr_put**(MPI_Comm comm, int keyval, void* attribute_val)

int **MPI_Attr_get**(MPI_Comm comm, int keyval, void **attribute_val, int *flag)

int **MPI_Keyval_free**(int *keyval)

int **MPI_Attr_delete**(MPI_Comm comm, int keyval)

int **Copy_fn**(MPI_Comm *oldcomm, int *keyval, void *extra_state,
        void *attribute_value_in, void **attribute_value_out, int *flag)

int **Delete_fn**(MPI_Comm *comm, int *keyval, void *attribute_value,
        void *extra_state)

Table 6.1
C bindings for new MPI calls needed by Ibcast, and related calls.

In some cases, a library may want to insure that the cached attribute information is propagated to new communicators created with `MPI_Comm_dup`. The version of Ibcast in Figure 6.2 does not do this, but a simple change is all that is required to add this feature. By changing one line of Ibcast, we can add the copy and delete callbacks:

```
#include "ibcast.h"
int ibcast_keyval = MPI_KEYVAL_INVALID; /* keyval for
                                          attribute cacheing */
int Ibcast(void *buf, int count, MPI_Datatype datatype, int root,
           MPI_Comm comm, Ibcast_handle **handle_out)
{
    Ibcast_syshandle *syshandle;
    Ibcast_handle    *handle;
    int                       flag, mask, relrank;
    int                       retn, size, rank;
    int                       req_no = 0;
    /* get info about the communicator */
    MPI_Comm_size ( comm, &size );
    MPI_Comm_rank ( comm, &rank );
    /* If size is 1, this is trivially finished */
    if (size == 1) {
      (*handle_out) = (Ibcast_handle *)0;
      return (MPI_SUCCESS);
    }
    /* first see if this library has ever been called. Generate new
       key value if not. */
    if(ibcast_keyval == MPI_KEYVAL_INVALID) {
      MPI_Keyval_create(NULL, NULL, &ibcast_keyval, NULL);
    }
    /* this communicator might already have used this collective
       operation, and so it would consequently have information
       of use to us cached on it. */
    MPI_Attr_get(comm, ibcast_keyval, (void **)&syshandle, &flag);
    if(flag == 0)  { /* there was no attribute previously cached */
        syshandle =
            (Ibcast_syshandle *)malloc(sizeof(Ibcast_syshandle));
        /* fill in the attribute information */
        syshandle->ordering_tag = 0; /* start with tag zero */
        MPI_Comm_dup(comm, &(syshandle->comm)); /* duplicate comm */
        /* attach information to the communicator */
        MPI_Attr_put(comm, ibcast_keyval, (void *)syshandle);
    }
```

Figure 6.2
The first part of the main library routine of Ibcast().

```
/* create a handle for this particular ibcast operation */
handle = (Ibcast_handle *)malloc(sizeof(Ibcast_handle));
handle->num_sends = 0;
handle->num_recvs = 0;
/* count how many send/recv handles we need */
mask    = 0x1;
relrank = (rank - root + size) % size;
while ((mask & relrank) == 0 && mask < size) {
  if ((relrank | mask) < size)
    handle->num_sends++;
  mask <<= 1;
}
if (mask < size)
  handle->num_recvs++;
/* allocate request and status arrays for sends and receives */
handle->req_array  = (MPI_Request *)
  malloc(sizeof(MPI_Request) * (handle->num_sends + handle->num_recvs));
handle->stat_array = (MPI_Status *)
  malloc(sizeof(MPI_Status) * (handle->num_sends + handle->num_recvs));
/* create "permanent" send/recv requests */
mask    = 0x1;
relrank = (rank - root + size) % size;
while ((mask & relrank) == 0 && mask < size) {
  if ((relrank|mask) < size)
    MPI_Send_init(buf, count, datatype, ((relrank|mask)+root)%size,
                  syshandle->ordering_tag, syshandle->comm,
                  &(handle->req_array[req_no++]));
  mask <<= 1;
}
if (mask < size)
  MPI_Recv_init(buf, count, datatype,
                ((relrank & (~ mask)) + root) % size,
                syshandle->ordering_tag, syshandle->comm,
                &(handle->req_array[req_no++]));
retn = Ibcast_work(handle);
/* prepare to update the cached information */
++(syshandle->ordering_tag); /* make bigger for next ibcast operation
                                to avoid back-masking */
(*handle_out) = handle;      /* return the handle */
return(retn);
}
```

Figure 6.3
The second part of the main library routine of Ibcast()

MPI_COMM_DUP(comm, newcomm, ierror)
        integer comm, newcomm, ierror

MPI_KEYVAL_CREATE(copy_fn, delete_fn, keyval, extra_state, ierror)
        external copy_fn, delete_fn
        integer keyval, extra_state, ierror

MPI_ATTR_PUT(comm, keyval, attribute_val, ierror)
        integer comm, keyval, attribute_val, ierror

MPI_ATTR_GET(comm, keyval, attribute_val, flag, ierror)
        integer comm, keyval, attribute_val, ierror
        logical flag

MPI_KEYVAL_FREE(keyval, ierror)
        integer keyval, ierror

MPI_ATTR_DELETE(comm, keyval, ierror)
        integer comm, keyval, ierror

FUNCTION COPY_FN(oldcomm, keyval, extra_state, attribute_value_in,
        attribute_value_out, flag)
        integer oldcomm, keyval, extra_state, attribute_value_in,
        attribute_value_out, flag

FUNCTION DELETE_FN(comm, keyval, attribute_value, extra_state)
        integer comm, keyval, attribute_value, extra_state
        logical flag

Table 6.2
Fortran bindings for new MPI calls needed by Ibcast, and related calls

```
/* first see if this library has ever been called. */
if(ibcast_keyval == MPI_KEYVAL_INVALID) {
  /* our first mission is to create the process-local keyval
     for this library, while specifying callbacks */
  MPI_Keyval_create(Ibcast_copy, Ibcast_delete,
                    &ibcast_keyval, NULL);

...
```

   (We also define the functions there that do the copy (`Ibcast_copy`, see Figure 6.6) and delete (`Ibcast_delete`, see Figure 6.7) to complete the modifications.) These changes will give the library the property that calls to `MPI_Comm_dup` and `MPI_Comm_free` on a communicator that has used `Ibcast` will behave as responsibly as possible about cleaning up memory.

```
#include "ibcast.h"
int Ibcast_work(Ibcast_handle *handle)
{
    /* if I don't have any recv's, start all my sends -- the root */
    if (handle->num_recvs == 0)
      MPI_Startall ( handle->num_sends, handle->req_array );
    /* start all my recv's */
    else
      MPI_Startall ( handle->num_recvs,
                     &handle->req_array[handle->num_sends] );
    return (MPI_SUCCESS);
}
```

Figure 6.4
The `Ibcast_work()` function, which does part of the broadcast for `Ibcast()`

   On systems that support threads or active messages, the ideas and code described above could be used to create a nonblocking reduce and a nonblocking barrier, as well as other collective calls not directly supported by the MPI Standard (see Chapter 10).

6.3   Linear Algebra on Grids

Many applications can be written in terms of the standard vector operations performed on a grid or mesh. One such example is the Poisson problem presented in Chapter 4. As we saw in that chapter, a major issue is the choice of data decomposition, that is, how the elements of the vectors are distributed across the processes. This section describes the design and implementation of MPI libraries that address some of the issues in providing efficient and flexible routines for vector operations on grids that will operate correctly with many different distributions of the elements. These libraries are initially "object based" and alternatively "object oriented." The object-based libraries make use of C data structures and therefore provide abstractions like vectors and data distributions. The object-oriented

```
#include "ibcast.h"
int Ibcast_wait(Ibcast_handle **handle_out)
{
    Ibcast_handle *handle = (*handle_out);
    int retn, i;
    /* A NULL handle means there's nothing to do */
    if (handle == (Ibcast_handle *)0)
      return (MPI_SUCCESS);
    /* If I wasn't the root, finish my recvs and
       start & wait on sends */
    if (handle->num_recvs != 0) {
      MPI_Waitall(handle->num_recvs,
                  &handle->req_array[handle->num_sends],
                  &handle->stat_array[handle->num_sends]);
      MPI_Startall ( handle->num_sends, handle->req_array );
    }
    /* Wait for my receive and then start all my sends */
    retn = MPI_Waitall(handle->num_sends, handle->req_array,
                       handle->stat_array);
    /* free permanent requests */
    for (i=0; i < (handle->num_sends + handle->num_recvs); i++)
        MPI_Request_free (&(handle->req_array[i]));
    /* Free request and status arrays and ibcast handle */
    free (handle->req_array);
    free (handle->stat_array);
    free (handle);
    /* Return a NULL handle */
    (*handle_out) = (Ibcast_handle *)0;
    return(retn);
}
```

Figure 6.5
The Ibcast_wait() function, which effects the "wait" for Ibcast()

```
/* copier for ibcast cached information */
void Ibcast_copy(MPI_Comm  *oldcomm, int *keyval,
     void *extra, void *attr_in, void **attr_out, int *flag)
{
  Ibcast_syshandle *syshandle = (Ibcast_syshandle *)attr_in;
  Ibcast_syshandle *new_syshandle;
  /* do we have a valid keyval */
  if ( ( (*keyval)     == MPI_KEYVAL_INVALID )          ||
       ( (*keyval)     != ibcast_keyval )               ||
       ( (syshandle    == (Ibcast_syshandle *)0) ) )
    return;
  /* create a new syshandle for the new communicator */
  new_syshandle =
    (Ibcast_syshandle *)malloc(sizeof(Ibcast_syshandle));
  /* fill in the attribute information */
  new_syshandle->ordering_tag = 0; /* start with tag zero */
  /* dup the "hidden" communicator */
  MPI_Comm_dup(syshandle->comm, &(new_syshandle->comm));
  /* return the new syshandle and set flag to true */
  (*attr_out) = (void *)new_syshandle;
  (*flag)      = 1;
}
```

Figure 6.6
The `Ibcast_copy()` function, which does copy-callback services for `Ibcast()`

libraries go one step further by exploiting inheritance and are consequently better able to optimize their run-time performance by making a number of decisions outside of inner loops. Typically, they do this with persistent objects that describe the details of a desired parallel computation.

6.3.1   Mappings and Logical Grids

Two basic abstractions help with data mapping. The first is a logical grid topology, which describes the names of processes and their relationships. This data structure is helpful for describing communication structures and data layout. Data layout itself is described by mapping functions, which describe transformations of indices of the data onto the logical grid topologies in each dimension. We will restrict our attention to two-dimensional logical grid topologies in this chapter.

```
/* destructor for ibcast cached information */
void Ibcast_delete(MPI_Comm *comm, int *keyval, void *attr_val,
                   void *extra)
{
  Ibcast_syshandle *syshandle = (Ibcast_syshandle *)attr_val;
  /* do we have a valid keyval */
  if ( ( (*keyval)    == MPI_KEYVAL_INVALID )          ||
       ( (*keyval)    != ibcast_keyval )               ||
       ( (syshandle   == (Ibcast_syshandle *)0) ) )
     return;
  /* free the "hidden" communicator and memory for syshandle */
  MPI_Comm_free ( &(syshandle->comm) );
  free (syshandle);
}
```

Figure 6.7
The `Ibcast_copy()` function, which does delete-callback services for `Ibcast()`

Logical 2-D Grid Topologies As we saw in Chapter 4, MPI provides a set of routines that can be used to create virtual topologies. The routines provided by MPI for creating Cartesian virtual topologies are not always applicable, however. In some cases, it may be necessary to decompose or split a communicator into parts based on a more general criterion. MPI provides the function `MPI_Comm_split` for this purpose. This function takes as input a communicator, a color, and a key. All processes with the same `color` are placed into the same new communicator, which is returned in the fourth argument. The processes are ranked in the new communicator in the order given by `key`; if two processes have the same key value, they retain the same relative ordering as in the old communicator.

As a simple example of the use of `MPI_Comm_split`, in Figure 6.9 we show an alternative way to generate a 2-D Cartesian topology. The data structure for the logical grid that this routine creates is shown in Figure 6.8.

int **MPI_Comm_split**(MPI_Comm oldcomm, int color, int key, MPI_Comm *newcomm)

Table 6.3
C binding for MPI routine used to make virtual topologies "by hand" in initial version of `la_grid_2d_new`.

```
typedef struct la_grid_2d
{
  int P, Q;  /* global shape of grid */
  int p, q;  /* local position on grid */

  MPI_Comm grid_comm; /* parent communicator */
  MPI_Comm row_comm;  /* row     communicator */
  MPI_Comm col_comm;  /* column communicator */

} LA_Grid_2d;
```

Figure 6.8
The 2-D logical grid structure

> **MPI_COMM_SPLIT**(oldcomm, color, key, newcomm, ierror)
>   integer oldcomm, color, key, group, ierror

Table 6.4
Fortran binding for MPI routine used to make virtual topologies "by hand" in initial version of la_grid_2d_new.

Multiple calls to `MPI_Comm_split` can be used to generate overlapping subgroup communicators, as we have done to get row- and column-communicators in Figure 6.9, where the topology constructor is presented.

Revisiting Grids Using MPI Topology Functions An alternative to `MPI_Comm_split` when using a Cartesian topology (created, for example, with `MPI_Cart_create`) is to use `MPI_Cart_sub`. This takes a communicator that has a Cartesian topology and returns a new communicator consisting of those processes that are in a hyperplane of the Cartesian topology of the input communicator. This hyperplane is described by the second argument; for each dimension in the original Cartesian topology, a true value indicates that that dimension remains in the Cartesian topology associated with the output communicator. One way to understand this is to think of a 2-D Cartesian topology, with rows numbered as the first dimension and columns the second. Then if `remain_dim = { 1, 0 }`, the output communicator represents the row containing the process; if `remain_dim = { 0, 1 }`, the output communicator represents the column containing the process. The use of `MPI_Cart_sub` to construct the row and column communicators for the virtual topology hierarchy is shown in Figure 6.10.

```
LA_Grid_2d *la_grid_2d_new(MPI_Comm comm, int P, Q)
{
  LA_Grid_2d *grid;
  MPI_Comm   row, col;
  int        my_rank, p, q;

  /* Determine row and column position */
  MPI_Comm_rank(comm, &my_rank);
  p = my_rank / Q;
  q = my_rank % Q;    /* pick a row-major mapping */

  /* Split comm into row and col comms */
  MPI_Comm_split(comm, p, q, &row); /* color by row, rank by column */
  MPI_Comm_split(comm, q, p, &col); /* color by column, rank by row */

  /* Make new grid */
  grid = NEW(LA_Grid_2d, 1);
  /* Fill in new grid structure */
  grid->grid_comm = comm;
  grid->row_comm  = row;
  grid->col_comm  = col;
  grid->P         = P;
  grid->Q         = Q;
  grid->p         = p;
  grid->q         = q;
  /* Return the newly built grid */
  return (grid);
}
```

Figure 6.9
The 2-D logical grid structure constructor

---

int **MPI_Cart_sub**(MPI_Comm oldcomm, int *remain_dims,
                     MPI_Comm *newcomm)

Table 6.5
C binding for MPI topology routine used in la_grid_2d_new_II.

```
#define N_DIMS 2
LA_Grid_2d *la_grid_2d_new_II(MPI_Comm comm, int P, Q)
{
  LA_Grid_2d *grid;
  MPI_Comm   comm_2d, row, col;
  int        my_rank, p, q;
  int dims[N_DIMS],          /* hold dimensions */
      local[N_DIMS],         /* local position */
      period[N_DIMS],        /* aperiodic flags */
      remain_dims[N_DIMS];   /* flags for sub-dimension computations */
  /* Generate a new communicator with virtual topology added: */
  dims[0] = P; period[0] = FALSE;
  dims[1] = Q; period[1] = FALSE;
  MPI_Cart_create(comm, N_DIMS, dims, period, TRUE, &comm_2d);
  /* map back to topology coordinates: */
  MPI_Comm_rank(comm, &my_rank);
  MPI_Cart_coords(comm_2d, my_rank, N_DIMS, &local);
  p = local[0]; q = local[1];  /* this is "my" grid location */
  /* Use cartesian sub-topology mechanism to get row/col comms: */
  remain_dims[0] = TRUE; remain_dims[1] = FALSE;
  MPI_Cart_sub(comm_2d, remain_dims, &row);
  remain_dims[0] = FALSE; remain_dims[1] = TRUE;
  MPI_Cart_sub(comm_2d, remain_dims, &col);
  grid = NEW(LA_Grid_2d, 1);  /* Make new grid */

  /* rest of the code is the same as before */
}
```

Figure 6.10
2-D topology hierarchy with Cartesian topology functions

```
MPI_CART_SUB(oldcomm, remain_dims, newcomm, ierror)
            integer oldcomm, newcomm, ierror
            logical remain_dims(*)
```

Table 6.6
Fortran binding for MPI topology routine used in la_grid_2d_new (revisited).

Mapping Functions and Distributions   Because we wish to provide flexible library routines, we let the user specify how data is laid out in the system. Specifically, we provide data mapping functions, particularly for common layouts (linear load balanced, scattered, and so on). Following the rules for these mappings, users can potentially add different mapping strategies for coefficients, but distributions we illustrate here will cover a lot of ground, and illustrate all our design goal of "data distribution independence."

```
typedef struct la_mapping
{
  int   map_type;         /* Used for quick comparison of mappings */

  void (*mu)(int I, P, N, void *extra, int *p, *i);
                          /* Mapping of I->(p,i) */
  void (*mu_inv)(int p, i, P, N, void *extra, int *I);
                          /* Inverse (p,i)->I:   */
  void (*local_len)(int p, P, N, void *extra, int *n);
                          /* # of coefficients mapped to each process: */

  void *extra;            /* for mapping-specific parameters */
} LA_Mapping;

/* some pre-defined mapping... */
extern LA_Mapping *LA_Mapping_Blk_Linear, *LA_Mapping_Blk_Scatter,
                  *LA_Mapping_Linear, *LA_Mapping_Scatter;
```

Figure 6.11
Definition of mapping function data structure

Single mappings aren't enough because they describe one-dimensional conversions between a global index space and local process naming for coefficients; they indicate which globally numbered coefficient goes where in a set of processes. For two-dimensional data structures (like matrices), we need two such mappings to describe how information maps onto a process topology. To meet this need, we devise a data structure, called a distribution, that we make particular to two dimensions but that could generalize for higher-dimensional grids, too.

Figure 6.12 illustrates the data structure that encompasses both the logical grid information and a pair of mappings, which proves sufficient to describe basic linear algebra.

```
typedef struct la_distrib_2d
{
  LA_Grid_2d  *grid;/* Base grid on which the distribution is based */
  LA_Mapping *row;  /* row mapping */
  LA_Mapping *col;  /* col mapping */

} LA_Distrib_2d;
```

Figure 6.12
Definition of mapping function data structure

6.3.2 Vectors and Matrices

Given the logical grids, mappings, and the two-dimension distributions based on them, we can now turn to distributed data structures for linear algebra.

Vectors In a 2-D logical grid topology, vectors may either be row- or column-oriented vectors. We assume that each row (respectively, column) vector is replicated over each row (respectively, column) of a logical grid. Figure 6.13 shows schematically how two row vectors might be distributed in a grid. In this example, each vector is broken into two subvectors and is distributed along the columns of the grid. Through replication, each process row has a complete copy of both vectors; see also [26, 68].

Vector Structure and Construction. Distributed vectors are defined by the data structure illustrated in Figure 6.14. As an instance of a distributed object, a vector contains information including both its global and its local length, a pointer to local real data storage, and a type field that indicates the choice of row or column distribution. In addition, the vector data structure references an underlying logical grid topology data structure and a data distribution. This latter information completes the specification of how vector coefficients are mapped and replicated over the topology.

Matrices Matrices on two-dimensional process grids are defined analogously to vectors, as depicted in Figure 6.15. A matrix is divided into submatrices, each with a local shape given by $m \times n$. The values of m and n generally differ in each process, just as the lengths of subvectors differ, in general, in each process. A matrix has a storage strategy, depending on whether it is row or column major. (The default constructor we use will make column-major local matrices; this detail remains an issue for fine optimizations of local memory access.) As with vectors, distributed

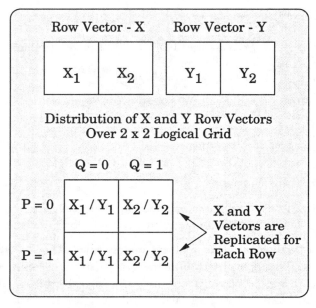

Figure 6.13
Layout of two row vectors over a 2 x 2 logical process grid. Column vectors are laid out in an analogous fashion, orthogonal to the row vectors.

matrices refer to an underlying logical process grid and distribution, through which they acquire the detailed information on topology shape and coefficient mapping.

6.3.3 Components of a Parallel Library

High-quality libraries must provide more than one version of a function that can perform efficiently over different conditions (we call such a set of methods a *poly-algorithm*). For example, we provide multiple versions of the vector sum and inner-product functions, both with the same sequential complexity. The "strided" version of these functions has a reduced computational load at the expense of more communication. Conversely, the "nonstrided" version is computationally more intensive but requires fewer messages because the algorithm exploits data redundancy; in the case of the vector sum (with compatibly stored data), no messages are needed at all. The most efficient function is determined by comparing issues such as message latency and bandwidth and floating-point performance, all with reference to the size of the vector and the logical grid dimensions P, Q. (The Upshot program and

```
typedef struct la_local_dvector
{
  int m;                 /* local vector length */
  double *data;          /* vector data */
} LA_Local_Dvector;

typedef struct la_dvector
{
  LA_Local_Dvector v;    /* Local vector */

  int M;                 /* full length of vector */
  int type;              /* row or column type */

  LA_Grid_2d    *grid;   /* logical grid information */
  LA_Distrib_2d *dis;    /* how to map data on grid */

} LA_Dvector;
```

Figure 6.14
Definition of the distributed vector on the logical grid

```
typedef struct la_local_dmatrix
{
        int     storage_type; /* Storage strategy (row/column-major) */
        int     m, n;         /* Local dimensions */
        double **data;        /* The local matrix, as set of pointers */
} LA_Local_Dmatrix;

typedef struct la_dmatrix
{
        LA_Local_Dmatrix a;   /* Local matrix */
        int     M, N;         /* Global dimensions of LA_Dmatrix. */

        LA_Grid_2d    *grid;  /* logical grid information */
        LA_Distrib_2d *dis;   /* how to map data onto grid */
} LA_Dmatrix;
```

Figure 6.15
The distributed matrix structure

some empirical modeling will help decide which function is best for a given case on a real system.)

Vector Sum   The vector sum is typically a noncommunicating operation provided the vectors being summed are stored compatibly, that is, corresponding coefficients appear in the same processes at aligned offsets. This is the simplest of the parallel vector operations possible on the distributed vectors. The operation to be performed is $\mathbf{z} := \alpha\mathbf{x} + \beta\mathbf{y}$ where α and β are real scalar constants. Good implementations handle special cases like $\alpha = 0$ and $\beta = 1.0$ for better performance. Even better implementations use sequential BLAS (for Basic Linear Algebra Subprograms [21, 20, 57]) when local vectors are long enough to make the cost of a subroutine call less important than the performance gain of an often-optimized sequential kernel.

Thus, a number of different versions of the vector sum must be available, and be selected appropriately for different situations. This is where the object-oriented and object-based approaches to the library design differ. For the object-oriented case, the user is forced to "commit" to certain operations in order to pre-evaluate all the data transformations, choices about use of BLAS, and so on. This approach makes these relatively expensive choices a one-time operation, and may even encourage further one-time overheads for better performance. The object-based versions, which are object-extensions to the familiar BLAS, have to test for errors, data layout, and so on, each time, making the overhead of general data layouts somewhat higher than the object-oriented versions. These concepts are illustrated in detail with the code and related documentation available in '`examples/libraries`' (Appendix D).

Inner Product   The inner product offers a similar set of challenges to those presented by vector sum; in addition to offering the choices of replicated and non-replicated work versions, the use or nonuse of underlying BLAS remains. Here, we illustrate a version of the code that utilizes the object-oriented approach. For this approach, a "dot product" object is created once, describing the dot-product relationship between two vectors. Whenever a dot product is needed, `(*xy->op)()` is performed. The absence of arguments here appears to be a deficiency, but is actually a sign that we have tightly optimized our code![2] We show the version that

---

[2]A "dangerous bend" of the object-oriented style of programming comes immediately. We are tempted to want operator overloading, so that the vectors and matrices are expressible as formulas and regain mathematical beauty; unfortunately, at least with existing C++ systems, overloading introduces overheads because of temporaries. In the C strategy used here, all temporaries are explicitly shown.

employs sequential BLAS, to remind the reader that we can access efficient local operations (in the limit of large enough data). See Figures 6.16 and 6.17.

Skew Inner product   The skew inner product combines the idea of vector redistribution and dot product into a single calculation, when the vectors are not distributed compatibly at the beginning of the operation. Specifically, it handles the case where one vector is a "row" vector, in any layout, and the other vector is a "column" vector. Until now, we have been assuming that the vectors are co-linear (either row or column) and of the same distribution.

Both object-based and object-oriented versions of this call appear in the software distribution. The nice feature of this routine is that the object-oriented version is needed to achieve the right computational complexity, because it is essential to organize the operations in each process once and for all.

Matrix-Vector Product   To illustrate the use of the vectors together with dense matrices, we have also included the equivalent object-based and object-oriented libraries for the dense matrix-vector product. Here the number of choices for data optimization grows; hence, if the vectors and matrices are distributed incompatibly, a large number of `if` statements have to be handled. For the object-oriented strategy, this is done once and for all. For the object-based approach, lots of conditional branching gets done with each call.

6.4   The LINPACK Benchmark in MPI

The LINPACK benchmark is a well-known numerical code that is often used to benchmark computers for floating-point performance. LINPACK itself is an example of a successful numerical library, and it is interesting to briefly discuss some aspects of a parallel version of this program. We note that there is an active effort to produce a parallel version of LINPACK's successor, LAPACK; this package is known as SCALAPACK (for Scalable LAPACK). We will discuss only a few of the issues involved in developing this code; a complete version can be found in 'libraries/linpack.f'.

The benchmark program solves the linear system $Ax = b$ for x, given a matrix A and right-hand-side vector b. The matrix A is *dense* (i.e, all of its elements are nonzero). The code solves this problem by computing a factorization of A into PLU; here, L is a lower-triangular matrix, U is an upper triangular matrix, and P is a permutation matrix. The permutation matrix represents the exchange of rows used in the *partial pivoting* algorithm that this code uses to improve numerical stability.

```
double ddot_stride(LA_Dvector *x, *y, int *error)
{
  int    i, start, stride, m;
  double local_sum = 0.0, sum, *x_data, *y_data;

  if (x->type != y->type)  /* Check for compatible types */
  {
      *error = MPI_FAILURE;
      return(0.0);
  }

  /* Determine the stride based on type */
  if (x->type == LA_GRID_ROW)
  {
    start = x->grid->p; stride = x->grid->P;
  }
  else
  {
    start = x->grid->q; stride = x->grid->Q;
  }

  /* Sum up my part (non-optimized) */
  m     = x->v->m;
  x_data = &(x->v->data[0]); y_data = &(y->v->data[0]);
  for (i =  start; i < m; i += stride)
    local_sum += x_data[i] * y_data[i];

  /* Get the sum of all parts */
  MPI_Allreduce(&local_sum, &sum, 1, MPI_DOUBLE, MPI_SUM,
                x->grid->grid_comm);

  /* Return result */
  *error = MPI_SUCCESS;
  return(sum);
}
```

Figure 6.16
Object-based, strided inner (dot) product on distributed vectors, without BLAS

```
void LAX_ddot_strided_blas(LA_Dvector_ddot_stride_binop *xy)
{
  int     start, stride;
  double local_sum = 0.0, sum;
  LA_Dvector *x, *y;

  /* Dereference the binary vector operands: */
  x = xy -> binop.x;  y = xy -> binop.y;

  /* Determine the stride based on type */
  start  = xy -> local_start;
  stride = xy -> local_stride;

  /* Sum up my part */
  blas_ddot(&(x->v->m), &(x->v->data[start]), &stride,
            &(y->v->data[start]), &stride);

  /* Get the sum of all parts, put result back in object */
  MPI_Allreduce(&local_sum, &(xy->result[0]), 1, MPI_DOUBLE, MPI_SUM,
                xy->binop.comm);
  /* Return result */
  xy -> binop.error = 0;
}
```

Figure 6.17
Object-oriented, strided inner (dot) product on distributed vectors, with BLAS

In order to determine the permutation, as each row of the matrix is used to generate the factorization, the row of the matrix that contains the largest element is needed. We assume that the rows (and columns) of the matrix may be distributed across the processes. To find this element, we can use the code in Figure 6.18. This makes use of the MPI_MAXLOC argument to MPI_ALLREDUCE; this routine returns just what we need (the maximum in the first element and the location of the maximum in the second element).

An interesting feature about this library is that once code is developed using a general communicator (instead of hard-wiring in MPI_COMM_WORLD), it immediately becomes useful on any subset of processes. Thus, if a parallel application is using task parallelism (dividing a job into tasks that may interact) and each of these tasks is itself parallel, then a parallel linear system solver library written in MPI can be

```
      DTEMP(1) = DABS( WORK( J, J ) )
      DTEMP(2) = MYROW

      CALL MPI_ALLREDUCE( DTEMP, DDUMMY, 2, MPI_DOUBLE_PRECISION,
     $      MPI_MAXLOC, COLCOMM )

      IPIVNODE = DDUMMY(2)
      IF ( DDUMMY(1) .EQ. 0.0D00 ) IPIVNODE = ICURROW
```

Figure 6.18
Code fragment for finding a pivot row

used by any or all of the tasks. Without communicators (more precisely, the group
component of the communicator), the library could not be used in this case.

6.5   Strategies for Library Building

The nonblocking broadcast example is an example of an asynchronous library. The
rest of this chapter concentrates on *loosely synchronous* parallel libraries.   By
loosely synchronous libraries, we mean libraries that are essentially single-program,
multiple data. They compute on analogous parts of a dataset, however complex or
irregular, and occasionally communicate. Perhaps this communication is collective;
perhaps it is just selective point-to-point transfers. In any event, the number of
messages produced and consumed is well characterized in advance for such libraries,
and most often, both the size and sources for all messages are anticipated at the time
the program is written. That processes may "get ahead" of other processes between
synchronizing communications is the reason for the term loosely synchronous [26].
Also included in this model is the idea that certain processes may send messages
and continue even though their counterpart has failed to complete a receive; for
this purpose, we use MPI send routines that are nonblocking.

   Particular strategies are now available to the library writer because of features
in MPI:

- Define persistent distributed structures, based on communicators.
- Duplicate communicators for safe communication space when entering calls to
parallel libraries (`MPI_Comm_dup`, `MPI_Comm_create`).

- Use MPI-defined virtual topology information to make algorithms easier to understand (e.g., `MPI_Cart_create`).
- Augment virtual topology technology as needed (e.g., topology hierarchies, as in Section 6.3.1).
- Use attribute caching when adding additional collective operations to a communicator (Section 6.2).

A number of mechanisms used in libraries before MPI to achieve correctness are no longer necessary and can be safely discarded:

- It is no longer necessary to publish tag usage by the library to avoid tag conflicts with user code. If the library uses its own communicator, both it and the user have access to a full range of tags.
- It is no longer necessary to make a parallel library mimic the behavior of a sequential library by synchronizing at the entry and exit of each parallel call in order to achieve quiescence. Communicators local to the library ensure that no library message will be intercepted by user code or vice versa.
- There is no need to restrict the library programming model to nonoverlapping process group assumptions, since communicators with overlapping groups pose no particular problem for MPI libraries.
- Many existing libraries work only over "all" processors (processes) of a user's allocation. With MPI it is easy to write a library so that it can use whatever group of processes is specified when it is called.

7 Other Features of MPI

This chapter describes the more advanced routines from the MPI Standard that have not arisen in the discussion so far. We use the opportunity to introduce several interesting example programs.

7.1 Simulating Shared-Memory Operations

Throughout this book we have been concentrating on the message-passing computational model. Some applications are more naturally written for a *shared-memory* model, in which all of the parallel machine's memory is directly available to each process. In this section we discuss what is necessary in order to provide the basic functionality of the shared-memory model in a distributed-memory environment, and what MPI routines might be used in doing so.

7.1.1 Shared vs. Distributed Memory

The essential feature of the message-passing model is that at least two processes are involved in every communication; send and receive operations must be paired. The essential feature of the shared-memory model is that any process can access all the memory in the machine. On a distributed-memory architecture, where each memory address is local to a specific processor, this means that each process must be able to access the local memory of other processes, without any particular action on the part of the process whose local memory is being read or written to.

In a sense, then, every processor (CPU plus memory) must be host to two different functions: a compute process that does the main work, and a data server process that provides access to that processor's memory to the other processes in the computation (see Figure 7.1). These two processes need not be separate MPI processes. In many cases the machine's operating system or message-passing software will not permit it, and in other cases the overhead of switching between the two processes is prohibitive.

Several solutions to this problem exist, depending on what level of extension to the message-passing model is offered by the underlying system. In Chapter 10 we describe the approaches that assume that there is at least *some* such extension: active messages, interrupt-driven receives, or threads, to provide the data management process. Here we assume that no such extension exists, and we have to do everything within the message-passing environment defined by MPI.

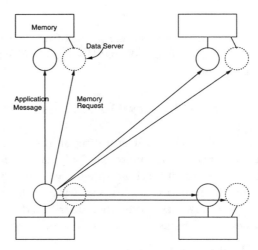

Figure 7.1
Sharing distributed memory

7.1.2   A Counter Example

We begin with the simplest possible case: simulating a single shared-memory location. Having a single "shared" variable that can be updated atomically by any
process is surprisingly useful. In a true shared-memory environment, the counter
is read and updated by normal memory operations, but the updating must be pro-
tected by a lock of some kind. In the message-passing environment, no lock is
needed because only one process is actually updating the memory location. Hence,
one easy way to implement the shared counter with MPI is to give one MPI process
the job of holding the counter and servicing requests to retrieve and update its value.
To make things particularly straightforward, let us suppose we wish to implement
something like the NXTVAL counter in the message-passing library TCGMSG. (See
Section 9.9 for a discussion of TCGMSG.) The function NXTVAL returns the value
of a built-in counter that is initialized to 0 at startup. Each retrieval of its value
increments the value by one. With many processes calling NXTVAL, it is guaranteed
that no two will ever retrieve the same value and that all values of the counter will
handed out consecutively, with no value being skipped.

We dedicate one process to being the "server" for this variable. It can be set
up much the same way in which we established the server for random numbers
in Chapter 3. Let us encapsulate the counter by defining of set of three routines
to manage it for the MPE library: MPE_Counter_create, MPE_Counter_free, and

Context	Group	Result
Same	Same	MPI_IDENT
	Same	MPI_CONGRUENT
Same		MPI_SIMILAR
		MPI_UNEQUAL

Table 7.1
Possible results for MPI_Comm_compare

MPE_Counter_nxtval. MPE_Counter_create will be a collective operation (must be called by all processes in a given communicator); it will split off one process of the communicator's group to hold the counter and return two new communicators. One communicator, counter_comm, will be used in calls to to MPE_Counter_nxtval; the other, smaller_comm, will be used by the remaining processes for the main computation. MPE_Counter_free cleans up these communicators and ends the server process function, terminating its original call to MPI_Counter_create. This strategy relies on the fact that MPI, unlike many other systems, supports collective and point-to-point operations on communicators based on arbitrary subgroups of processes. Thus, the communicator smaller_comm is just as capable as the communicator passed to MPI_Counter_create, except that it has one less process available.

This client-server computation is easy enough that we can include all the necessary code here. MPE_Counter_create is shown in Figure 7.2. MPE_Counter_nxtval is shown in Figure 7.3. MPE_Counter_free is shown in Figure 7.4. It is also a collective operation. The process with rank 0 in the counter's communicator sends a message to the counter process to make it call MPE_Counter_free as well.

We use MPI_Comm_compare to make sure that the server process does not attempt to free the communicator whose group it is not a member of. This routine compares two communicators by comparing the groups and contexts that make up a communicator. Since there are four combinations, there are four possible results. The result of the comparison has one of the values shown in Table 7.1.

7.1.3 The Shared Counter Using Polling Instead of an Extra Process

The disadvantage of the implementation we have just described, of course, is that one process is "wasted" minding the counter when it could perhaps be used in computation. To get around this disadvantage, this process must do useful work and manage the counter simultaneously. One way to do so within the restrictions of the message-passing mode, where all communication requires explicit receives,

```
int MPE_Counter_create( oldcomm, smaller_comm, counter_comm )
MPI_Comm  oldcomm,  *smaller_comm,  *counter_comm;
{
    int counter = 0;
    int message, done = 0, myid, numprocs, server, ranks[1];
    MPI_Status status;
    MPI_Group oldgroup, smaller_group;

    MPI_Comm_size(oldcomm, &numprocs);
    MPI_Comm_rank(oldcomm, &myid);
    server = numprocs-1;      /*    last proc is server */
    MPI_Comm_dup( oldcomm, counter_comm ); /* make one new comm */
    MPI_Comm_group( oldcomm, &oldgroup );
    ranks[0] = server;
    MPI_Group_excl( oldgroup, 1, ranks, &smaller_group );
    MPI_Comm_create( oldcomm, smaller_group, smaller_comm );
    MPI_Group_free(&smaller_group);

    if (myid == server) {          /* I am the server */
        while (!done) {
            MPI_Recv(&message, 1, MPI_INT, MPI_ANY_SOURCE,
                     MPI_ANY_TAG, *counter_comm, &status );
            if (status.MPI_TAG == REQUEST) {
                MPI_Send(&counter, 1, MPI_INT, status.MPI_SOURCE,
                         VALUE, *counter_comm );
                counter++;
            }
            else if (status.MPI_TAG == GOAWAY) {
                done = 1;
            }
            else
                fprintf(stderr, "bad tag sent to MPE counter\n");
        }
        MPE_Counter_free( smaller_comm, counter_comm );
    }
}
```

Figure 7.2
MPE_Counter_create

```
int MPE_Counter_nxtval(counter_comm, value)
MPI_Comm counter_comm;
int *value;
{
    int server,numprocs, myid;
    MPI_Status status;
    MPI_Comm_size( counter_comm, &numprocs );
    MPI_Comm_rank( counter_comm, &myid);
    server = numprocs-1;
    MPI_Send(NULL, 0, MPI_INT, server, REQUEST, counter_comm );
    MPI_Recv(value, 1, MPI_INT, server, VALUE, counter_comm,
            &status );
    return(0);
}
```

Figure 7.3
MPE_Counter_nxtval

```
int MPE_Counter_free( smaller_comm, counter_comm )
MPI_Comm *smaller_comm;
MPI_Comm *counter_comm;
{
    int myid, numprocs, result;
    MPI_Comm_rank( *counter_comm, &myid );
    MPI_Comm_size( *counter_comm, &numprocs );
    /* Make sure that all requests have been serviced */
    if (myid == 0)
        MPI_Send(NULL, 0, MPI_INT, numprocs-1, GOAWAY, *counter_comm);
    MPI_Comm_free( counter_comm );
    if (smaller_comm) {
        MPI_Comm_Compare( *smaller_comm, MPI_COMM_NULL, &result );
        if (result == MPI_UNEQUAL) {
            MPI_Barrier(smaller_comm);
            MPI_Comm_free( smaller_comm );
        }
    }
    return(0);
}
```

Figure 7.4
MPE_Counter_free

---

int **MPI_Comm_compare**(MPI_Comm comm1, MPI_Comm comm2, int *result))

int **MPI_Rsend**(void* buf, int count, MPI_Datatype datatype, int dest, int tag,
          MPI_Comm comm)

int **MPI_Iprobe**(int source, int tag, MPI_Comm comm, int *flag,
          MPI_Status *status)

int **MPI_Probe**(int source, int tag, MPI_Comm comm, MPI_Status *status)

Table 7.2
C bindings for MPI routines in counter example

MPI_COMM_COMPARE(comm1, comm2, result, ierror)
          integer comm1, comm2, result, ierror

MPI_RSEND(buf, count, datatype, dest, tag, comm, ierror)
          <type> buf(*)
          integer count, datatype, dest, tag, comm, ierror

MPI_IPROBE(source, tag, comm, flag, status, ierror)
          logical flag
          integer source, tag, comm, status(MPI_STATUS_SIZE), ierror

MPI_PROBE(source, tag, comm, status, ierror)
          integer source, tag, comm, status(MPI_STATUS_SIZE), ierror

---

Table 7.3
Fortran bindings for MPI routines in counter example

is to periodically probe the system to see whether a request for "counter service" has arrived. If a message *has* arrived, then the message is received and responded to; otherwise the computation is resumed. The check can be carried out with a call to MPI_Iprobe, which determines whether messages have arrived that match a source and tag given as arguments. The difference between using MPI_Test and using MPI_Iprobe is that MPI_Test is associated with a specific nonblocking send or receive operation that created a request. In particular, in the case of the receive, this means that the buffer has already been supplied by the user program. MPI_Iprobe (and its blocking version, MPI_Probe), on the other hand, are not associated with a particular request. Rather, they check for receipt of messages arriving with certain characteristics. To periodically check for counter requests and service them, then, the application program periodically calls

```
    MPE_Counter_service( comm )
```

where comm is the communicator built for use by the counter. Let us suppose that this time we let process 0 be responsible for the counter and define COUNTER as the tag to be used in counter-related communication. The code for MPE_Counter_service is shown in Figure 7.5. Assorted generalizations are of course possible (multiple counters, separate comunicators), but we show here just the simplest case.

```
    MPE_Counter_service( MPI_Comm comm )
    {
        static int counter = 0;
        int requester, flag;
        MPI_Status status;
        int flag;
        do {
           MPI_Iprobe(MPI_ANY_SOURCE, COUNTER, comm, &flag, &status );
           if (flag) {
               requester = status.MPI_SOURCE;
               MPI_Recv(NULL, 0, MPI_INT, requester, COUNTER, comm );
               counter++;
               MPI_Send(&counter, 1, MPI_INT, requester,
                        COUNTER, comm );
               }
           }
        while (flag);
    }
```

Figure 7.5
MPE_Counter_service

The programmer is responsible for seeing that this routine gets called often enough by the server process to service requests. One way to do this might be to use the profiling interface described in Section 7.6 to intercept MPI calls and probe for messages. The requests themselves are made with

```
    MPI_Send( NULL, 0, MPI_INT, 0, COUNTER, comm );
    MPI_Recv( &val, 1, MPI_INT, 0, COUNTER, comm );
```

Note the explicit known server and tag. The `count` field in the send is 0 because there is no data associated with the request; the tag is enough. Note that we also could have used `MPI_Sendrecv` here.

7.1.4 Shared Memory on Distributed-Memory Machines

In the preceding two sections, "shared memory" has consisted of a single value held by a single process. At this point, however, it is not difficult to see how to generalize the concept to treat all, or nearly all, the machine's memory as shared. If multiple processes per processor are allowed, then we can use the approach of Section 7.1.2, where the memory of each node is managed by a separate process. If they are not, or we cannot tolerate the overhead of constantly switching processes on a single processor, then we can use the approach of Section 7.1.3, at the expense of having to call the service routine often enough to provide timely service to requests. It is precisely the desire to avoid both of these drawbacks (multiple processes per node or frequent calls to a "polling" routine) that has motivated the approaches that go beyond the message-passing model. We touch on these in Chapter 10.

There is one way in which we might be able to improve the performance of the mechanism we have used here. We note that whenever a process requests data from another one, it knows that the request will be answered. Similarly, the "server" process knows that every request is expecting a reply. This means that the request for data, which earlier had the form

```
MPI_Send
MPI_Recv
```

can be recoded as

```
MPI_Irecv
MPI_Send
MPI_Wait
```

On some architectures, such as the Intel Paragon and the TMC CM-5, the protocol that takes place between sending and receiving processes can be greatly simplified if the sending process can assume that the matching receive has already been posted. The reason the protocol can be simpler is that if the sending side knows that a buffer has been supplied (this is the main function of `MPI_Irecv`), any negotiations between the processes over buffer space can be bypassed. MPI provides a special form of the send for this situation. If the sender is assured that the receive has already been posted, then it may use `MPI_Rsend`. (The "R" is for "receiver ready," the MPI Standard calls this kind of send a "ready send".) The MPI implementation may treat this as a normal send (the semantics are the same as those of `MPI_Send`) but is allowed to optimize the protocol if it can. If the corresponding receive is *not* posted, then this is treated as a programmer error, and MPI's behavior is undefined in this case. Thus the request for data is now of the form

```
MPI_Irecv
MPI_Rsend
MPI_Wait
```

7.2   Application: Full-Configuration Interaction

Ab initio chemistry attempts to compute chemical results from the first principles of the quantum theory of charged particles and their interactions. Solution of the Schrödinger equation leads to linear algebra problems that are amenable to solution on parallel computers. Several of the techniques discussed above are used in an actual production chemistry code, currently running on the Intel Delta and being ported to MPI.

Full-configuration interaction (FCI) provides the *exact* solution of the electronic Schrödinger equation within the initial algebraic approximation of finite 1-particle basis set. The only errors present in an FCI result derive from either the underlying finite one-particle basis set or approximations in the nonrelativistic, Born-Oppenheimer Hamiltonian. The ability to compute FCI wave functions thus confers the ability to adjudicate among all approximate methods (e.g., SCF, many-body methods, and truncated CI*) and, by comparison with experiment, permits assessment of deficiencies in the one-particle basis set and the Hamiltonian approximations.

In the largest application to date, which is also the largest full-CI calculation successfully completed, included 94,930,032 configurations, or 418,639,400 determinants. Methane ($r = 1.085600$Å) in a cc-p VDZ basis set was run in a C_{2v} subgroup of T_4, again with a frozen canonical SCF core orbital. This is just one point in a series of calculations. Details are given in [46].

The particular code described here uses "shared memory" in two different ways. First, on the Intel Delta, it uses Intel's `hrecv` to allow each process to serve as a data server for other processes. This program uses all the processing power and all the memory of the 512-node Delta, but there is no locality to the computation. That is, a single process may require access to data from any other node in the course of its work. When it does so, it calculates where the data is that it needs, posts a receive, and sends a request. The other process receives it with a preposted

hrecv, and sends it back with an Intel "force-type" message. This corresponds to
the use of MPI_Rsend.

Second, the workload is distributed through access to a shared counter, of the
type we have used as an example in this section. In TCGMSG, which this code
was originally written in, it uses NXTVAL, implemented on the Delta with hrecv.

7.3 Advanced Collective Operations

In the book so far, we have introduced new features of MPI as a consequence of
trying to create a parallel algorithm, code, or library. At this stage, a few routines
remain that we haven't needed in our palette of examples. Since these routines are
important, and may be just what is needed to get the job done, we present them
here all at once.

7.3.1 Data Movement

MPI provides many operations for collective data movement. We have already
seen MPI_Bcast and the gather routines. In addition to these, MPI provides the
opposite of gather, called scatter (MPI_Scatter and MPI_Scatterv, and a kind of
"all scatter" call alltoall (MPI_Alltoall and MPI_Alltoallv). These are illustrated
in Figure 7.6.

7.3.2 Collective Computation

We have already seen several collective computation routines;
MPI_Reduce performs a reduction of data from each process onto the specified root
process. We have already seen the use of MPI_SUM to sum up entries from all of
the processes in a communicator. MPI provides a number of additional operations,
shown in Table 7.4, that can be used with any of the collective computation routines.
Most of these are self-explanatory. The last two, MPI_MAXLOC and MPI_MINLOC, are
similar to MPI_MAX and MPI_MIN except that they also return the rank of the process
where the maximum or minimum was found (if several processes have the maximum
or minimum, the rank of the first one is returned). The datatype that is used for
MPI_MAXLOC and MPI_MINLOC contains both the value and the rank; see the MPI
Standard or the model-implementations man pages on MPI_MAXLOC and MPI_MINLOC
for more details.

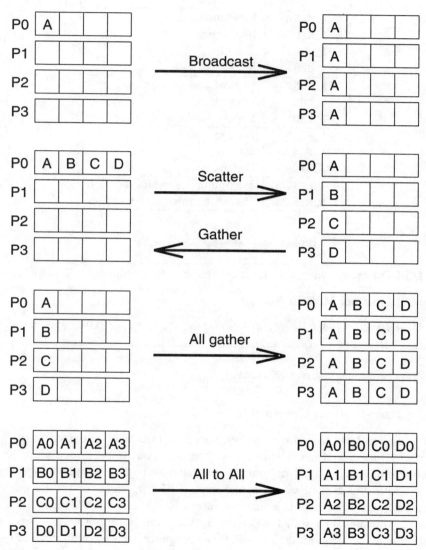

Figure 7.6
Schematic representation of collective data movement in MPI

MPI Name	Operation
MPI_MAX	Maximum
MPI_MIN	Minimum
MPI_PROD	Product
MPI_SUM	Sum
MPI_LAND	Logical and
MPI_LOR	Logical or
MPI_LXOR	Logical exclusive or (xor)
MPI_BAND	Bitwise and
MPI_BOR	Bitwise or
MPI_BXOR	Bitwise xor
MPI_MAXLOC	Maximum value and location
MPI_MINLOC	Minimum value and location

Table 7.4
Predefined operations for MPI collective computation

---

int **MPI_Op_create**(MPI_User_function *function, int commute, MPI_Op *op)

int **MPI_Op_free**(MPI_Op *op)

int **User_function**(void *invec, void *inoutvec, int *len, MPI_Datatype *datatype)

Table 7.5
C bindings for defining collective computation

7.3.3 User-Defined Operations

MPI also allows you to define your own operations that can be passed to the collective computation routines. For example, you may want to perform a more complex arithmetic operation (e.g., arguments are matrices to be multiplied together). A new operation is defined by using the routine MPI_Op_create; the output (third argument) of this routine is a new operation (in C, of type MPI_Op) that can be passed to routines such as MPI_Allreduce. There are two input values; the first is a function and the second indicates whether the operation is commutative. The form of the function is the same for C and Fortran; the bindings are shown in Tables 7.5 and 7.6. A user-defined operation is deleted by calling MPI_Op_free.

The second argument to MPI_Op_create, allows you to indicate that the operation is not commutative; that is, **a op b** does not give the same results as **b op**

MPI_OP_CREATE(function, commute, op, ierror)
           external function
           logical commute
           integer op, ierror

MPI_OP_FREE(op, ierror)
           integer op, ierror

int **User_function**(invec, inoutvec, len, datatype)

<type> invec(*),inoutvec(*)
integer len, datatype

Table 7.6
Fortran bindings for defining collective computation

a. Matrix multiplication is a well-known example of a noncommutative operation. The presence of the commutative flag allows an MPI implementation more freedom in determining the order in which it compute the result.

7.3.4 Other Collective Operations

MPI provides two more collective operations that users may find valuable. One is `MPI_Scan`. This is much like an `MPI_Allreduce` in that the values are formed by combining values contribute by each process and that each process receives a result. The difference is that the result returned by the process with rank r is the result of operating on the input elements on processes with rank $0, 1, \ldots, r$. If the operation is `MPI_SUM`, `MPI_Scan` computes all of the partial sums.

The other is `MPI_Reduce_scatter`. The effect of this routine is to combines a `MPI_Reduce` and a `MPI_Scatterv`. This routine can be used to perform multiple `MPI_Reduce` operations concurrently, and, in a sophisticated MPI implementation, can run faster than using `MPI_Reduce` and `MPI_Scatterv`.

7.4 Intercommunicators

Despite the convenience of communicators discussed thus far, a more general form of communicators, specifically targeted for group-to-group communication, proves a useful addition to MPI. Such "extended communicators" are called *intercommunicators* in the standard, and the regular communicators discussed thus far are more formally called *intracommunicators*. MPI defines a minimal number of operations for these intercommunicators; these operations are, however, a powerful starting point for group-to-group communication. (See also [70] for some discussion on extensions to MPI's intercommunicators.)

Figure 7.7 illustrates the relationship of processes and groups in an intercommunicator. Each intercommunicator contains a local group and a remote group. Accessor functions (mainly used by library routines) permit queries about whether a communicator is an intercommunicator, via MPI_Comm_test_inter, and access to information about the remote group, via MPI_Comm_remote_size and MPI_Comm_remote_group. The local group, of which the owner of the intercommunicator is always a member, is accessible with the usual commands MPI_Comm_size and MPI_Comm_group, as before.

The remote group is the destination of messages sent with MPI_Send and its relatives. When sending a message, one names processes in the remote group by rank. When receiving a message, a process is ranked according to its rank in the local group. These groups are not normally allowed to overlap; that is, no process in the remote group may also be part of the local group[1]. At present, only point-to-point communication is defined on intercommunicators, in addition to special operations used to construct and destroy them. These operations, mentioned above, are summarized for C in Table 7.7, and for Fortran in Table 7.8. The most commonly used function is MPI_Intercomm_create; regular MPI_Send and MPI_Recv calls are valid with an intercommunicator as their argument, as well as the usual intracommunicator already introduced.

Though general collective operations are not currently defined for intercommunicators, it is possible to turn an intercommunicator into an intracommunicator, with MPI_Intercomm_merge. This command provides a means to get an intracommunicator suitable for use with collective operations (as well as point-to-point operations). This operation is also summarized in the two tables just mentioned.

NXTVAL Revisited. Earlier in this chapter, we defined a client-server computation to provide the NXTVAL counter service. It turns out that using intercommunicators is another way to implement this service, and actually simplifies the coding of some features. Therefore, we've reimplemented the earlier service, as displayed in Figures 7.8, 7.9, and 7.10. While the service provided is equivalent, the bookkeeping of an intercommunicator is simpler, because the remote group of the clients is a server, at known rank 0. As before, the clients get their own "smaller_comm"

---

[1]There are exceptions to this requirement. In a multithreaded environment, processes may be duplicated in both the local and remote groups without deadlock.

```
int MPI_Comm_test_inter(MPI_Comm comm, int *flag)

int MPI_Comm_remote_size(MPI_Comm comm, int *size)

int MPI_Comm_remote_group(MPI_Comm comm, MPI_Group *group)

int MPI_Intercomm_create(MPI_Comm local_comm, int local_leader,
          MPI_Comm peer_comm, int remote_leader, int tag,
          MPI_Comm *newintercomm)

int MPI_Intercomm_merge(MPI_Comm intercomm, int high,
          MPI_Comm *newintracomm)
```

Table 7.7
C bindings for intercommunicator routines

```
MPI_COMM_TEST_INTER(comm, flag, ierror)
          integer comm, ierror
          logical flag

MPI_COMM_REMOTE_SIZE(comm, size, ierror)
          integer comm, size, ierror

MPI_COMM_REMOTE_GROUP(comm, group, ierror)
          integer comm, group, ierror

MPI_INTERCOMM_CREATE(local_comm, local_leader, peer_comm,
          remote_leader, tag, newintercomm, ierror)
          integer local_comm, local_leader, peer_comm, remote_leader, tag,
          newintercomm, ierror

MPI_INTERCOMM_MERGE(intercomm, high, intracomm, ierror)
          integer intercomm, intracomm, ierror
          logical high
```

Table 7.8
Fortran bindings for intercommunicator routines

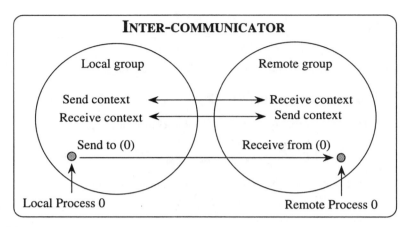

Figure 7.7
Schematic of an MPI intercommunicator

in which to work; unlike the earlier examples, `counter_comm` is an intercommunicator. The only interaction that makes sense is for the server to communicate with the clients (and the clients with the server) when referring to `counter_comm`. This provides a nice separation from any communication that might have been intended in `oldcomm` (which might have well been `MPI_COMM_WORLD`).

This simple example, while introducing the use of intercommunicators, does not demonstrate the convenience that they bring when both groups have, in general, more than one process. This provides a clean way to implement "parallel-client, parallel-server" computations [69].

To give more of a flavor for intercommunicators, we conclude by outlining two interesting services that could be supported by them: first, peer-oriented intercommunicators to allow separately devised "modules" to be interfaced at a higher level (an abstraction of an atmospheric/ocean model communication); second, a bulletin-board system analogous to the Linda tuple space [14].

Atmospheric/Ocean Intercommunication. A Grand Challenge application that is often discussed is modeling the ocean and atmosphere in a single, comprehensive code. Several groups are developing such codes, or evolving them from their sequential counterparts—often the atmospheric and oceanic codes are developed separately, with the intent to couple them at a higher level later on and to transfer boundary information at the ocean-atmosphere boundary via messages.

```
#define ICTAG 0
int MPE_Counter_create_ic(MPI_Comm oldcomm, *smaller_comm, *counter_comm)
{
    int counter = 0;
    int message, done = 0, myid, numprocs, server;
    int color, remote_leader_rank;
    MPI_Status status;
    MPI_Comm oldcommdup, splitcomm;

    MPI_Comm_dup(oldcomm, &oldcommdup); /* for safety, copy used only here */
    MPI_Comm_size(oldcommdup, &numprocs);
    MPI_Comm_rank(oldcommdup, &myid);
    server = numprocs-1;        /* last proc is server */

    color = (myid == server);  /* split into server and rest */
    MPI_Comm_split(oldcomm, color, myid, &splitcomm);

    /* build intercommunicator using bridge w/ oldcommdup */
    if(!color) { /* I am not the server */
        /* 1) the non-server leader process is chosen to have rank "0"
              in the peer comm. oldcommdup != rank of server
           guaranteed that this leader "0" has rank "0" in both
           oldcommdup and in this splitcomm too, by virtue of
           MPI_Comm_split
           2) the server has rank "server" in the peer comm. oldcommdup */

        remote_leader_rank = server; /* rank of server in oldcommdup */
        *smaller_comm = splitcomm;  /* return this new, smaller world */
    }
    else
        remote_leader_rank = 0; /* rank of non-server leader in oldcommdup */

    MPI_Intercomm_create(splitcomm, 0, oldcommdup, remote_leader_rank,
                         ICTAG, counter_comm);
    MPI_Comm_free(&oldcommdup); /* not needed after Intercomm_create */

    /* rest of code unchanged from before... */
}
```

Figure 7.8
MPE_Counter_create using intercommunicators

```
#define SERVER_RANK 0
int MPE_Counter_nxtval_ic(MPI_Comm counter_comm, int *value)
{
    MPI_Status status;
    /* always request/receive services from
        intercomm (remote) rank=0 */
    MPI_Send(NULL, 0, MPI_INT, SERVER_RANK, REQUEST, counter_comm );
    MPI_Recv(value, 1, MPI_INT, SERVER_RANK, VALUE, counter_comm,
                &status );
    return(0);
}
```

Figure 7.9
MPE_Counter_nxtval using intercommunicators

```
#define SERVER_RANK 0
int MPE_Counter_free_ic(MPI_Comm *smaller_comm, *counter_comm)
{
    int myid;
    MPI_Comm_rank( *smaller_comm, &myid );
    MPI_Barrier( *smaller_comm );
    if (myid == 0)
        MPI_Send(NULL, 0, MPI_INT, SERVER_RANK, GOAWAY,
                    *counter_comm);

    MPI_Comm_free( counter_comm );
    MPI_Comm_free( smaller_comm );

    return(0);
}
```

Figure 7.10
MPE_Counter_free using intercommunicators

Intercommunicators are natural for this situation. The separate codes can both work with intracommunicators, allowing them to be developed and tested separately. The intercommunicator for the ocean will have as its local group the ocean's processes, just as they appear in the intracommunicator used for ocean-only messages. Similarly, the intercommunicator for the atmosphere will have as its local group the atmosphere's processes. The remote group for the ocean will be the atmospheric processes that interface on the ocean, and vice versa. Other strategies are possible too, depending on the details of the communication across the boundary.

Building a Bulletin Board (or Linda-Tuple Space). A group of parallel data servers is another possibility with intercommunicators. The Linda tuple-space model provides a bulletin board of data that can be accessed by name, in the style of a virtual shared memory. In order to get reasonable scalability with of this strategy, multiple processes will have to be involved in the process of serving these requests.

Obvious operations are to place a named object into the space, to retrieve its value, or to retrieve its value and remove it. A process that is a client of the bulletin board service would have as its local group itself, or itself and others who are receiving the same class, or priority of service. The remote group for such clients is the set of servers (or subset of servers) that is allowed to post and retrieve information.

A key facet of these requests is that the clients should not know *where* the data is, or have to specify where it should be stored. Rather, a request will be made, possibly to a master server, which will then scatter the request. One of the servers will provide the service. The communication isolation of an intercommunicator helps with the possibility that the client receive a response from any of the servers, not just the server that took the client's original request.

7.5 Heterogeneous Computing

Heterogeneous computing refers to using a collection of computers of different types as a parallel computer. In many settings, a powerful parallel computer can be constructed by connecting workstations together. If workstations from several vendors are combined, the workstations may not share a common format for data. For example, the order of bytes within an integer may differ. Systems may even use different numbers of bytes to represent integers and floating-point values.

MPI has been designed to operate correctly in this environment. MPI ensures that if data is sent and received with MPI datatypes with the same type signature, then the correct data will be received (if the data is representable on both the sender and the receiver). No special steps need be taken to port an MPI program to a heterogenous parallel computer. Note also that this flexibility can be provided by an MPI implementation at no cost on a homogeneous system; this helps to encourage the creation of programs that are truly portable between dedicated MPPs and workstation clusters.

7.6   The MPI Profiling Interface

The MPI Forum recognized that profiling and other forms of performance measurement were vital to the success of MPI. At the same time, it seemed far too early to standardize on any particular performance measurement approach. Common to all approaches, however, is the requirement that something particular happens at the time of every MPI call, for example, to take a time measurement, or write a log record, or perform some more elaborate action.

The MPI Forum decided, therefore, to include in MPI a specification for how it would be possible for anyone, even without the source code for the MPI implementation, to intercept calls to the MPI library and perform *arbitrary* actions.

The trick is to perform this interception of calls at link time rather than compile time. The MPI specification requires that every MPI routine be callable by an alternative name. In particular, every routine of the form MPI_xxx must also be callable by the name PMPI_xxx. Moreover, users must be able to provide their own versions of MPI_xxx.

This scheme allows users to write a limited number of "wrappers" for the MPI routines and perform whatever actions they wish in the wrappers. To call the "real" MPI routine, they address it with its PMPI_ prefix. For example, suppose that we wished to create logfiles automatically instead of explicitly as we did in Chapter 3. Then we might write our own version of, say, MPI_Bcast, as shown in Figure 7.11.

We then need only ensure that our version of MPI_Bcast is the one used by the linker to resolve references to it from the application code. Our routine calls PMPI_Bcast to do the normal work. So the sequence of libraries presented to the linker is as shown in Figure 7.12.

The MPE logging routines require an initialization of their data structures. This can be provided just by having a "profile" version of MPI_Init, as shown in Figure 7.13.

Similarly, a profiling version of MPI_Finalize can be used to do any termination processing, such as writing out log files or printing statistics accumulated during the individual calls to profiled versions of the MPI routines.

Various profiling libraries are likely to want to enable user control of some of their functions at run time. A simple example is the MPE_Stoplog and MPE_Startlog that we defined in Chapter 3. The problem for the profiling interface is that the

```
int MPI_Bcast( buf, count, datatype, source, comm )
void *buf;
int count, source;
MPI_Datatype datatype;
MPI_Comm comm;
{
    int result;

    MPE_Log_event( S_BCAST_EVENT, Bcast_ncalls, (char *)0 );
    result = PMPI_Bcast( buf, count, datatype, source, comm );
    MPE_Log_event( E_BCAST_EVENT, Bcast_ncalls, (char *)0 );
    return result;
}
```

Figure 7.11
Profiling version of MPI_Bcast

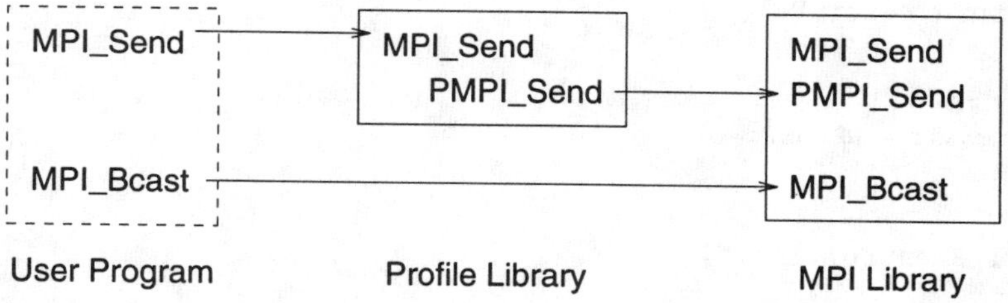

Figure 7.12
Resolution of routines when using profiling library

types of control are likely to vary widely from one profiling library to another. The solution is to define a single MPI profiling control routine, MPI_Pcontrol, with a variable length argument list. The first argument is assumed to be a level number, used to control the amount or type of profiling that is to occur. The amusing feature about this routine is that it is not defined to do anything. But a profiling library writer can redefine it, just as he redefines other MPI routines. For example, to provide the MPE_Stoplog and MPE_Startlog functions to the automatic MPE logging profiling library, one could do something like the following:

```
int MPI_Init( argc, argv )
int *argc;
char ***argv;
{
    int procid, returnVal;
    returnVal = PMPI_Init( argc, argv );
    MPE_Initlog();
    MPI_Comm_rank( MPI_COMM_WORLD, &procid );
    if (procid == 0) {
        MPE_Describe_state( S_SEND_EVENT, E_SEND_EVENT,
                            "Send", "blue:gray3" );
        MPE_Describe_state( S_RECV_EVENT, E_RECV_EVENT,
                            "Recv", "green:light_gray" );

        ...
    }
    return returnVal;
}
```

Figure 7.13
Profiling version of MPI_Init

```
MPI_Pcontrol(int flag);
{
    if (flag)
        MPE_Startlog();
    else
        MPE_Stoplog();
}
```

int **MPI_Pcontrol**(const int level, . . .)

Table 7.9
C binding for MPI profiling control

The beauty of this arrangement is that the supplier of the profiling library need not provide profiling versions of any routines other than those in which he is interested.

With the model implementation of MPI come at least three profiling libraries that use the MPI profiling interface.

MPI_PCONTROL(level)
                    integer level

Table 7.10
Fortran binding for MPI profiling control

- The first is extremely simple. It merely uses `MPI_Wtime` to measure the time spent in each call to the corresponding `MPI_` routine.
- The second creates MPE logfiles, which can be examined with a variety of tools, such as Teeshot. This profiling library was used to create the logfile data used to examine communication alternatives in Chapter 4.
- The third profiling library implements a simple form of real-time program animation, using the MPE graphics library to show process states and message traffic as it happens. A single frame looks roughly like Figure 7.14.

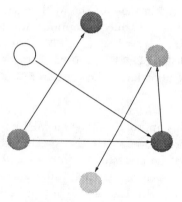

Figure 7.14
Program animation created with MPI profiling interface

Once the style of profiling has been chosen, of course, most of what goes into the profiled version of each routine is the same. It is not difficult to develop a meta-profiling mechanism that automates the wrapping of all, or a specific subset, of the MPI routines at once, provided that the action taken for each routine is the same.

7.7   Error Handling

Error handling and error recovery are important and difficult issues. Errors can be the result of user mistakes (e.g., invalid arguments), hardware errors (e.g., power supply failure), resource exhaustion (e.g., no more memory), or bugs in the base software. MPI provides some facilities for handling error reporting, particularly by libraries.

7.7.1   Error Handlers

MPI associates an error handler with each communicator. When an error is detected, MPI calls the error handler associated with the communicator being used; if there is no communicator, `MPI_COMM_WORLD` is used. When `MPI_Init` is called, the initial (default) error handler is one that causes the program to abort (i.e., all processes exit). Most MPI implementations will print an error message as well.

Instead of aborting on an error, MPI can return an error code. In Fortran, this is the `ierror` argument in most of the MPI routines; in C, this is the return value of the MPI function. The only exceptions are `MPI_Wtime` and `MPI_Wtick`. MPI provides two predefined error handlers: `MPI_ERRORS_ARE_FATAL` (the default) and `MPI_ERRORS_RETURN`. `MPI_ERRORS_RETURN` causes the MPI routines to return an error value instead of aborting. The routine `MPI_ERRHANDLER_SET` is used to change the error handler.

The error codes returned, with the exception of `MPI_SUCCESS`, are defined by each MPI implementation. This approach allows an MPI implementation to encode additional data into the error code. MPI also specifies a small set of error *classes*: small integers that divide the errors codes into a small number of categories. For example, for an error class such as `MPI_ERR_TAG`, the error code could encode information on what was wrong with the tag value (e.g., too big? too small?) and the MPI routine that detected the error. The error classes are shown in Table 7.11.

The difference between `MPI_ERR_UNKNOWN` and `MPI_ERR_OTHER` is that `MPI_ERROR_STRING` can return useful information about `MPI_ERR_OTHER`. The error class `MPI_ERR_UNKNOWN` can be used by an MPI implementation for unexpected situations, such as an error return from code that the MPI implementation itself uses.

To convert an error code into a error class, one uses `MPI_Error_class`. As an example, consider this code:

MPI_SUCCESS	No error
MPI_ERR_BUFFER	Invalid buffer pointer
MPI_ERR_COUNT	Invalid count argument
MPI_ERR_TYPE	Invalid datatype argument
MPI_ERR_TAG	Invalid tag argument
MPI_ERR_COMM	Invalid communicator
MPI_ERR_RANK	Invalid rank
MPI_ERR_REQUEST	Invalid request (handle)
MPI_ERR_ROOT	Invalid root
MPI_ERR_GROUP	Invalid group
MPI_ERR_OP	Invalid operation
MPI_ERR_TOPOLOGY	Invalid topology
MPI_ERR_DIMS	Invalid dimension argument
MPI_ERR_ARG	Invalid argument of some other kind
MPI_ERR_UNKNOWN	Unknown error
MPI_ERR_TRUNCATE	Message truncated on receive
MPI_ERR_OTHER	Known error not in this list
MPI_ERR_INTERN	Internal MPI error
MPI_ERR_LASTCODE	Last standard error code

Table 7.11
Error classes defined by MPI

```
/* Install a new error handler */
MPI_Errhandler_set( MPI_COMM_WORLD, MPI_ERRORS_RETURN );
/* Send a message to an invalid destination */
errcode = MPI_Send( ..., dest=-1, .... );
if (errcode != MPI_SUCCESS) {
    MPI_Error_class( errcode, &errclass );
    if (errclass == MPI_ERR_RANK) {
        puts( "Invalid rank in call to MPI_Send" );
        }
    }
```

All MPI implementations provide a way to translate an MPI error code (*not* error class) into a string. The routine MPI_Error_string takes an error code and a user-provided string buffer and returns a description of the error in the

string, along with the length of the text in the string. The string buffer must be
`MPI_MAX_ERROR_STRING` in size.

For example, instead of using `MPI_Error_class` in the example above, we could
use

```
...
if (errcode != MPI_SUCCESS) {
    MPI_Error_class( errcode, &errclass );
    if (errclass == MPI_ERR_RANK) {
        char buffer[MPI_MAX_ERROR_STRING];
        int  resultlen;
        MPI_Error_string( errcode, buffer, &resultlen );
        puts( buffer );
        }
    }
```

7.7.2 User-Defined Error Handlers

MPI also allows the user to define additional error handlers.

A user-defined error handler has the form

```
void user_function( MPI_Comm *, int *, ... )
```

The first argument is the communicator of the operation; the second is the error code. Pointers are used so that Fortran programmers may write MPI error
handlers without resorting to C. Additional arguments are available to C programmers through a "stdargs" interface; the meaning of these is defined by each MPI
implementation.

Often, it is desirable to temporarily replace one error handler with another one.
For example, in Fortran we can use:

```
call MPI_Errhandler_get( comm, old_handler, ierr )
call MPI_Errhandler_set( comm, new_handler, ierr )
<.... code .... >
call MPI_Errhandler_set( comm, old_handler, ierr )
```

For Fortran users to be able to do this, the error handler must be an object that can
be assigned to a variable. Since Fortran has no variable type that can be assigned
the pointer to a function, an MPI error handler is an opaque object that is created
and freed much like an `MPI_Request`. The routine `MPI_Errhandler_create` creates
an MPI error handler that Fortran and C users can assign to a variable.

Error handlers are attached to a communicator (so that a library that uses its own communicator can have its own error handler). Once an error handler is created, it can be attached to a communicator with `MPI_Errhandler_set`. The error handler for a communicator can be retrieved with `MPI_Errhandler_get` and freed with `MPI_Errhandler_free`.

Error handlers are inherited from the parent communicator. That is, when a new communicator is created with a function such as `MPI_Comm_dup`, the error handler in the new communicator is set to be the same one as the input communicator. Thus, to change the "global" error handler, one might change the error handler associated with `MPI_COMM_WORLD` before any other communicators are created (for example, right after the `MPI_Init` call).

Users should be careful with error handlers. An MPI program that encounters an error may not be continuable; that is, once an error has occurred, the user should terminate the program (see the next section). User-defined error handlers can be used to ensure that program termination proceeds in an orderly way and that important information is preserved. For example, a user-defined error handler might flush all file output buffers and write out some information on the cause of the error.

7.7.3 Terminating MPI Programs

To force an MPI program to exit, MPI provides the function `MPI_Abort`. This function has two arguments: the communicator of tasks to abort, and the error code that should, where possible, be returned to the calling environment (for example, by `exit(code)` or `stop code`).

An implementation is always free to abort all processes; that is, it can act as if the communicator argument was `MPI_COMM_WORLD`. The presence of the communicator argument is intended for compatibility with future extensions of MPI that may include dynamic process management.

7.8 Environmental Inquiry

In writing portable programs, it is often necessary to determine some implementation limits. For example, even a sequential program may need to know how many open files it can have. In many cases, this information is available only from the documentation of the system; this documentation may be incorrect or out of date. MPI provides access to some of the implementation limits through predefined at-

```
int MPI_Abort(MPI_Comm comm, int errorcode)

int MPI_Errhandler_create(MPI_Handler_function *function,
            MPI_Errhandler *errhandler)

int MPI_Errhandler_set(MPI_Comm comm, MPI_Errhandler errhandler)

int MPI_Errhandler_get(MPI_Comm comm, MPI_Errhandler *errhandler)

int MPI_Errhandler_free(MPI_Errhandler *errhandler)

int MPI_Error_string(int errorcode, char *string, int *resultlen)

int MPI_Error_class(int errorcode, int *errorclass)
```

Table 7.12
C bindings for error handling

```
MPI_ABORT(comm, errorcode, ierror)
            integer comm, errorcode, ierror

MPI_ERRHANDLER_CREATE(function, handler, ierror)
            external function
            integer errhandler, ierror

MPI_ERRHANDLER_SET(comm, errhandler, ierror)
            integer comm, errhandler, ierror

MPI_ERRHANDLER_GET(comm, errhandler, ierror)
            integer comm, errhandler, ierror

MPI_ERRHANDLER_FREE(errhandler, ierror)
            integer errhandler, ierror

MPI_ERROR_STRING(errorcode, string, resultlen, ierror)
            integer errorcode, resultlen, ierror
            character*(*) string

MPI_ERROR_CLASS(errorcode, errorclass, ierror)
            integer errorcode, errorclass, ierror
```

Table 7.13
Fortran bindings for error handling

tribute keys defined for the communicator `MPI_COMM_WORLD` (see Section 6.2 for information about attribute keys).

Currently, there are only three predefined attribute keys:

`MPI_TAG_UB` Largest message tag value (smallest is zero)

`MPI_HOST` Rank in `MPI_COMM_WORLD` of host process, if any

`MPI_IO` Which process can do I/O (see below)

In some parallel processing systems, there is a distinguished process called the *host*. The value of `MPI_HOST` is the rank of this process in `MPI_COMM_WORLD`. If there is no host process, the value `MPI_PROC_NULL` is used.

MPI makes some requirements for how system operations are provided *if* they are provided. For example, any system operation, whether it be (in C) a `malloc` or a `printf` or (in Fortran) an `open` or `write`, must operate independently of other processes. This means that all I/O is independent *if it can be performed at all*. To determine whether I/O is available, one uses the attribute key `MPI_IO`. The value associated with this key can be `MPI_ANY_SOURCE`, indicating that any and all processes can perform I/O; `MPI_PROC_NULL`, indicating that no process can perform I/O; or a rank of a process that can perform I/O.

The definition of "perform I/O" is that any of the language-specified I/O operations are allowed. For example, for C users, this means, for example, that `printf` and `scanf` are supported. For Fortran, this means that `read` (including `read *`, ...) and `print` are supported. If a system cannot provide the full functionality of the language-specified I/O, it is required to return `MPI_PROC_NULL` as the value of the key `MPI_IO`. (This does not mean that the system can not provide any I/O; just that it must return `MPI_PROC_NULL` if it can not provide all of the language-specified I/O. On some systems, providing access to standard input is not possible; these systems must return `MPI_PROC_NULL`.)

Note that because the key values are defined by MPI, future versions of MPI can define additional key values. In addition, each MPI implementation may define key values that refer to a particular implementation. As a hypothetical example, an implementation might provide `MPIV_REQUESTS` (`MPIV` for MPI vendor) that would give the number of `MPI_Requests` that can be active at any time.

7.8.1 Processor Name

It is often helpful to be able to identify the processor on which a process is running. Having the program provide the names of the processors on which the program has run is much more reliable than having the user remember to do so. In MPI, the

```
int MPI_Get_processor_name(char *name, int *resultlen)

int MPI_Initialized(int *flag)
```

Table 7.14
C bindings for inquiry functions

```
MPI_GET_PROCESSOR_NAME(name, resultlen, ierror)
            character*(MPI_MAX_PROCESSOR_NAME) name
            integer resultlen, ierror

MPI_INITIALIZED(flag, ierror)
            logical flag
            integer ierror
```

Table 7.15
Fortran bindings for inquiry functions

routine `MPI_Get_processor_name` performs this task. It also returns the length of the string. The buffer provided to this routine should be at least `MPI_MAX_PROCESSOR_STRING` characters long.

7.8.2   Is MPI Initialized?

We pointed out in Chapter 3 that `MPI_Init` had to be called before any other MPI routine, and that it could be called at most once by each process. These requirements can cause problems for modules that wish to use MPI and are prepared to call `MPI_Init` if necessary. To solve this problem, MPI has one routine that can always be called, even if `MPI_Init` has not been called. The routine, `MPI_Initialized`, returns a flag whose value is true if `MPI_Init` has been called and false otherwise.

7.9   Other Functions in MPI

The routines that we have not discussed fall into seven categories:

• Routines to create new groups from an existing group or groups:
`MPI_Group_incl`, `MPI_Group_range_incl`, `MPI_Group_range_excl`,
`MPI_Group_union`, `MPI_Group_intersection`, and `MPI_Group_difference`.

- Routines to get information about a group: `MPI_Group_compare`, `MPI_Group_size`, `MPI_Group_rank`, and `MPI_Group_translate_ranks`.
- Determine the type of virtual topology: `MPI_Topo_test`.
- Routines to manipulate Cartesian virtual topologies: `MPI_Cartdim_get`, `MPI_Cart_rank`, and `MPI_Cart_map`.
- Routines to manipulate graph virtual topologies: `MPI_Graph_create`, `MPI_Graphdims_get`, `MPI_Graph_neighbors_count`, `MPI_Graph_neighbors`, and `MPI_Graph_map`.
- Routines to cancel a point-to-point operation `MPI_Cancel` and `MPI_Test_cancelled`.
- Miscellaneous point-to-point routines: `MPI_Bsend_init`, `MPI_Get_elements`, `MPI_Ibsend`, `MPI_Issend`, `MPI_Irsend`, `MPI_Rsend_init`, `MPI_Sendrecv_replace`, `MPI_Ssend_init`, `MPI_Testsome`, and `MPI_Waitsome`.

Though these routines did not find a natural place in our book, they may be just what you need. For example, the routines for manipulating virtual topologies may provide exactly the operations needed for a PDE application on a complicated mesh. We encourage you to consider these routines when developing an application.

7.10   Application: Computational Fluid Dynamics

The following application illustrates the usefulness of user-defined virtual topologies and collective communication over these virtual topologies, all within a computational fluid dynamics code. It illustrates the use of operations on communicators to define topologies not provided directly by MPI. The computation of flow regimes over complex configurations involves the numerical solution of a system of coupled nonlinear partial differential equations known as the Navier-Stokes equations. Researchers in the CFD lab at the Mississippi State University NSF Engineering Research Center for Computational Field Simulation have developed an implicit, finite-volume code (known as UNCLE) for solving the unsteady three-dimensional incompressible Euler and Navier-Stokes equations using an artificial compressibility approach [74, 73, 77]. The flow solver can be used in a variety of applications ranging from maneuvering underwater vehicles to centrifugal compressors.

This code uses dynamic multiblock grids with relative motion in order to account for complex moving geometries. Key elements of the solution method include high-resolution, flux-based, upwind finite-volume approximations in time-varying transformed coordinates and a multiple-pass solution algorithm based on discretized Newton relaxation [77]. The equations in the fully coupled unsteady form are solved using third-order spatial differencing for both steady and unsteady flows and second-order time differencing for unsteady flows. Relaxation at each time step is carried out using a simple symmetric Gauss-Seidel sweeps. Turbulent flows are simulated using the Baldwin-Lomax turbulence model.

Large memory requirements and run times severely restrict the size and complexity of the problems that can be handled using the sequential version of the code. Therefore, the need was identified for a scalable portable parallel version that could take advantage of existing and emerging parallel platforms. The message-passing interface required for the parallel implementation had to support collective operations within user-defined groups as well as provide safe communication contexts for overlapping sets of collective operations.

7.10.1   Parallel Formulation

The parallel formulation employs spatial decomposition of the overall grid into subblocks that are assigned to separate processes [63]. To exploit coarse-grained parallelism and message passing, the implicit subiteration algorithm was modified at block interfaces to provide a block-decoupled algorithm. This decoupled algorithm utilizes Gauss-Seidel relaxation sweeps within each process but is effectively explicit at block boundaries, allowing parallel solution for all blocks. The solution at points shared by neighboring processes is updated between each subiteration by means of a message exchange.

The implementation of the Baldwin-Lomax turbulence model [3] introduces additional complexity into the parallel implementation of the flow code. This mainly affects the set-up phase of the solution process. The model requires the normal derivative of the tangential velocity at all impermeable surfaces in order to calculate the turbulent viscosity. This derivative is calculated in any block that includes an impermeable surface. The values of the derivatives then are propagated along the blocks that lie on any of the computational domain axes that begin with or terminate in an impermeable boundary. The blocks that satisfy the above condition are grouped together to share the derivative information. The turbulence model further requires the calculation of the maxima and minima of quantities that are distributed among the blocks of the above group.

The time-dependent equations in Cartesian coordinates are transformed into general curvilinear coordinates while introducing the artificial compressibility terms into the equations. The coordinate transformation essentially maps the arbitrary shape of the region of interest to a computational domain that is a rectangular parallelepiped. The solution procedure consists of two different phases. The first involves setting up a linear system using appropriate flux formulation and lineariza-

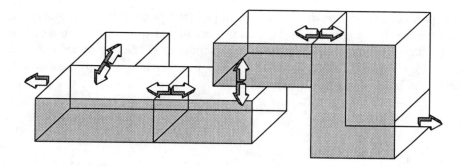

Figure 7.15
Multiblock grid of physical domain for CFD problem

tion techniques. The second phase is the solution of the linear system. The size of the system is equal to four times the number of grid points in the domain and could be of order 10^4–10^6 unknowns for realistic problems. However, the coefficient matrix of the linear system is extremely sparse and is generally solved using iterative methods. From the parallel processing point of view, the set-up phase is easily parallelizable, having local data dependencies and being confined to at most 13-point stencils for three-dimensional problems.

The mapping of the physical domain into a single rectangular parallelepiped is often not possible for complex geometries. This problem is resolved by resorting to what are known as multiblock grids, where the physical domain is partitioned appropriately before being mapped into a number of rectangular three-dimensional domains that share common faces. This is shown in Figure 7.15. The linear system in each block is solved using symmetric Gauss-Seidel iterations with boundary information being exchanged at the end of each forward and backward iteration [73].

Key areas of the parallel implementation include (a) initialization of the flow field, (b) duplication of stored data for points near block interfaces, (c) exchange of data during subiterations, for points having duplicated storage, and (d) treatment of line searches along coordinates emanating from solid boundaries, which arise from the particular algebraic turbulence model used. These issues are discussed below.

7.10.2   Parallel Implementation

In the parallel implementation of this code [63], the domain is partitioned into a number of nearly equally sized subdomains, each of which is assigned to a different process. The local data dependencies at the boundary of each block are taken into account by a two-cell-deep layer of buffer cells whose values are updated from the appropriate block as shown in Figure 7.16.

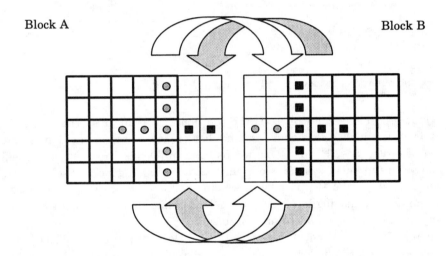

Figure 7.16
Information interchange between grid blocks in CFD application

These values are used for setting up and solving the linear system. Each node independently performs Gauss-Seidel iterations and exchanges information through point-to-point messages. Thus each block goes through the sequence of operations shown in Figure 7.17.

The data duplication and updating at the block boundaries are implemented using the MPI_Sendrecv routine. Since this is a locally blocking routine, tight synchronization is achieved among the blocks. A message is exchanged after each

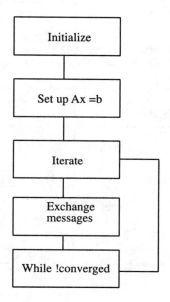

Figure 7.17
Simple flowchart of algorithm for CFD application

forward and backward sweep of the symmetric Gauss-Seidel iteration as shown in Figure 7.18.

The connectivity of the processes gives rise to a Cartesian virtual topology having empty nodes in it. Each process is tagged using an ordered triplet P,Q,R that represents its coordinate on the virtual Cartesian grid. These coordinates are then used to define communicators for processes that are oriented along any of the three axes of the grid. This technique involves repeated use of the `MPI_COMM_SPLIT`, by using the values of the coordinate triplet at the `color` value. For example, in creating the communicator in the second coordinate, we could use

```
call MPI_COMM_SPLIT( MPI_COMM_WORLD, p+r*p_max, q, q_comm, ierror )
```

The communicators that are defined in this way form the basis for all the collective operations needed for implementing the turbulence model.

The details of the parallel turbulence model implementation are shown in Figure 7.18. The blocks with the shaded borders have impermeable boundaries and

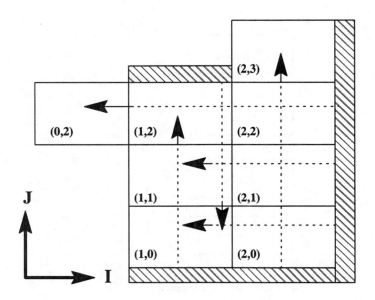

Figure 7.18
Communication pattern for CFD application with turbulence model

therefore calculate the velocity derivatives. The values of the derivative are then
broadcast to the blocks through which the arrows pass. This is done using the
`MPI_BCAST` routine within an appropriately defined communicator. Thus each ar-
row represents a separate process group and its associated communicator. A global
`MPI_ALLREDUCE` operation using the local minimum and maximum leaves the global
minimum and maximu with each process that participates.

This application illustrates how MPI can simplify the coding of a complex application. The key simplifications that result come from the use of virtual topologies
and collective communication with the virtual topologies. Although the researchers
chose to use their own virtual topologies in this case, the availability of communicators, and the ease of building subset communicators with `MPI_COMM_SPLIT` made
programming easy. This application would be extremely difficult on a system that
was strictly a point-to-point message-passing interface without contexts of message
passing.

8 Implementing MPI

A proposed standard library interface like MPI will provide little benefit unless it attracts implementors. To give them a running start, we describe in this chapter a design strategy for MPI implementation. This strategy allows for portability of large parts of the code implementing MPI while allowing tailoring of part of the code for maximum efficiency on individual parallel architectures. Looking at the implementation also reveals the motivation for some of the MPI design decisions. This motivation might be missed if one considered the library design only from the viewpoint of programmer convenience and failed to take into account the interface between the MPI library and the underlying message-passing hardware. The idea is to separate the complicated part of an MPI implementation (managing communicators, derived datatypes, topologies, etc.) from the part that makes contact with the communications device. The upper layers can remain open and portable, while various implementations of the abstract device on various real devices enables vendors to take advantage of their own proprietary algorithms and hardware.

Although we describe here a software architecture that facilitates the implementation of the MPI library, in fact the "device interface" described here can be used as a platform for the portable implementation of other message-passing systems as well. MPI provided a powerful motivation for this design by imposing simultaneous requirements of portability and efficiency. Today's (and tomorrow's) parallel machines and networks possess great diversity in their communication hardware, yet MPI is expected to deliver peak performance on all of them.

A much more detailed and specific description of this design can be found in [37]. We have tested the approach given here in the implementation for the model MPI system described in [22] and in Appendix B.

8.1 Introduction

The goal is to define an abstract device (ADI) on which a high-level message-passing application programmer interface (API) such as MPI can be implemented. An important requirement is to support a variety of instantiations of this device, from low-level FIFO's and streams to high-level libraries such as IBM's EUI-H, the Intel NX communication library, or portable libraries like Chameleon, p4, or PVM. Implementations of an API can thus consist almost entirely of portable code; dependencies on the low-level transport layer are encapsulated in the implementation of the abstract device. What we have most in mind are low-level devices provided by individual MPP and workstation network vendors; thus, a primary consideration is that this abstract-device approach not contribute any execution-time overhead to the real device. A wide variety of possible device protocols are envisioned. The design suggested here attempts to retain flexibility by listing a set of macros that are to be defined by each side of the interface but invoked by the other side. In other words, each side provides services to the other.

The original motivation for this work was the challenge of providing an implementation of MPI [24] that was both portable and efficient. Although MPI is a relatively large specification, the device-dependent parts are small. By implementing MPI using the ADI, we could provide code that could be shared among many implementations. Efficiency could be obtained by vendor-specific proprietary implementations of the abstract device. For this approach to be successful, the semantics of the ADI must not preclude maximally efficient instantiations using modern message-passing hardware. While this ADI has been designed to provide a portable MPI implementation, there is nothing about this part of the design that is specific to the MPI library; this definition of an abstract device can be used to implement any high-level message-passing library.

The design of the ADI is made relatively complex because we wish to allow for but not require a range of possible enhanced functions of the device. For example, the device may implement its own message-queuing and data-transfer functions. In addition, the specific environment in which the device operates can strongly affect the choice of implementation, particularly with regard to how data is transferred to and from the user's memory space. For example, if the device code runs in the user's address space, then it can easily copy data to and from the user's space. If it runs as part of the user's process (for example, as library routines on top of a simple hardware device), then the device and the API can easily communicate, calling each other to perform services. If, on the other hand, the device is operating as a separate process and requires a context-switch to exchange data or requests, then it can be very expensive to switch between processes, and it becomes important to minimize the number of such exchanges by providing all information needed with a single call.

In order to understand the design, it is useful to look at some abstract devices for other operations, for example, for graphical display or for printing. Most graphical displays provide for drawing a single pixel at an arbitrary location; any other graphical function can be built using this single, elegant primitive. However, high-performance graphical displays offer a wide variety of additional functions, ranging from block copy and line drawing to 3-D surface shading. One approach for allowing an API (application programmer interface) to access the full power of the most sophisticated graphics devices without sacrificing portability to less capable devices is to define an abstract device with a rich set of functions, and then provide software emulations of any functions not implemented by the graphics device. We will use the same approach in defining our message-passing ADI.

A message-passing ADI must provide four sets of functions: specifying a message to be sent or received, moving data between the API and the message-passing hardware, managing queues of pending messages, and basic information about the execution environment (e.g., the number of tasks). The ADI will provide all of these functions; however, we expect that many message-passing hardware systems will not provide queue management or elaborate data-transfer abilities. These functions will be emulated through the use of auxiliary routines that we will define here.

The structure of this chapter is as follows. We break down the functions of the ADI into

- Sending and receiving
- Data transfer
- Queueing
- Other device-dependent functions

Of course, these features are not independent. We tie them together by illustrating their interaction with a set of scenarios, in which we step through the sequence of actions of the API (think of it as the application program), the ADI (the MPI implementation), and the device (the software-firmware-hardware). Since low-level handshaking protocols are specified by the device, it is bound to be a hardware-software combination. As communication coprocessors become more widely used, more and more of the device's functionality is absorbed into what we refer to as "hardware" even though we mean system software running in a communication coprocessor.

We do not discuss any of the issues related to providing reliable communications, buffer protocols, or the implementation of the API side of the interface. We assume that the global (or collective) operations are implemented with the point-to-point operations, so our ADI has no global operations. This is an area for further development; we expect to add support for collective operations in the future.

8.2 Sending and Receiving

Sending a message from one process to another is the simplest operation; as we will see, the sending side of this is simpler than the receiving side.

8.2.1   Sending a message

Table 8.1 shows one possible scenario from the point where the user calls a nonblocking send routine (at the top) to when the user completes the nonblocking send.

User Program	MPI Implementation	Device
MPI_Isend		
	create device data structures; call device layer to start send operation	
		initiate send operation (or may just notify destination that message is available)
	return	
(User code)	...	...
		interrupt; message sent; mark send completed
	post send completed in MPI data structures	
(User code)	...	...
MPI_Test		
	MPI data structures show send completed	
MPI_Wait		
	deallocate device data structures; return	

Table 8.1
Nonblocking send followed by wait

The API part of this process is responsible for setting up the initial request and for converting user requests into the correct ADI requests. The ADI is responsible for transmitting the message. Note that the ADI and API work together to transfer the actual data; this strategy allows the API to provide a richer set of data layouts (for example, structures or vectors with regular stride) that are not supported by the ADI. Also note that we don't specify the protocol used by the ADI to actually transfer the message; this allows the ADI to optimize the protocol for different cases.

8.2.2 Receiving a Message

Receiving a message is much like sending one (the most important differences are discussed in Section 8.4 on the message queues). The progress of a nonblocking receive is shown in Table 8.2. A comparison with Table 8.1 shows that the only significant difference is the "check unexpected queue"; this handles the case of the data having arrived before the user posts the receive for the message.

User Program	MPI implementation	Device
MPI_Irecv		
	check unexpected queue (suppose not found); create device data structures; call device layer to start receive operation	
		post receive at device level
	return	
(user code)	...	...
		(message arrives, interrupt calls device) transfers data; mark receive completed
MPI_Test		
	check MPI data structures for status; return	
MPI_Wait		
	waiting on a particular receive (could transfer control to device layer or could poll); return	

Table 8.2
Nonblocking receive

8.3 Data Transfer

Transferring data from the API through the ADI to another process is a critical part of any device interface design. Unless great care is taken, an interface may require that data be copied several times before being dispatched or received. In addition, the user's data may not occupy contiguous locations in memory; any full-featured API (such as MPI) will provide a way for the user to specify how the data is laid out, and the ADI and API together must arrange to move it efficiently.

In describing the data transfer functions, we first describe those that relate to contiguous data. We require only that the ADI handle contiguous data, but we make provisions for ADI's that can handle more elaborate data layouts. However, our interface is designed so that data that is noncontiguous in the API can be transferred by providing the ADI with contiguous data. The design is complicated by the fact that we are striving to eliminate unnecessary memory motion; this objective requires several different ways of moving data between the API and the ADI.

The API is required to decompose any complex data layouts into layouts that the ADI can manage. The ADI may need to make multiple calls to the API to transfer data in this case. The ADI should attempt to minimize the number of transfers, and, where possible, do them directly without using the transfer routines provided by the API.

8.3.1   Transfers to and from the ADI

When a message is received, the ADI must transfer the data to the API in the location that the API user has specified. There are several ways to do this; the best choice depends on the exact situation. The easiest is for the ADI simply to use the known location of the destination data and for the ADI to transfer the data directly. If, for example, the data is contiguous, then before the receive is posted, a routine can be called to set the location into which the data should be stored. The ADI then can use this information to transfer the data into the user's program.

A more general interface that is capable of handling arbitrary data layouts is provided by having the ADI ask the API to perform the actual transfers. This allows the API to provide arbitrarily complex datatypes without requiring the ADI to handle them. One approach is to provide a way to transfer the data on demand; details can be found in [37]. Another approach is to have the ADI hand the API a contiguous buffer that the API packs or unpacks as required. This allows the ADI to transfer the message without any further exchanges with the API; this may be important if the ADI runs in a separate process and a context switch is needed every time control is exchanged between the ADI and API.

8.3.2   Noncontiguous Data

An ADI that can directly handle more general layouts of data can provide enhanced performance, particularly on high-performance systems where data can be moved between processes at rates similar to the rate that data can be moved to and from local memory. Our ADI design allows an ADI to provide this functionality and enable the API to adapt itself to the ADI. An ADI that can handle more sophisticated datatypes can define the appropriate macros to notify the API of which datatypes the ADI can handle directly.

To handle noncontiguous data, the ADI needs to know the layout of the data and the size of each element; for heterogeneous systems, it must also know the datatype. This data is provided in the `datatype` field of the `Request`.

If the datatype is too complicated for the ADI (for example, it is a complex structure), then the API can force the ADI to use the routines for transferring contiguous data.

8.4   Message Queuing

In a message-passing system, there are two queues: pending receives and unexpected messages (ones that have been delivered, at least in part, but for which the API has not yet issued a matching receive). Both the API and the ADI interact with these queues. For example, when the API issues a nonblocking receive, an element is added to the posted receive queue. When the ADI receives a message that matches this posted receive, the ADI must modify that entry in the posted-receive queue to mark that the message has been received. Because the ADI may operate asynchronously (for example, as the result of an interrupt), great care must be taken to ensure that the ADI and API do not attempt inconsistent modifications to the queues. There are a number of solutions to this problem, including the use of critical sections and multiple queues; the solution that we have chosen is to give the ADI sole responsibility for the queues. In other words, when the API needs to investigate any of the queues, it asks the ADI to do so for it. The ADI is then responsible for ensuring that all operations on the queues are safe. Since most basic message-passing devices do not provide any queue management, we provide a suite of routines that can be used to provide the required functions. All that the ADI implementor must do is to ensure that the ADI implements a critical section around queue accesses if the ADI operates asynchronously.

8.5 Unexpected Messages

The device must be able to react when messages arrive for which no receive has been posted. Such a scenario is shown in Table 8.3. The first event is the arrival of a message at the device; since no receive has been posted for it, it is an "unexpected" message. Contrast this with Table 8.2.

User Program	MPI Implementation	Device
(user code)	. . .	. . . (message arrives) MPI layer called
	place matching information in unexpected queue	transfer message into unexpected queue at this point, or defer data transfer (to buffer on sender, for example). Assume it defers.
	. . .	. . .
MPI_Irecv	check unexpected queue and find message; request device to complete receive	
		fetch message; transfer into user space
MPI_Test	return "not completed"	
		mark receive completed
MPI_Test	return "completed"	

Table 8.3
Message arrives; receive is posted later

In this case, the device must notify the ADI layer that the message has arrived, so that the ADI can update its data structures to represent that fact. Then either the message can be transferred in its entirety to the unexpected queue, or the receive can be deferred for later completion, when the MPI_Recv is eventually called by the application program.

8.6   Device Capabilities and the MPI Library Definition

Earlier we commented that considering the device interface illuminates some of the design decisions in MPI. Any message-passing library imposes a certain view of the characteristics of the devices it is intended for. MPI was carefully designed to impose as few restrictions as possible, thus allowing implementations that take full advantage of modern, powerful communications hardware.

For a simple example, consider the case of `MPI_Probe`, the blocking "probe" function. Recall that MPI also has a nonblocking version, `MPI_Iprobe`. Not all message-passing libraries support probe at all, and those that do tend to supply only the nonblocking version, since the blocking one can be implemented at the user level by calling the nonblocking one in a loop. However, this "busy waiting" is not really acceptable in a multithreaded or even multiprogramming environment. If the library supplies the blocking probe as well, then the implementation can use whatever resources it may have, such as an intelligent communication controller, to free the CPU while waiting for a message.

Similarly, from the programmer's point of view there is no *need* for the (blocking) function `MPI_Recv`, since its functionality can be obtained with `MPI_Irecv` followed by `MPI_Wait`. On the other hand, the library can make more efficient use of the device if it does not have to return to the user halfway through the operation. Another case in point is the use of a datatype parameter on all MPI communication calls, rather than using `MPI_Pack` and `MPI_Unpack` together with sending untyped data. Explicit packing and unpacking, while sometimes necessary, forces a memory copy operation that usually is not.

Other parts of the MPI library, such as `MPI_Waitany`, clearly could be implemented at the user level, and thus are not necessary in order for the programmer to implement an algorithm. Eliminating them would make MPI a smaller and simpler library. On the other hand, it would also eliminate opportunities for optimization by the communications layer. One reason that MPI is a relatively large library is that the MPI Forum deliberately sacrificed the notion of a "minimalist" library for enabling high performance.

9 Dusty Decks: Porting Existing Message-Passing Programs to MPI

It is a sign of the maturity of parallel computing that there already exist many explicitly parallel application programs written for the message-passing model. Old programs needing to be ported to new hardware and software platforms used to be called "dusty decks." Now they are more respectfully called "legacy applications." In this chapter we describe how to port such programs to MPI. In general, porting will be straightforward, because MPI is for the most part a functional superset of existing message-passing libraries. Therefore the changes to existing programs will be largely syntactical changes and, in some cases, can be done automatically.

This chapter emphasizes the need for the MPI Standard by illustrating how similar in semantics, yet different in syntax, the various message-passing systems are. It also illustrates the range of extra facilities that have been found useful by the users of these systems. Including the best of all of these facilities has contributed to the size of the MPI specification.

We will describe how to make minimal modifications to existing message-passing programs so that they will run on MPI-based systems. In most cases the most straightforward translations will provide improved performance on systems with well-tuned MPI implementations. Further performance gains may be possible by taking advantage of MPI features not found in the original programming system, but that will not be our main focus here. We nonetheless recommend that users consider such changes as an important second phase of using MPI.

We first consider message-passing libraries provided by the vendors: Intel NX, IBM EUI libraries, and Thinking Machines CMMD. These systems represent high-performance libraries that have been customized for particular platforms. We then look at public-domain message-passing libraries. These are precursors of MPI in that they were designed to be portable, but their design has in most cases been driven by particular research projects, and they have not had the benefit of the broad-based design process that produced MPI. They have, on the other hand, contributed many research ideas that have been incorporated into MPI, and they have provided an initial impetus to parallel computing in general by offering early mechanisms by which users could write portable parallel code. In particular, we describe how to port programs written for PVM, PARMACS, p4, TCGMSG, Chameleon, and Zipcode. Because PVM is so widely used (both versions 2.4.x and 3.2.x) on workstation networks, we devote special attention to moving both styles of PVM programs to MPI.

For each of the libraries we describe, we will organize the presentation as follows.

Basics Initialization and cleanup, identifying one's self and one's peers, and basic (blocking) send and receive

Miscellaneous Functions Nonblocking send and receive operations, wait, test, probe, status information, and error handling

Collective operations Synchronizing processes, collective data movement and computations, process subgroups

MPI Counterparts of Other Features Special features in the library that have MPI counterparts

Features not in MPI Special features in the library that do not have MPI counterparts

Process Startup Features outside MPI, but worth considering and comparing

Translation Tools programs to aid in conversion to MPI.

In the sections on process startup, we will describe the particular method used by the library at hand. We note that MPI provides no mechanism for process startup. It was decided during the MPI design process that

- On parallel machines, vendor-specific mechanisms were currently too diverse to coerce into a single style.
- On workstation networks, the problems of process startup and management were intertwined with the difficulties of workstation management and parallel job queueing, which were being addressed by a variety of both proprietary and public-domain systems. (DQS is one example of such a system.) These systems are being designed to interface to a number of different parallel programming systems being run on the networks, including MPI.

The systems summarized here, however, all did have to provide a startup mechanism, and we describe each in its place.

9.1   Intel NX

NX is Intel's message passing library. It is called NX/2 on Intel iPSC/2 and iPSC860 computers, and sometimes called NX/M on the Intel Delta and Paragon. We describe the common features of recent versions of the system.

The Basics

Table 9.1 shows the correspondences between basic NX functions and their MPI counterparts. The table shows Fortran bindings for both NX and MPI; the C translations are similar.

(most programs start in parallel)	`MPI_INIT(...,ierr)`
(no special exit code)	`MPI_FINALIZE(ierr)`
`me = mynode();`	`MPI_COMM_RANK(MCW,all_of_me,ierr)`
`mep = myptype();`	
`np = numnodes()`	`MPI_COMM_SIZE(MCW,np,ierr)`
`csend(tag,buf,count,`	`MPI_SEND(buf, count, MPI_BYTE,`
`    dest,destp)`	`    dest, tag, MCW)`
`crecv(tag,buf,count)`	`MPI_RECV(buf, count, MPI_BYTE,`
	`    MPI_SRC_ANY, tag, MCW, status)`
`crecvx(tag,buf,count,`	`MPI_RECV(..., MPI_BYTE,`
`  src,srcp,status)`	`    src,...,status)`

Table 9.1
Translating NX to MPI: basic functions. "`MCW`" is short for `MPI_COMM_WORLD` in the table.

NX has both traditional and new-style calls (with **x** at the end of the names). The **x**-style calls are more general, support both tag- and source-matching, and universally include the secondary node name, the "ptype," which is a means of distinguishing multiple processes per processor. For our purposes, the source pairs (`src,srcp`) and destination pairs (`dest,destp`) correspond to ranks. For many applications, and for older NX codes, all the ptype's are zero.

Miscellaneous Functions

Good correspondence exists between nonblocking NX and MPI point-to-point communication, as we can see from Table 9.2. For error handling, NX provides access through prepended underscore versions of most routines that return success/failure; these are documented in the Intel manual. Furthermore, while MPI provides different communication modes with variations of send (e.g., `MPI_RSEND`), NX accomplishes "ready send" with "force types," which are the available tags 1,073,741,824–1,999,999,999. Also, NX reserves all message tags above 1,000,000,000, except for the force types. Force type messages don't match up against wildcard tag selection (`tag=-1` in Intel calls), to help provide some guarantee that messages don't end up in the wrong buffer.

```
isend(...)        MPI_ISEND(.., MPI_BYTE,..)
irecv(...)        MPI_IRECV(.., MPI_BYTE,..)
iprobe(tag)       MPI_IPROBE(MPI_SRC_ANY,tag,comm,flag,status,
                  ierr)
cprobe(tag)       MPI_PROBE(...)
cprobex(...)      MPI_PROBE(...)
msgwait(...)      MPI_WAIT(...)
msgcancel(...)    MPI_CANCEL(...)
```

Table 9.2
Translating NX to MPI: miscellaneous functions

Collective Operations

Several but not all of the MPI collective operations are provided in NX but, crucially, without subgroups in NX. Table 9.3 shows a sampling of the correspondences. In Table 9.3, the tag used by the pseudo-broadcast gsendx() must be unique to

```
gsync()                          MPI_BARRIER(MCW,ierr)
gsendx(excltag,buf,count,        MPI_BCAST(buf,count,datatype,
  root,group,groupsize)
                                 comm_of_group,ierr)
gopf(sbuf,count,rbuf,op)         MPI_ALLREDUCE(sbuf,rbuf,count,
                                 datatype,op,MCW)
gd[high,low](sbuf,count,rbuf)    MPI_ALLREDUCE(sbuf,rbuf,count,
                                 MPI_DOUBLE,MPI_[MAX,MIN],MCW)
gd[sum,prod](sbuf,count,rbuf)    MPI_ALLREDUCE(sbuf,rbuf,count,
                                 MPI_DOUBLE,MPI_[SUM,PROD],...)
gcol(sbuf,slen,rbuf,rlen,count)  MPI_ALLGATHERV(sbuf,scount,
                                   datatype,rbuf,rcount,
                                   displs,recvtype,MCW)
gcolx(sbuf,all_lens,rbuf)        MPI_ALLGATHER(sbuf,scount,
                                   datatype,rbuf,
                                   rcount,datatype,MCW)
```

Table 9.3
Translating NX to MPI: collective operations; MCW is short for MPI_COMM_WORLD. Only a sampling of the NX collective routines are shown.

prevent mixups with other messages; gsendx() is matched with crecv(), irecv(), or `hrecv()` at the receiver. The x-suffix to `gcolx()` refers to the fact that each process knows the size of all elements going to be concatenated, whereas for `gcol()` only each local node knows this information beforehand. The use of `sbuf` and `rbuf` shown in Table 9.3 is not precise; Intel calls require extra storage for received data for operations, but actually place the final result over `sbuf`, unlike MPI routines, which use both `sbuf` and `rbuf` but place the result in `rbuf`.

MPI Counterparts of Other Features

MPI provides several other calls that also appear in NX. Some of these are shown in Table 9.4.

```
csendrecv(...)      MPI_SENDRECV(...)
isendrecv(...)      MPI_ISEND(...); MPI_IRECV(...);
host = myhost()     MPI_ATTR_GET(MPI_COMM_WORLD, MPI_HOST, &host);
```

Table 9.4
Translating NX to MPI: mapping other features of NX.

Features not in MPI

MPI does not support interrupt-driven messages, such as those that appear in both NX and CMMD. The identifying feature of these interrupt messages is that a user handler is provided, and this handler is called when such a message is received. This makes interrupt messages essentially equivalent to coarse-grained "active messages." These calls are extremely useful for creating virtual shared memory in the absence of a true multithreaded capability on a compute node.

In addition, NX provides access to basic parallel I/O capability. It has a number of synchronous and asynchronous calls related to file I/O, which are sandwiched into the NX library. MPI does not currently define any parallel I/O calls.

Process Startup

Earlier versions of NX supported dynamic process management, particularly the version for iPSC/860 and earlier; the `load()` call exemplifies this support. With the Paragon came the re-introduction of dynamic process support. NX on the Paragon also has extensive calls for dynamic partition management.

9.2   IBM EUI

EUI, also known as MPL, is IBM's product for message passing on the SP1 and SP2 parallel machines.

The Basics

Table 9.5 shows the correspondences between basic EUI functions and their MPI counterparts. The table shows Fortran bindings for both EUI and MPI; the C translations are similar; EUI C calls are all lower case and replace MP_ with mpc_. We omit most arguments for this conversion, because they can be easily inferred from the way in which the EUI (and respective MPI) calls are used.

(programs start in parallel)	MPI_INIT(...,ierr)
(no special exit code)	MPI_FINALIZE(ierr)
MP_GETRANK(...)	MPI_COMM_RANK(...)
MP_GETSIZE()	MPI_COMM_SIZE(...)
MP_BSEND(...)	MPI_SEND(...)
MP_BRECV(...)	MPI_RECV(...)

Table 9.5
Translating EUI to MPI: basic functions

Miscellaneous Functions

There is also substantial compatibility between nonblocking EUI and MPI point-to-point communication, as can be seen in Table 9.6

MP_SEND(...)	MPI_ISEND(.., MPI_BYTE,..)
MP_RECV(...)	MPI_IRECV(.., MPI_BYTE,..)
MP_WAIT(...)	MPI_WAIT(...)
MP_STATUS(...)	MPI_TEST(...)

Table 9.6
Translating EUI to MPI: miscellaneous functions

Collective Operations

EUI has a relatively complete set of collective operations, defined on groups and subgroups, all working from the allgrp, which is directly analogous to

MPI_COMM_WORLD's group. In Table 9.7, each EUI call with a group argument is to

MP_SYNC()	MPI_BARRIER(...)
MP_BCAST()	MPI_BCAST(...)
MP_COMBINE(...)	MPI_ALLREDUCE(...)
MP_SCATTER(...)	MPI_SCATTER(...)
MP_GATHER(...)	MPI_GATHER(...)
MP_PREFIX(...)	MPI_SCAN(...)
MP_CONCAT(...)	MPI_ALLGATHER(...)
MP_INDEX(...)	MPI_ALLTOALLV(...)

Table 9.7
Translating EUI to MPI: collective operations

be replaced with a corresponding communicator in MPI, so conversion is obvious.

MPI Counterparts of Other Features

MP_GROUP(...)	(MPI Group Setlike Operations)
MP_PARTITION(...)	MPI_COMM_SPLIT(...)
MP_PACK(...)	MPI_PACK(...)
MP_UNPACK(...)	MPI_UNPACK(...)
MP_STOPALL(...)	MPI_ABORT(...)

Table 9.8
Translating EUI to MPI: mapping other features of EUI

EUI's collective operations can operate over subgroups.

Features Not in MPI

EUI provides access not only to the ranks of processes, but to their "task ID" for providing low-level translations. This provision is specifically disallowed in MPI. Furthermore, EUI provides a number of task inquiry operations not found in MPI.

Process Startup

The IBM SP1 manages process creation statically, outside the scope of its message-passing system. Thus, like MPI, EUI has no process management functionality.

9.3 TMC CMMD

CMMD is the message-passing system supported on the Thinking Machines CM-5. It in turn is implemented on top of the CMAM active message library. CMMD has gone through a number of major revisions; to date, the major versions have all had incompatibilities. We discuss here version 3.0.

The Basics

Table 9.9 shows the correspondences between the basic MPI routines and CMMD. CMMD provides a number of different send and receive modes; we have made one of several possible correspondences in this table.

(programs start in parallel)	`MPI_INIT(...)`
(no special exit code)	`MPI_FINALIZE(ierr)`
`me=CMMD_self_address()`	`MPI_COMM_RANK(MPI_COMM_WORLD,me,ierr)`
`np=CMMD_partition_size()`	`MPI_COMM_SIZE(MPI_COMM_WORLD,np,ierr)`
`CMMD_send_block(...)`	`MPI_SEND(.., MPI_BYTE,...)`
`CMMD_receive_block(...)`	`MPI_RECV(.., MPI_BYTE,...)`

Table 9.9
Translating to MPI: basic functions

Miscellaneous Functions

CMMD provides both blocking and nonblocking operations. The nonblocking communication ("async") routines provide a handler that can be called when the message arrives; the MPI idiom for this is a blocking operation in a separate thread. CMMD mcbs are somewhat like a combination of MPI's `MPI_Request` objects and `MPI_Status` objects. CMMD has a `CMMD_all_msgs_wait()`; but it takes no arguments and refers to all messages globally, and hence can not be used in libraries (unless they clearly restrict the user's ability to use CMMD).

CMMD provides for "virtual channels." MPI has no direct counterpart, but for many situations, MPI's persistent requests (created with, e.g., `MPI_Send_init`) and "ready send" mode (`MPI_Rsend`) provide similar functionality.

Another view of the buffering choices made by CMMD is that `MPI_Rsend` can be thought of as the MPI counterpart of `CMMD_send_block`; users porting *to* CMMD may wish to bear this in mind.

```
CMMD_send_and_receive(...)    MPI_Sendrecv(...)
CMMD_send_block_v(...)        MPI_Send(...,vector-datatype,...)
CMMD_msg_pending(...)         MPI_Iprobe(..)
CMMD_msg_sender()             status.MPI_SOURCE
CMMD_msg_tag()                status.MPI_TAG
CMMD_bytes_received()         MPI_Get_count(&status,MPI_BYTE,&len)
CMMD_send_async(...)          MPI_Isend(...)
CMMD_receive_async(...)       MPI_Irecv(...)
CMMD_send_noblock(...)        MPI_Send(...)
CMMD_msg_done(mcb)            MPI_Test(&request,&status)
CMMD_msg_wait(mcb)            MPI_Wait(&request,&status)
```

Table 9.10
Translating to MPI: Miscellaneous functions

Collective Operations

The CM-5 has special hardware to perform some collective operations; the design of the CMMD collective operations reflects this.

```
CMMD_bc_to_nodes(...)         MPI_BCAST(...,MCW)
CMMD_receive_bc_from_node(...)
CMMD_scan_int(...)            MPI_SCAN(...,1,MPI_INT,...,MCW)
CMMD_reduce_double(...)       MPI_ALLREDUCE(...,1,
                                   MPI_DOUBLE,...,MCW )
CMMD_reduce_v(...)            MPI_ALLREDUCE(...)
CMMD_concat_with_nodes(...)   MPI_ALLGATHER(...)
CMMD_sync_with_nodes()        MPI_BARRIER(MCW)
```

Table 9.11
Translating CMMD to MPI: collective functions; MCW is short for MPI_COMM_WORLD.

The CMMD scan routines can be *segmented*; MPI can accomplish the same effect by using multiple contexts.

CMMD collective routines can be applied only to all processes; no subsets are possible.[1]

---

[1] It is possible to use CMMD_reset_partition_size to permanently decrease the number of processes, but this procedure is not reversible and is effectively redefining the CMMD equivalent of MPI_COMM_WORLD.

MPI Counterparts of Other Features

```
CMMD_error(format,args...)   printf(...);
                             MPI_Abort(0,MPI_COMM_WORLD);
```

Table 9.12
Translating to MPI: special functions

CMMD provides some timers that measure the time taken by a user program; the *elapsed time* field of these timers is roughly equivalent to the time given by MPI_Wtime. It is difficult for libraries to use these timers because they are identified by a single integer and any part of a program may reset them. There is no "registry" mechanism or other way for a routine to discover which timers are already being used.

Features Not in MPI

CMMD contains an active messages interface (it is in fact implemented on top of it) that is available to sophisticated users. The interface includes routines to copy data (CMAML_scopy and CMAML_pcopy) and routines such as CMAML_rpc to send remote procedure calls.

CMMD includes some I/O features. In particular, CMMD I/O operations can be collective as well as independent; the CMMD mode CMMD_local matches the requirements of MPI for non-message-passing operations.

Process Startup

Programs start automatically; the setup is handled essentially at link time by linking with special initialization code. This process is relatively transparent to the user. The number of nodes is chosen by selecting a partition; if an application needs fewer nodes than the smallest partition it can call CMMD_reset_partition_size.

9.4   Express

Express is a commercial portable set of tools and utilities designed for parallel processing, sold by ParaSoft. It provides not only message passing and collective operations, but also a rich tuning and debugging environment. There are tools for managing I/O and parallel graphics. Here we focus just on the message-passing library, and, for variety, show the C bindings instead of Fortran. The routines described here come from Version 3.0 of the C User's Guide [17].

The Basics

```
exparam(&env)        MPI_Init(...)
me = env.procnum     MPI_Comm_rank(MPI_COMM_WORLD,&me)
np = env.nprocs      MPI_Comm_size(MPI_COMM_WORLD,&np)
exread(...)          MPI_Send(.., MPI_BYTE,...)
exwrite(...)         MPI_Recv(.., MPI_BYTE,...)
```

Table 9.13
Translating Express to MPI: basic functions

Miscellaneous Functions

The nonblocking operations in Express have an extra integer argument, shown as status in Table 9.14, which is set to -1 at the initiation of the operation, which can be tested to determine whether the operation is complete. At completion, it is set to the number of bytes sent or received.

```
exsend(...,&status)       MPI_Isend(.., MPI_BYTE,..)
exreceive(...,&status)    MPI_Irecv(.., MPI_BYTE,..)
(status < 0) ?            MPI_TEST(...)
```

Table 9.14
Translating Express to MPI: miscellaneous functions

Collective Operations

Express has a simple set of collective operations, and supports subgroups. The single operation **excombine** is used for nearly all of them; the user supplies the specific function to be used in the operation. Arguments to **excombine** specify a list of processes that are to participate in the operation. The result is always distributed back to all the processes who participated. A reserved value (ALLNODES) specifies all the processes.

MPI Counterparts of Other Features

Express does have features for dealing with a virtual topology of processes. These are currently limited to grid topologies. Some of the capabilities of MPI datatypes are provided by the **exvread** and **exvwrite** functions for sending and receiving noncontiguous data.

```
exsync(...            MPI_Barrier(...)
exbroadcast(...)      MPI_Bcast(...)
excombine(...,op,...) MPI_Allreduce(...,op,...)
```

Table 9.15
Translating Express to MPI: Collective Operations

Features not in MPI

Express is an entire environment for parallel programming, not just a message-passing system. Thus it contains many features that have not been addressed by MPI, including graphics, debugging, and some aspects of parallel I/O.

Process Startup

There are facilities for starting processes very simply (`cubix -n10` to start 10 processes, for example) or to load files explicitly under program control. There is complete support for the "host-node" system model.

9.5   PVM 2.4.x

PVM 2.4.x (normally 2.4.1 or 2.4.2) is an important intermediate version of a library of message-passing models developed at Oak Ridge National Laboratory, University of Tennessee, and Emory University by Vaidy Sunderam, Al Geist, Jack Dongarra, Robert Manchek, and others (see [34]). PVM stands for "Parallel Virtual Machine," heralding its support for process management, heterogeneous clusters, and message passing. PVM 2.4.2 and earlier versions run on heterogeneous networks of workstations and on front ends of parallel machines, whereas PVM 3.0 and later also support some parallel machines. Version 2.4.x's message-passing aspects are quite simple, and translation to MPI should consequently be straightforward. In the next section, we detail porting from PVM 3.2.x to MPI separately, since PVM 2.4.x and 3.2.x are different. For more information, see [30].

The Basics

Table 9.16 shows the correspondences between basic PVM 2.4.x functions and their MPI counterparts. The table shows Fortran bindings for both PVM 2.4.x and MPI; the C translations are similar. We show only certain of the arguments to each routine; the correspondences for the others can be readily inferred.

`enroll()`	`MPI_INIT(...)`
`leave()`	`MPI_FINALIZE(ierr)`
`whoami(...,me)`	`MPI_COMM_RANK(MPI_COMM_WORLD,me,ierr)`
`pstatus(np,...)`	`MPI_COMM_SIZE(MPI_COMM_WORLD,np,ierr)`
`snd(...), vsnd(...)`	`MPI_SEND(.., buf_type,...)`
`rcv(...), vrcv(...)`	`MPI_RECV(.., buf_type,...)`

Table 9.16
Translating PVM 2.4.x to MPI: basic functions

In PVM 2.4.x, the `enroll()` call may be omitted in favor of `whoami()` if the program was "initiated" by PVM; the corresponding call to `MPI_INIT()` is not optional. The call to `leave()` is optional as well (when processes have been started by a call to `initiate()` or `initiateM()`), but its counterpart, `MPI_FINALIZE()` is never optional. The call `pvm_mstat()` provides further information. (see [34]). (In Table 9.16, the "`buf_type`" argument in `MPI_SEND()` and `MPI_RECV()` refers either to a simple type like `MPI_BYTE` or `MPI_INTEGER` or to a more complex data type, covered below.)

The PVM design makes no claims about buffering, though the most widely distributed implementation provides significant (though not infinite) buffering. PVM users who depend on the buffering in the implementation can use the buffered sends (`MPI_Bsend`) of MPI.

The functions `rcvmulti` and `vrcvmulti`, which are capable of enumerating acceptable message tags, can be emulated in several ways with MPI. The preferred means is to use multiple contexts of communication if wild-carded source and/or tag (`MPI_ANY_SOURCE`, `MPI_ANY_TAG`) should prove insufficient to distinguish messages in a single context. Since MPI provides both source and tag selectivity, removing `rcvmulti()` and `vrcvmulti()` calls does not usually pose a practical problem of conversion.

Places where "components" are used in PVM 2.4.x correspond roughly to groups in MPI, and groups are encapsulated in communicators. Hence, functionality achieved with components in PVM 2.4.x can be emulated. Since not all PVM 2.4.x calls refer to the component consistently, however, there is no one-to-one mapping of calls. PVM 2.4.x "instance numbers" correspond roughly to MPI process ranks in a group.

We have simplified the discussion of sending operations so far by neglecting the fact that the `snd()` and `vsnd()` calls must always be preceded with an `initsend()` command and commands to pack the single send buffer of a process. There is an analog in MPI to this procedure, which we will discuss later in this section. For now it is sufficient to say that for sending contiguous data of any one type, MPI needs only a single send command to prepare, convert, and dispatch data.

Miscellaneous Functions

PVM 2.4.x does not have a nonblocking receive. It does have a "probe" function and a "probemulti" function. The former is directly replaceable by an MPI call, while the latter follows logic analogous to that described above for replacing `rcvmulti`. Note that the output role of `source` (represented by the value `MPI_ANY_SOURCE` in

```
probe(tag)        MPI_IPROBE(MPI_ANY_SOURCE,tag,MPI_COMM_WORLD,
                     flag,status)
pvm_error(str)    MPI_ABORT(comm, val)
```

Table 9.17
Translating PVM 2.4.x to MPI: miscellaneous functions

Table 9.17) has no counterpart in PVM 2.4.x.

Collective Operations

PVM 2.4.x provides a few collective operations. A rough correspondence to the functions of MPI is shown in Table 9.18.

```
barrier("name",n)  MPI_BARRIER(comm,ierr)
snd(...,-1,...)     MPI_BCAST(buf,count,datatype,root,comm,ierr)
```

Table 9.18
Translating PVM 2.4.x to MPI: collective operations

PVM 2.4.x has no counterpart to the a wide variety of global data-movement routines in MPI. In addition, PVM 2.4.x does not have subgroups, but has more fuzzy components (a process in PVM 2.4.x belongs to one component, whereas an MPI process can belong to an arbitrary number of groups and hence to an arbitrary number of communication contexts). Note that the broadcast operation in PVM is really a multisend; whereas in MPI messages sent with `MPI_BCAST` are received with `MPI_BCAST`. The sender is specified by the `root` parameter; the other processes receive. The semantics of a PVM 2.4.x barrier are much different from those of an MPI barrier, in that MPI barriers are over a specific group and synchronize, whereas PVM 2.4.x barriers wait for any **n** processes to call the function, with possible race conditions. The PVM 2.4.x `waituntil()` and `ready()` event functions are not implementable strictly as MPI functions. MPI has no non-blocking collective communications; these must be implemented via thread extensions.

MPI Counterparts of Other Features

Communication among heterogeneous machines in PVM 2.4.x is provided by packing and unpacking functions that apply to the single send and receive buffers on each process. The first pack command is always preceded by `initsend()`. Only one pending send is permitted in PVM 2.4.x because of the single send buffer.

In MPI every *send* has a datatype argument, so we have the correspondences shown in Table 9.19. The table shows the case where single datatypes are sent in PVM 2.4.x. The corresponding receives are shown in Table 9.20.

```
putnshort(data,len); snd(...)      MPI_SEND(...,MPI_SHORT,...)
putnint(data,len); snd(...)        MPI_SEND(...,MPI_INT,...)
putnlong(data,len); snd(...)       MPI_SEND(...,MPI_LONG,...)
putnfloat(data,len); snd(...)      MPI_SEND(...,MPI_FLOAT,...)
putndfloat(data,len); snd(...)     MPI_SEND(...,MPI_DOUBLE,...)
putncplx(data,len); snd(...)       MPI_SEND(...,MPI_COMPLEX,...)
putndcplx(data,len); snd(...)      MPI_SEND(...,
                                     MPI_DOUBLE_COMPLEX,...)
putbytes(data,len); snd(...)       MPI_SEND(...,MPI_BYTE,...)
putstring(data); snd(...)          MPI_SEND(...,MPI_CHARACTER,...)
```

Table 9.19
Translating PVM 2.4.x to MPI: heterogeneous and synchronous communication (sends)

PVM 2.4.x has support for most, and MPI support for all, the basic datatypes supported by the host language, whether Fortran or C. In converting string transmissions from PVM to MPI, the correspondence between `putstring()` and the use of `MPI_CHARACTER` is not exact, in that the send must elect to send or not send the null termination when it sizes the character array. (The detailed issues of Fortran character strings vs. character arrays and substrings are thorny, as described in the MPI Standard [23, Chapters 2 and 3].)

A number of `putxxx()` calls can be posed before the `snd()`; the corresponding `rcv()` is then followed by a number of `getxxx()`s. This can be emulated in MPI as well, but not without the use of a packing/unpacking mechanism described in Section 5.2.5.

```
rcv(...); getnshort(data,len)    MPI_RECV(...,MPI_SHORT,...)
rcv(...); getnint(data,len)      MPI_RECV(...,MPI_INT,...)
rcv(...); getnlong(data,len)     MPI_RECV(...,MPI_LONG,...)
rcv(...); getnfloat(data,len)    MPI_RECV(...,MPI_FLOAT,...)
rcv(...); getndfloat(data,len)   MPI_RECV(...,MPI_DOUBLE,...)
rcv(...); getncplx(data,len)     MPI_RECV(...,MPI_COMPLEX,...)
rcv(...); getndcplx(data,len)    MPI_RECV(...,
                                     MPI_DOUBLE_COMPLEX,...)
rcv(...); getbytes(data,len)     MPI_RECV(...,MPI_BYTE,...)
rcv(...); getstring(data)        MPI_RECV(...,MPI_CHARACTER,...)
```

Table 9.20
Translating PVM 2.4.x to MPI: heterogeneous and synchronous communication (receives)

Features Not in MPI

Key features in PVM 2.4.x that are not in MPI are as follows:

- Global events and barriers, as described earlier,
- Interactive process management as described in the following section,

Process Startup

Parallel programs written using PVM 2.4.x are started by running the first instance of the program (or the master program executable, if the slaves and master have different executables) in a normal Unix way, after the master PVM daemon has also been started as a regular Unix process. The first process then starts the other processes via an `initiate()` or `initiateM()` call, which specify locale by architecture and name, respectively. The virtual machine is specified to PVM 2.4.x through a "hostfile" with a specific format (see [34, Section 9]), and a default location in the user's directory structure. Note that the `enroll()` that appears in the master program does *not* start the PVM master daemon. The daemon must be started beforehand; it in turn subsequently starts slave daemons. The master daemon may be run interactively, particularly when passwords are needed to achieve startup on remote nodes, or the user wants to observe the behavior of processes (see Section 6.2 of [34]). MPI has not specified any analogous portable mechanism for either process startup or dynamic management.

9.6   PVM 3.2.x

PVM 3.2.x (the most recent as of this writing is 3.2.6) is the currently supported version of the PVM library described in the preceding section [30]. Unlike PVM 2.4.x, PVM 3.0 and higher have support for specific parallel machines as well as for heterogeneous networks of workstations. Furthermore, the Version 3 release constituted a complete redesign of the system. Yet, version 3.2.x's message-passing aspects remain quite simple, and translation to MPI should consequently be straightforward, just as for PVM 2.4.x and p4.

The Version 3 release uses a new, more systematic naming convention for functions and constants. In C, pvm_ is prepended to all the names of routines to avoid the many potential conflicts in short, common names. In Fortran, this is modified to pvmf.

The Basics

Table 9.21 shows the correspondences between basic PVM 3.2.x functions and their MPI counterparts. The table shows Fortran bindings for both PVM 3.2.x and MPI; the full C translations are similar. We show only certain of the arguments to each routine; the correspondences for the others can be readily inferred. Group arguments for PVM 3.2.x correspond to the dynamic group concept added in this Version 3 release. In MPI, the communicator would hold a corresponding static group. Use of dynamic addition or subtraction of processes after an initial group formulation is not within the MPI model and requires a more complex porting strategy than what which is shown in Table 9.21. Intercommunicators provide one alternative means for handling complex group management in MPI. (The rank of a task and the number of tasks can also be determined without using the PVM group operations at the time the PVM processes are started. We will not discuss this approach here.)

PVM 3 has replaced the notion of "components" and "instances" with TIDs (task IDs) and dynamic process groups. This change makes porting to MPI somewhat simpler than with the earlier versions of PVM, unless dynamic groups are used extensively. Furthermore, PVM 3 has replaced the restriction of single buffers with multiple buffers, each identified by its "bufid." PVM 3 buffers are created, deleted and selected; these operations are unneeded in MPI. As before, buf_type refers to a simple type like MPI_DOUBLE or MPI_BYTE, or to a more complex datatype as we discussed for the PVM 2.4.x conversion process above; we return to this again below.

```
pvmfmytid(mytid)           MPI_INIT(...)
pvmfexit(info)             MPI_FINALIZE(ierr)
pvmfgetinst(grp,mytid,me)  MPI_COMM_RANK(comm,me,ierr)
pvmfgsize(grp,np)          MPI_COMM_SIZE(comm,np,ierr)
pvmfsend(tid,tag,info)     MPI_SEND(.., buf_type,...)
pvmfrecv(tid,tag,bufid)    MPI_RECV(.., buf_type,...)
```

Table 9.21
Translating PVM 3.2.x to MPI: basic functions

Miscellaneous Functions

PVM 3.2.x has both "probe" and nonblocking receive. Note that PVM's non-blocking receive is not like MPI's `MPI_Irecv`; rather is combines the effects of `MPI_Iprobe` and `MPI_Recv`.

```
pvmfnrecv(src,tag,bufid)   MPI_IPROBE(...);
                           if(flag) MPI_RECV(...);
pvmfprobe(src,tag,bufid)   MPI_IPROBE(src,tag,
                              MPI_COMM_WORLD,flag,status)
pvmfperror(str,info)       MPI_ABORT(comm, val)
```

Table 9.22
Translating PVM 3.2.x to MPI: miscellaneous functions

Collective Operations

To get access to most of PVM 3.2.x's collective operations, one needs to use dynamic groups. The `pvmfmcast()` call (corresponding to `snd(...,-1,...)` in PVM 2.4.x) still maps to an MPI broadcast. The problem with dynamic groups, unlike MPI's static groups, is that there are race conditions associated with "joining" and "leaving" these groups (since a dynamic group is a distributed data structure, it may be out of date in some processes unless it is synchronized properly). Assuming one is careful to form a group and then barrier synchronize, Table 9.23 gives an accurate picture of how to map from PVM 3.2.x's groups to MPI communicators. Note that the tag argument of PVM 3.2.x's broadcast has no corresponding entry in MPI.

pvmfmcast(ntask,tids,tag,info)	MPI_BCAST(buf,count,datatype, root,comm,ierr)
pvmfbcast(grp,tag,info)	MPI_BCAST(buf,count,datatype, root,comm,ierr)
pvmfbarrier(grp,count,info)	MPI_BARRIER(comm,ierr)

Table 9.23
Translating PVM 3.2.x to MPI: collective operations

MPI Counterparts of Other Features

Communication among heterogeneous machines in PVM 3.2.x is provided by packing and unpacking functions that apply to the current-send and specified-receive buffers on each process. The first pack command is normally preceded by pvmfinitsend() (when pvmfmkbuf()/pvmffreebuf are used, pvmfinitsend() may not be necessary). Multiple pending sends are possible.

In MPI every *send* has a datatype argument; this matches PVM's use of different routines for different types of data.

PVM 3.2.x has support for most of the the basic datatypes supported by the host language, whether Fortran or C. In converting string transmissions from PVM to MPI, it should be noted that the correspondence of PVM's STRING and the use of MPI_CHARACTER is not exact, as stated above under PVM 2.4.x's section.

Features Not in MPI

Key features in PVM 3.2.x that are not in MPI are as follows:

- Interactive process management as described in the following section
- Routines for adding and deleting hosts from the virtual machine dynamically (in addition to dynamic process management)

Process Startup

Parallel programs written using PVM 3.2.x are started by running the first instance of the program (or the master program executable, if the slaves and master have different executables) from the Unix shell, after the master PVM daemon has also been started as a regular Unix process. The first process then starts the other processes via a pvmfspawn() call, which can specify location either by architecture or by machine name. The virtual machine is specified to PVM 3.2.x through a "hostfile" with a specific format (see [6]), and a default location in the user's directory structure. Note that the `pvmfmytid()` that appears in the master program does *not* start the PVM master daemon. The daemon must be started beforehand (perhaps as a separate program, running interactively in a separate window); it in turn subsequently starts slave daemons. The PVM console may be run interactively and interacts with the daemons; this feature is particularly useful when passwords are needed to achieve startup on remote nodes or when the user wishes to observe the behavior of processes (see [6]). There is also a group server for dynamic group management, which gets started automatically if needed. In contrast, MPI has not specified any analogous portable mechanism for process startup or dynamic management.

Tools

A recent master's project report by Fei Cheng of Mississippi State University illustrates how one can reasonably unify the existing PVM 3.2.x application programmer interface (API) with the MPI API. An internal upgrade of PVM is demonstrated (using two complementary strategies) in order to support contexts and static groups [15]. In about a person-month's work, Cheng implemented a large subset of the November, 1993 MPI specification[24], while allowing most existing PVM 3.2.x calls to work alongside MPI calls in user applications. There are plans to make this software available by anonymous ftp once it is made fully MPI standard compliant (most likely by leveraging the MPI model implementation and by providing a "patch" utility for existing PVM source code). This software technology differs a bit from the abstract device interface approach of Gropp and Lusk (that allows the model implementation to run on top of PVM 3.2.x) in that a dual API results with Cheng's strategy. Both PVM 3.2.x and MPI will show through to the application; in the long run, PVM calls would be changed to MPI calls to evolve a legacy application to be fully MPI compliant.

9.7   p4

p4 is a library for both shared-memory and message-passing models, developed at Argonne National Laboratory [12] by Ralph Butler and Ewing Lusk. Its message-passing part is quite simple, and translation to MPI should consequently be straightforward.

The Basics

Table 9.24 shows the correspondences between basic p4 functions and their MPI counterparts. The table shows Fortran bindings for both p4 and MPI; the C translations are similar. We show only certain of the arguments to each routine; the correspondences for the others should be easy to infer.

```
p4init()              MPI_INIT(...)
p4cleanup()           MPI_FINALIZE(ierr)
me = p4myid()         MPI_COMM_RANK(MPI_COMM_WORLD,me,ierr)
np = p4ntotids()      MPI_COMM_SIZE(MPI_COMM_WORLD,np,ierr)
p4send(...)           MPI_SEND(.., MPI_BYTE,...)
p4recv(...)           MPI_RECV(.., MPI_BYTE,...)
```

Table 9.24
Translating to MPI: basic functions

The p4 library uses in/out arguments for source and tag. In MPI, the output part of these is replaced by the single argument **status**, from which the tag, sender, and length of the received message can be retrieved.

The C version of **p4recv** can be passed a null buffer pointer to indicate that no buffer is being provided and that the system should acquire one that fits the message that is received. This is useful in situations where the length of a message cannot be inferred from its tag. In MPI, **MPI_Iprobe** can be used to provide this functionality, since the length of the message waiting to be received can be extracted from the **status** argument. In place of the buffer pointer, the p4 user can specifically manage buffers with **p4_msg_alloc** and **p4_msg_free**.

Miscellaneous Functions

P4 does not have a nonblocking send or receive. It does have a "probe" function.

```
p4probe(tag,src,flag)   MPI_IPROBE(src,tag,comm,flag,status,ierr)
p4error(str,val)        MPI_ABORT(comm,val,ierr)
p4softerrs(new,old)     MPI_ERRHANDLER_SET(ierr)
p4clock(),p4ustimer()   MPI_WTIME(ierr)
```

Table 9.25
Translating p4 to MPI: miscellaneous functions

The function `MPI_Probe` is a blocking call; therefore the MPI call that matches the semantics of `p4probe` is `MPI_Iprobe` instead. Note also that the output roles of `tag` and `source` have been replaced by the `status` argument in `MPI_Iprobe`. For error handling, p4 provides only the options provided by MPI's `MPI_ERRORS_FATAL` and `MPI_ERRORS_RETURN`. MPI provides also the capability for a library to provide its own error handler. Finally, the routine `MPI_Wtime` provides a high-resolution timing facility and substitutes for both the low-resolution `p4clock` and the high-resolution `p4ustimer`.

Collective Operations

Many but not all of the MPI collective operations are provided in p4. Table 9.26 shows the correspondences.

```
p4globarr(tag)                    MPI_BARRIER(MPI_COMM_WORLD,ierr)
p4brdcast(type,data,count,..)     MPI_BCAST(buf,count,datatype,)
                                      root,comm,ierr)
p4globop(tag,buf,count,           MPI_REDUCE(sendbuf,recvbuf,
  size,op,datatype,count,)            datatype,op,root,comm,ierr)
```

Table 9.26
Translating p4 to MPI: collective operations

MPI has a wide variety of global data-movement routines, which have no counterpart in p4. In addition, p4 does not have subgroups. Note that p4's broadcast operation is really a multisend; messages sent with `p4brdcast` are received with `p4recv`, whereas in MPI messages sent with `MPI_BCAST` are received with `MPI_BCAST`. The sender is specified by the `root` parameter; the other processes receive.

MPI Counterparts of Other Features

Communication among heterogeneous machines in p4 is provided by `p4_sendx`, which has an extra, single-datatype argument. In MPI every *send* has a datatype argument, so we have the correspondences shown in Table 9.27. None of the MPI derived datatypes are necessary to translate p4 programs, since p4 programs support transmission only of contiguous buffers.

In p4 one can request an acknowledgment of a message by using `p4_sendr` or `p4_sendrx`. Although there is not an exact correspondence, much of the same functionality can be obtained in MPI by using `MPI_SSEND` and its relations; in both cases execution of the sender is halted until it is certain that a matching receive

```
p4sendx(...,P4INT,...)     MPI_SEND(...,MPI_INT,...)
p4sendx(...,P4LNG,...)     MPI_SEND(...,MPI_LONG,...)
p4sendx(...,P4FLT,...)     MPI_SEND(...,MPI_FLOAT,...)
p4sendx(...,P4DBL,...)     MPI_SEND(...,MPI_DOUBLE,...)
p4sendx(...,P4NOX,...)     MPI_SEND(...,MPI_BYTE,...)
p4brdcastx(....)           MPI_BCAST(...)
p4sendr(...)               MPI_SSEND(...)
```

Table 9.27
Translating p4 to MPI: heterogeneous and synchronous communication

has taken place. MPI has support for all of the datatypes supported by the host language, in either Fortran or C.

Features Not in MPI

MPI has no support for the shared-memory mode supported by p4 with its monitor datatype and library of predefined monitors. We anticipate that the need for a shared-memory programming model will be at least partly provided by threads and MPI's thread safety. The cluster model, in which processes that share memory communicate via message passing, is part of p4 but not of MPI. In the future, MPI together with a thread library may replace the p4 cluster model.

Process Startup

Parallel programs written using p4 and running on networks of machines are started by running the first instance of the program (or the master program executable, if the slaves and master have different executables) in a normal Unix way. The first process then starts the others, using the function **p4crpg** to read the contents of a file (the "procgroup file") and determine which executables should be started and where. On various parallel machines vendor-specific mechanisms are required, and the procgroup file must match them. MPI has not specified any portable mechanism for process startup.

9.8   PARMACS

PARMACS [13, 48] is a portable message-passing system widely used in Europe, originally developed by Rolf Hempel at GMD. It is now distributed commercially by Pallas GmbH. Originally a set of **m4** macro definitions for adding message-passing

statements to Fortran, it is now (as of Version 6.0) a subroutine library for both
C and Fortran. PARMACS made particular contributions to MPI in the area of
process topologies.

The Basics

In Figure 9.28 we show only the Fortran bindings; the C bindings are similar. PAR-
MACS provides an explicit host/node model of computation, realized, for example,
on the Intel IPSC/860. MPI programs do not need to have explicit "host" code, but
an inquiry function can be used to determine which process is the "host" if there
is one. Table 9.28 gives the MPI routines that correspond to the basic PARMACS
primitives.

```
PMINIT(...)         MPI_INIT(...)
PMEND()             MPI_FINALIZE()
me = PMYPID()       MPI_COMM_RANK(MPI_COMM_WORLD,&me)
np = PMNRPS()       MPI_COMM_SIZE(MPI_COMM_WORLD,&np)
ho = PMHPID()       MPI_GET_HOST()
PMSND(...)          MPI_SEND(.., MPI_BYTE,..)
PMRCV(...)          MPI_RECV(.., MPI_BYTE,..)
```

Table 9.28
Translating PARMACS to MPI: basic functions

Miscellaneous Functions

PARMACS does not have a nonblocking send or receive. It does have a "probe"
function. It and some of the other functions are shown in Table 9.29.

```
PMWAIT(...)         MPI_WAITANY(...)
PMPROB(...)         MPI_IPROBE(src,tag,comm,flag,status)
PMSERR(code,str)    MPI_ERROR_STRING(code,str,rlen)
PMTIME()            MPI_WTIME()
```

Table 9.29
Translating PARMACS to MPI: miscellaneous functions

Collective Operations

PARMACS does not have global data-movement or collective-computation routines. It does provide a global process tree that sets up the communication structure for user-defined collective operations. PARMACS does have a global synchronization routine. Table 9.30 shows the correspondence with MPI. Note that one supplies

PMBARR(barr_id)	MPI_BARRIER(comm)

Table 9.30
Translating PARMACS to MPI: global synchronization

a tag on the PMBARR call. This corresponds to the use of a (possibly nondefault) communicator in the MPI version, although it would be one whose associated group included all processes.

MPI Counterparts of Other Features

PARMACS has a number of features in common with MPI, shown in Table 9.31. PARMACS supports communication among heterogeneous machines, by means of the PMFORM function. With this function the user specifies the contents of the message being sent with the next PMSND. If the data representations differ between sender and receiver, the information specified by PMFORM is used to perform the translation. Thus, data is copied or translated only if necessary. The source data to be sent may have mixed type. The components must be made up of a set of contiguous chunks, however. The corresponding functionality in MPI is proveded by MPI_TYPE_STRUCT, where the components are built using MPI_TYPE_CONTIG. Note that the concept of *next message* is not thread safe and has thus been avoided in MPI whereas thread safety has not been a design goal of PARMACS.

The best way to mimic the PARMACS behavior in MPI is to save the message format information, as with the PMFORM call, and to send this information together with the message instead of the next PMSND. The message is received with data type MPI_PACKED, and MPI_UNPACK is used to unpack the message.

PMFORM(...)	MPI_UNPACK(...)
PMSNDR(...)	MPI_SSEND(...)
PMRCVR(...)	MPI_RECV(...)

Table 9.31
Translating PARMACS to MPI: heterogeneous and synchronous communication

In PARMACS one can request an acknowledgment of a message by using `PMSNDR`. Although there is not an exact correspondence, much of the same functionality can be obtained in MPI by using `MPI_SSEND` and its relations; in both cases execution of the sender is halted until it is certain that a matching receive has taken place. In PARMACS, such a message must be received with `PMRCVR`; in MPI, messages send with `MPI_SSEND` are received with a normal `MPI_RECV`.

The most outstanding feature of PARMACS is its support for process topologies. Most of the topology features in MPI are inherited from PARMACS. What are called "torus" topologies in PARMACS are called "cart" (for "Cartesian") topologies in MPI. Table 9.32 shows the correspondences.

`PMPGRP(...)`	`MPI_GRAPH_CREATE(...)`
`PMPTOR(...)`	`MPI_CART_CREATE(...)`
`PMQMAP(...)`	`MPI_TOPO_TEST`
`PMQGRP(...)`	`MPI_GRAPH_GET`
`PMQTOR(...)`	`MPI_CART_GET`
`PMLKUP(...)`	`MPI_CART_RANK`
`PMGLTR(...)`	collective functions

Table 9.32
Translating PARMACS to MPI: process topologies

Features Not in MPI

Some of the PARMACS topology management functions do not have MPI counterparts. The agglomerate-torus and de-agglomerate-torus functions are examples. Their main purpose is the efficient support of multigrid solvers in PDE applications, whereas MPI has no special features to support any particular application area.

Process Startup

PARMACS postulates a host-node model, and so its process startup mechanisms involve separate initialization of the host process and the node processes. MPI does not make this distinction, and in fact does not specify how processes come into existence.

Tools

The distributors of PARMACS are planning to develop PARMACS-to-MPI software that would largely automate the process of translating their application base of programs that use PARMACS into MPI programs.

9.9 TCGMSG

The "TCG" in TCGMSG [44] stands for the Theoretical Chemistry Group at Argonne National Laboratory, where Robert Harrison first began developing the system. It is now widely used in the international computational chemistry community. TCGMSG has a slightly restricted semantics for its otherwise familiar message-passing primitives. These restrictions allow it to achieve extreme efficiency on high-performance parallel computers, while still enabling execution on workstation networks.

The Basics

Table 9.33 shows the MPI routines corresponding to the basic functions in TCGMSG.

```
PBEGINF()        MPI_INIT(...)
PEND()           MPI_FINALIZE()
me = NODEID()    MPI_COMM_RANK(MPI_COMM_WORLD,me,ierr)
np = NNODES()    MPI_COMM_SIZE(MPI_COMM_WORLD,np,ierr)
SND(...,1)       MPI_SSEND(.., MPI_BYTE,..)
RCV(...,1)       MPI_RECV(.., MPI_BYTE,..)
```

Table 9.33
Translating TCGMSG to MPI: basic functions

The final argument in `SND` and `RCV` determines whether the communication is synchronous or not. The TCGMSG model supports only synchronous or asynchronous (nonblocking) sends, although the behavior is for the synchronous send to be buffered into an ordinary blocking send if buffering is available, in which case it behaves like an `MPI_SEND` instead. Wild cards in receive operations are allowed for process identifiers, but not on tag values. This situation is true also for `PROBE`.

Miscellaneous Functions

TCGMSG also provides nonblocking communication routines and timing functions, and some error-handling mechanisms. Table 9.34 shows the corresponding MPI routines.

```
SND(...,0)          MPI_ISEND(.., MPI_BYTE,..)
RCV(...,0)          MPI_IRECV(.., MPI_BYTE,..)
WAITCOM(...)        MPI_WAIT(...)
PROBE(...)          MPI_IPROBE(src,tag,comm,flag,status)
PARERR(code,str)    MPI_ERROR_STRING(code,str,rlen)
TCGTIME()           MPI_WTIME()
MTIME()             MPI_WTIME()
```

Table 9.34
Translating TCGMSG to MPI: miscellaneous functions

Collective Operations

TCGMSG provides basic collective operations. The corresponding MPI routines are shown in Table 9.35.

```
SYNCH(tag)                      MPI_BARRIER(comm)
BRDCAST(type,data,count,root)   MPI_BCAST(buf,count,datatype,
                                  root,comm,ierr)
IGOP(tag,buf,count,size,        MPI_REDUCE(sendbuf,recvbuf,count,
  op,datatype)                    datatype,op,root,comm,ierr)
IDOP(tag,buf,count,size,        MPI_REDUCE(sendbuf,recvbuf,count,
  op,datatype)                    datatype,op,root,comm,ierr)
```

Table 9.35
Translating TCGMSG to MPI: collective operations

There are two collective computation routines, one for integer operations and one for double-precision floating-point operations. The operations are +, *, max, min, absmax, and absmin. These have MPI counterparts except for absmin and absmax, which can be added to MPI through user-supplied operations. The integer operations include bitwise or and bitwise and. MPI has these operations, and bitwise xor as well.

MPI Counterparts of Other Features

In order to send and receive messages in a heterogeneous environment, one or's the tag field with a constant to indicate the data type.

```
SND(tag | type,...)    MPI_SEND(..,datatype,..)
RCV(tag | type,...)    MPI_RECV(..,datatype,..)
EVON(), EVOFF()        MPI_PCONTROL
```

Table 9.36
Translating TCGMSG to MPI: heterogeneous communication and event logging

TCGMSG provides an event-logging capability for producing files that performance tools can read to create statistical or graphical representations of the events that occurr during the execution of the parallel program. MPI does not provide a specific interface of this type, but rather a generic mechanism for intercepting MPI calls, by which anyone can attach any profiling tools to any conforming MPI implementation.

Features not in MPI

One unusual feature of TCGMSG is its provision of an absolutely minimal shared memory item (one integer). The TCGMSG function NXTVAL returns the next value of a counter. It is guaranteed that no two calls will return the same value and that all values will be eventually returned, in order. On machines such as Intel or IBM SP1 (EUIH) with interrupt-driven receives, the highest numbered process registers an interrupt handler to provide the necessary services. On other machines the process that runs the parallel command is actually a TCGMSG process numbered higher than any application process. It provides NXTVAL service.

This feature cannot be implemented strictly within the message-passing model. The MPE library implements it on some machines where a version of the second method is available. On other machines, threads can be used to implement this feature.

TCGMSG also has a parallel file copying command, called PCOPY, that is useful for broadcasting a file from the local disk of one process to the local disks of other processes. This command is PCOPY. No I/O commands are part of MPI.

Process Startup

TCGMSG provides a simple, portable mechanism for starting a set of parallel processes. The **parallel** command (a C program) invokes whatever command is

required to start a fixed number of processes on a parallel computer, and invokes
rsh to start processes on networks of workstations.

Tools

Translation of TCGMSG programs into MPI programs is straightforward, with the
exception of **NXTVAL**, which is heavily used by the TCGMSG community. To supply
the functionality of **NXTVAL**, an additional function must be supplied, such as the
one in the MPE library (See Section 7.1).

9.10   Chameleon

Chameleon is a lightweight message-passing system that provides a common interface to a variety of popular message-passing systems, including both proprietary
vendor-specific systems and portability systems. Chameleon is designed to provide
the maximum performance; many of the functions, particularly the point-to-point
operations, are implemented with compile-time macros. In fact, it is often possible
to use Chameleon to generate "native" code by taking the output of the preproces-
sor. Chameleon made particular contributions to MPI in the area of point-to-point
communication modes and datatypes. Chameleon provides support for both C and
Fortran applications.

The Basics

Table 9.37 shows the MPI routines corresponding to the basic functions in Chameleon.

```
PIiInit(...)           MPI_Init(...)
PIiFinish()            MPI_Finalize()
me = PImytid           MPI_Comm_rank(MPI_COMM_WORLD,&me)
np = PInumtids         MPI_Comm_size(MPI_COMM_WORLD,&np)
PIbsend(...,datatype)  MPI_Send(.., datatype,..)
PIbrecv(...,datatype)  MPI_Recv(.., datatype,..)
```

Table 9.37
Translating Chameleon to MPI: basic functions

Chameleon supports only contiguous messages of a single datatype but does
support heterogeneous systems with a datatype argument. Table 9.38 shows the
correspondence between Chameleon and MPI datatypes.

MSG_OTHER	MPI_BYTE
MSG_INT	MPI_INT
MSG_LNG	MPI_LONG
MSG_SHRT	MPI_SHORT
MSG_FLT	MPI_FLOAT
MSG_DBL	MPI_DOUBLE

Table 9.38
Translating Chameleon to MPI datatype

Miscellaneous Functions

Chameleon supports nonblocking operations and an operation similar to the MPI "ready send." One difference is that when the ready-send mode is used, Chameleon requires that both the send and receive modes match; MPI allows any receive to match any mode of send.

PInsend(...)	MPI_Isend(...)
PIwsend(...)	MPI_Wait(...)
PInrecv(...)	MPI_Irecv(...)
PIwrecv(...)	MPI_Wait(...)
PInsendrr(...)	MPI_Irsend(...)
PIbprobe(...)	MPI_Probe(...)
PInprobe(...)	MPI_Iprobe(...)
PIcrecv(...)	MPI_Cancel(...)
PIcsend(...)	MPI_Cancel(...)
PInstatus(...)	MPI_Test(...)
SYGetElapsedTime()	MPI_Wtime()
PINodeName(...)	MPI_Get_processor_name(...)

Table 9.39
Translating Chameleon to MPI: miscellaneous functions

Collective Operations

Chameleon supports a rich set of collective operations, including operations on arbitrary groups of processes. Some of these, including the operations to form groups of processes, are shown in Table 9.40.

newps=PSPartition(key,oldps)	MPI_Comm_split(oldcomm,color,key, newcomm)
ps=PSCreate(name)	MPI_Group_incl(old,n,list,group)
PSAddMember(ps,list,n)	MPI_Comm_create(old,group,new)
PSCompile(ps)	
PSDestroy(ps)	MPI_Comm_free(&comm)
size = PSnumtids(ps)	MPI_Comm_size(ps,&size)
rank = PSmytid(ps)	MPI_Comm_rank(ps,&rank)
PIgsync(procset)	MPI_Barrier(comm)
PIbcastSrc(buf,count,root, procset,datatype)	MPI_Bcast(buf,count,datatype, root,comm)
PIgxop(buf,len,work,procset)	MPI_Allreduce(sendbuf,recvbuf, size,MPI_op,datatype)

Table 9.40
Translating Chameleon to MPI: operations on process sets

MPI Counterparts of Other Features

Chameleon provides a message tag request system to ensure that libraries are using different message tags. This works only as long as all parts of the code use this mechanism. MPI provides a better way to do this through the use of communicators. The Chameleon routines that provide the tag requests are shown in Table 9.41.

Chameleon also provides extensive correctness and performance debugging features when used with the profiling version of the Chameleon libraries. These provide built-in features that MPI can provide through the profiling interface. The preferred method for controlling these features in Chameleon is through a command-line interface.

Chameleon contains a few routines for manipulating virtual topologies for both 2-D Cartesian meshes and binary trees. MPI has corresponding routines for meshes, but for the binary trees MPI would have to use the general graph topologies.

ltag=PIGetTags(ps,n)	Create a new communicator
PIReturnTags(ps,n,ltag)	Free that communicator

Table 9.41
Translating Chameleon to MPI: counterparts of other functions

Features Not in MPI

Chameleon includes some routines for parallel I/O. Chameleon also allows a knowledgeable user to change the algorithms used for the collective operations.

Process Startup

Chameleon provides a simple and consistent process startup mechanism. Chameleon programs are started (on most systems) just as if they were regular uniprocessor programs. Command-line arguments are used to specify the number of processors, particular processors, and resource limits on the program (such as the number of CPU seconds or page faults). On many systems, running a Chameleon program appears no different from running any uniprocessor program. This interface is inherited by the model MPI implementation described in Appendix B.

Tools

Chameleon provides some tools for translating to MPI that are based on the `m4` macro processor. These tools have been used to help generate the Intel version of the model MPI implementation. To convert a file from Chameleon to MPI, the user simply uses the command

```
inlinecomm -mpi filename
```

this changes `filename` to use MPI calls instead of Chameleon calls. It is only an approximation, however; the output should be checked by hand.

9.11   Zipcode

Zipcode [70, 71, 72] is a portable message-passing system originally developed by Anthony Skjellum at Caltech. Zipcode made particular contributions to MPI in the area of process groups, contexts, and intracommunicators (though they have different names and some detailed differences in Zipcode). Zipcode also postulated a form of virtual topologies, but the form of PARMACS topologies was adopted by MPI. The support of diverse collective operations with group scope is another aspect of Zipcode that has also moved into MPI. Like PARMACS, Zipcode usually operates under the assumption of a host-node model of computation.

Porting between Zipcode and MPI is easy because they both have contexts, groups, and communicators, though with some differences.

The Basics

Zipcode as currently released has only a C binding, because of its use of dynamic message management for point-to-point messaging, following the Reactive Kernel/Cosmic Environment style of message management [66, 67]. Zipcode follows the CrOS III model of collective operations, in a generalized form [71]. Zipcode provides an explicit host/node model of computation available, for example, on the Intel Delta and Paragon, and BBN TC-2000 Butterfly. In contrast, MPI programs do not need to have explicit "host" code, but an inquiry function can be used to determine which process is the "host" if there is one. Table 9.42 gives the MPI routines that correspond to the basic Zipcode primitives. In the most general model, a Zipcode program includes a "Postmaster General" process that provides safe contexts of communication when communicating groups start "mailers" (called intracommunicators in MPI). MPI achieves safe contexts through a cooperative synchronization that does not require a "context server" of the form used by Zipcode.

Zipcode is based on "classes" of mail, each associated with a different naming strategy for processes (often a virtual topology). Consequently, the receipt selectivity of each class of Zipcode mail is different, because different amounts of information are available to inform the recipient of what the message contains. Most Zipcode classes have source selectivity, but not tag selectivity, since this proves quite sufficient for many applications. Other classes have both forms of selectivity. For simplicity, throughout we show the messaging primitives for the 3D grid abstraction class, called G3. A G3 class (unlike MPI's topologies) automatically contains recursively defined topologies for the plane children, and the plane children in turn have row/column children (G1).

Semantically, a Zipcode *receive* allocates a message like a "malloc," while a Zipcode *send* is analogous to a "free" with the side-effect that the message appears at its destination. A Zipcode program never needs to know the length of a message prior to accepting it, something that is not provided by any MPI receive mode.

Miscellaneous Functions

Zipcode has a nonblocking send and receive. It does not have a non-blocking "probe" function because its receive returns NULL if no message has arrived. It and some of the other functions are shown in Table 9.43.

```
Zip_Init(...)              MPI_Init(...)
Zip_exit()                 MPI_Finalize()
g3_pqr(comm,p,q,r)         MPI_Cart_coords(comm,rank,3,pqr)
g3_PQR(comm,P,Q,R)         MPI_Cart_get(comm,3,dims,...)
g3_send(comm,ltr,p,q,r)    MPI_Cart_rank(comm,pqr,rank);
                           MPI_Send(.., MPI_BYTE,..,comm,ierr)
                           free((void *)ltr)

ltr =
   g3_recvb(comm,p,q,r)

                           MPI_Cart_rank(comm,pqr,rank);
                           MPI_Probe(.., MPI_BYTE,...);
                           ltr = (char *)malloc(len*sizeof(char));
                           MPI_Recv(.., MPI_BYTE,...,comm,ierr)
```

Table 9.42
Translating Zipcode to MPI: basic functions

```
g3_recv(comm,ltr,p,q,r)    MPI_Cart_rank(comm,pqr,rank);
                           MPI_Iprobe(..,MPI_BYTE,...,flag,..);
                           if(flag) ltr=(char *)malloc(...);
                           if(flag) MPI_Recv(...,MPI_BYTE,...);
```

Table 9.43
Translating Zipcode to MPI: miscellaneous functions

Collective Operations

Zipcode has a number of collective-computation routines, but not as extensive as MPI. Table 9.44 shows the correspondence.

```
g3_fanin(comm,...,rootp,rootq,...)    MPI_Reduce(...,comm)
g3_fanout(comm,...,rootp,rootq,...)   MPI_Bcast(...,comm)
g3_combine(comm,...)                  MPI_Allreduce(...,comm)
g3_prefix(comm,...)                   MPI_Scan(...,comm)
zip_sync(comm)                        MPI_Barrier(comm)
```

Table 9.44
Translating Zipcode to MPI: selected collective operations

MPI Counterparts of Other Features

Zipcode supports packing and unpacking of data through "invoices," which are a form of datatype, also supported by other systems. Zipcode has selected a printf-style mechanism for creating such datatypes; it permits variable-sized objects and user-defined types, but currently does not support recursive definitions. The use of invoices with Zipcode's "pack" point-to-point and collective operations provides the user with insulation from heterogeneous conversion worries. Table 9.45 shows the correlations with MPI, in brief.

```
zip_pack(...)          MPI_Pack(...)
zip_unpack(...)        MPI_Unpack(...)
zip_pack_send(...)     MPI_Send(...datatype,)
zip_pack_recv(...)     MPI_Recv(...datatype,)
g3_pack_combine(...)   MPI_Allreduce(...)
```

Table 9.45
Translating Zipcode to MPI: heterogeneous communication

Zipcode also supports a mechanism for Cartesian subgridding, analogous to `MPI_Cart_sub` and `MPI_Comm_split` (see [71]).

Features Not in MPI

Zipcode topologies are more closely tied to message passing than in either MPI or PARMACS. Furthermore, Zipcode is tied to the model of a topology as a hierarchical family of intracommunicators. This is done automatically to support the communication over subgroups that is likely for a Cartesian topology.

As pointed out above, Zipcode supports dynamic memory allocation for point-to-point messages, while using user-specified buffers (as MPI does) for collective communication. In the "pack" modes, the operations for Zipcode use invoices and encapsulate heterogeneous conversion.

Process Startup

Zipcode provides the process management support for which there is no analog in MPI.

Tools

The distributors of Zipcode are planning to develop a Zipcode-to-MPI port that will allow Zipcode programs to operate on top of MPI, while defining versions of Zipcode invoices for MPI to simplify the use of MPI datatypes.

9.12   Where to Learn More

In this chapter, we have outlined porting strategies for a number of existing vendor and portability systems. Additional information about porting and about detailed features of the other systems is available. The Internet newsgroups *comp.parallel*, *comp.parallel.pvm*, and *comp.parallel.mpi* provide access to up-to-the-minute discussions on message-passing systems, including details of real experience with porting. See also the discussion in Appendix D for other ways to access information on MPI as well as many of the systems described in this chapter on the Internet.

10 Beyond Message Passing

As we've discussed all along, MPI is a de-facto standard library (and notation) specification for supporting the message-passing model of parallel computation. The MPI Forum interpreted its mission broadly (not without considerable discussion), and "message passing" in MPI includes not only many varieties of point-to-point communication, but also contexts, groups, collective operations, and process topologies, and profiling and environmental inquiry functions. Making MPI a large specification has widened the scope of its applicability.

On the other hand, programmers are already starting to experiment with facilities that extend beyond the message-passing model. Vendors are starting to provide such features as part of their operating environments, whereas these features were previously included only in research systems; the most notable example is threads, discussed further below. Some of these these facilities are closely related to message passing and deserve mention here in order to clarify their relationship to MPI and perhaps open the discussion on how the MPI Standard itself might be expanded to include them.

In this chapter, we focus on three broad topics:

- **Generalizing the notion of process.** The MPI process model implicitly characterizes MPI processes as existing statically and having disjoint address spaces. The *thread* model postulates "lightweight" processes that come into and go out of existence quickly and that share memory with one another. This has important implications for message passing and for parallel performance.

- **Generalizing the notion of message passing.** The idea here is to explore ways that a process can cause events to occur on another process or processor without sending a message that the other process must explicitly receive, such as a remote signal or remote memory copy.

- **Generalizing the notion of computation.** As parallel machines have become larger, many applications based on scalable algorithms for their core computations have seen their bottlenecks shift from computation and interprocess communication to input and output of data. New parallel computers have parallel hardware in the file system, but what a "parallel file" *means* or what parallel I/O should be in general is still an open research question.

We will consider these areas in turn.

10.1 Dynamic Processes

The MPI specification describes the effects of calls made to MPI subroutines after each process calls `MPI_Init` and before it calls `MPI_Finalize`. In particular, it is silent on the topic of how processes come into existence. In current systems, a wide variety of mechanisms are in use: specialized program startup programs and scripts, custom daemons running on other processors, remote shells, and other mechanisms. The reason MPI does not address this problem is that it is complicated and there is no consensus about common methods, particularly among vendors.

To start a process, one must specify at least an executable file and a processor on which to run it. Although the examples in this book typically show the same program (executable file) being executed by all processes, in what is called the SPMD (single program, multiple data) model, this is not required by MPI, and a different program text may be run by each process.

Bringing new processes into existence is only the first part of what needs to be done. It is also necessary to establish communication between new and previously existing processes. In MPI terms, this means that a communicator must be provided that includes at least one of the "old" processes and one of the "new" processes. Note that MPI addresses this problem currently by

- omitting the definition of how processes are created,
- disallowing new processes to be born or die after the call to `MPI_Init`, and
- providing the communicator `MPI_Comm_world`.

To allow dynamic process creation, we need a way to bring the processes into existence and provide the "bridging" communicator between "old" and "new." Several reasonable alternative mechanisms exist.

First, let us sidestep the problem of how to specify the programs, files, and other data associated with starting processes on processors by postulating a string (in an as-yet-undefined format) that will specify this information. The string may come from the command line, a file, or some other source. Then the new function

```
MPI_Spawn( char *string, MPI_Comm oldcomm, MPI_Comm *newcomm )
```

would be a collective operation by the processes in `oldcomm` that spawns processes as specified in `string` and returns a new communicator whose group contains the processes in `oldcomm` and also the new processes. There are alternatives, of course, such as having the new communicator contain only one of the new processes, but that seems awkward to us.

There are also alternatives to consider on the side of the new collection of processes just created. It seems reasonable that they should come into existence with their own `MPI_COMM_WORLD` that includes only the newly created processes. This approach is consistent with the way processes are ordinarily born in the current MPI standard, with no particular knowledge of how they were created. But in order for them to communicate with the original set of processes, they need to acquire a communicator that includes one or more of the processes in the "original" group. One possibility is a function like

```
MPI_Spawn_comm( MPI_Comm oldcomm, MPI_Comm *newcomm )
```

that would return a new communicator containing all of the processes in both communicators. If the processes were not spawned by any other MPI set of processes, then the new communicator could be set to `MPI_COMM_NULL`.

An interesting special case of this arrangement arises when the original communicator contains a single process. (MPI specifies a predefined communicator called `MPI_COMM_SELF`, which when used by any process refers to a communicator whose group contains only that process.) Then we have a host-node process model that is used on certain parallel machines. In this model, one process is designated the *host*; the other processes are called *node* processes. Node processes are responsible for most of the computation and collective operations are defined for them. The host process usually does not participate in SPMD-oriented collective operations, but can communicate with the nodes via send and receive. This is just the model we have defined above, where the node processes are spawned by a host process.

This model is slightly at odds with MPI's current way of dealing with the host-node model, in which both host and nodes processes are assumed to be in `MPI_COMM_WORLD`. In this case the host process, if it exists, can be identified by

```
MPI_Attr_get( MPI_COMM_WORLD, MPI_HOST, &host_rank )
```

`MPI_HOST` is one of the predefined attribute values (see Section 7.8). Then the host can be excluded to form a new communicator containing only the nodes.

A different, more modular approach is to employ intercommunicators. On the spawning side, the processes call call `MPI_Spawn`. `MPI_Init` is called by the spawned nodes, creating their `MPI_COMM_WORLD`, and completing the protocol with the spawning nodes. (Intercommunicators are defined in Section 7.4.) In this case even stricter isolation is preserved; no "expanded" communicator is returned by `MPI_Spawn`. Rather, `MPI_Spawn` returns an intercommunicator. On the spawning side, the local group of the intercommunicator is the group that did the spawning; the remote group is the group that was spawned, namely, the group associated with

`MPI_COMM_WORLD` in the new processes. On the spawned side, `MPI_Spawned_comm`, called by the newly created processes, returns an intercommunicator with the local group set to the `MPI_COMM_WORLD` of the new processes and the remote group set to the group that did the spawning. The two communicators share a common context, so that messages can be exchanged among all the process using them.

At this point, the two groups, each with its own non-overlapping `MPI_COMM_WORLD`, can elect to form an ordinary (intra) communicator by collectively calling `MPI_Intercomm_merge`. Each group calls it with the intracommunicators described above and gets back an intracommunicator whose group contains all of the processes. Currently, `MPI_Intercomm_merge` is the only collective operation defined on intercommunicators. However, there is nothing to prevent other operations to be defined as well, either by layering on top of MPI, or by later inclusion in the standard.

10.2   Threads

Throughout this book we have referred constantly to *processes* as the entities that communicate with one another. A process may be defined loosely as an address space together with a current state consisting of a program counter, register values, and a subroutine call stack. The fact that a process has only one program counter means that it is doing only one thing at a time; we call such a process *single threaded*. Multiple processes may be executed on a single processor through timesharing, so in some sense the processor is doing more than one thing at a time, but the process isn't.

Both vendors and users are experimenting with a generalization of this situation in which processes have multiple program counters (with associated register values and stacks) sharing the process's address space. The (program counter, register set, stack) triple is called a *thread* and is very much like a process in its own right except that it does not have an address space of its own.

The motivation is to allow a concurrent programming model within a single process, with very rapid switching of control of the CPU from one thread to another enabled because little or no memory management is involved.

Individual threads are not visible outside of the process. In other words, MPI communication among multithreaded processes does not address individual threads; the threads of a process can perform MPI operations on behalf of their processes. Using threads in conjunction with message passing can be extremely convenient, for several reasons:

- Threads provide a natural implementation of nonblocking communication operations. A thread can be created to do a blocking receive operation. As long as this blocks only the thread and not the process, it has the effect of a nonblocking receive. The same applies to sends.

- Threads provide a natural way to implement operations required for the "shared-memory" operations we discussed in Chapter 7. A separate set of threads, one for each process, can use its own communicator to handle the data management functions on behalf of a process while a "main" thread in each process performs the main computation.

- Threads can increase the convenience and efficiency of the implementation of collective operations.

- Threads are becoming the parallel programming model of choice for "symmetric multiprocessing" shared-memory machines.

- Threads can help improve performance by helping to make highly latent systems more "latency tolerant."

In order for threads to be used in conjunction with a message-passing library, however, it is necessary that the library be designed to work well with the threads. This property is called *thread safety*. Thread safety means that multiple threads can be executing message-passing library calls without interfering with one another. Thread *unsafety* occurs when the message-passing system is expected to hold certain parts of the process state and it is impossible to hold it for more than one thread at a time. For example, some libraries use the concept of "the most recently received message" to avoid passing a status argument stored on the process's stack. That is, it is expected that user code will look something like

```
recv(msg, type);
src = get_src();
len = get_len();
```

This approach works in the single-threaded case, but in the multithreaded case, several receives may be in progress simultaneously, and when get_src is called, it may not be clear for which message it is supposed to return the source. MPI solves this particular problem by returning the source as part of the status object, which normally resides on the stack of a specific thread. This problem of a resource that is owned by the message-passing library instead of by the user thread can arise in the case of other data structures as well, such as message buffers, error fields, or "current" contexts. MPI has been carefully engineered to be thread-safe in its semantics, and implementors are encouraged to provide thread-safe implementations, so that MPI can work hand-in-hand with thread libraries.

In addition to the requirement that MPI be thread-safe, there is also a requirement that the thread library be aware of the MPI to the extent that execution of a blocking operation will cause the current thread to yield control to another thread in the process rather than cause the process to block. When a message arrives, a thread waiting for it should be made runnable again. Furthermore, when a system call is made, the operating system should block only the thread that made the call, not all threads, or much of the flexibility of user-level threads is lost.

The issue of threads has been widely discussed and implemented in slightly different ways by various vendors. Fortunately, a standardization effort is under way, and the POSIX standard P1003.4a [52], also known as *Pthreads*, seems likely to become the most widely used definition for threads.

Threads are also becoming a widely used programming paradigms for shared-memory multiprocessors, which are now appearing from a number of vendors. MPI can be used to program networks of such machines precisely because it is thread-safe. (A higher-level paradigm for programming with the thread model is *monitors*, discussed in [8].)

10.3   Action at a Distance

The most characteristic feature of the message-passing model is that one process cannot access the memory of another process without its explicit consent: send has no effect without a corresponding receive. This isolation of processes increases modularity and arguably makes message-passing programs easier to debug than those in which processes can access one another's memory directly. On the other hand, sometimes a process would like to cause some event on another processor, typically to access its memory, without involving the other process.

In a true shared-memory machine, the process of accessing remote memory is transparent; a process does not even know which accesses are "local" and which are "remote." One of the first extensions to message-passing distributed-memory machines was the *interrupt-driven receive*. This extension, pioneered by Intel, is discussed in Section 9.1. The idea is that an interrupt handler is associated with a message tag; when a matching message arrives, the user-defined interrupt handler is called. After the interrupt is serviced, control is returned to wherever it was when the interrupt occurred. Thus the methods of Section 7.1.3 could be used without the need for polling. The code to receive and respond to a request for the counter value, or for memory access in general, can reside in an interrupt handler. One can also think of the interrupt-handler code as taking place in a separate thread.

A more elaborate mechanism is provided by *active messages*. Active messages are described in [75] and form the low-level communication mechanism on the TMC CM-5. An active message is one whose arrival triggers the execution of a specific subroutine in the target process. Active messages are sometimes used to initiate *remote memory copying*, in which data is moved from one process's address space to another's by the action of only one process. On the CM-5, a restriction that makes this possible is the requirement that each process be executing the exact same code, so that addresses refer to the same objects on all processors. Because active messages cause the execution of code on the destination processor, they can be costly if this forces a context-switch, particularly for parallel machines built with commodity RISC processors. Another complication facing the programmer is the need to coordinate the active messages. In data-parallel applications, however, active-messages can be an attractive approach.

10.4   Parallel I/O

Parallel I/O means providing access by a collection of processes to external devices. The most common device is an external disk containing a file system; however, other devices include tape systems, graphical displays, and real-time signal sources.

Many of these external devices are themselves parallel, often for the same reason that a parallel processor is used. For example, the speed at which data can be moved on and off of a spinning disk necessitates the use of arrays of disks in order to get data transfer rates of more than about 10 MB/sec.

This situation leads to a problem with files. Many programmers (and the Unix operating system) view files as a single stream of bytes, making it difficult to exploit parallelism in this mode. Therefore, much current research has considered various kinds of file layout organized by parallel objects [18, 62, 19, 29]. Existing I/O systems for parallel computers have tended to concentrate on providing access to the file system at a fairly low level; users often need to know details of disk-blocking and read-write caching strategies to get acceptable performance.

Fortunately, MPI datatypes provide a powerful way to describe data layouts; MPI's communicators provide an effective means of organizing the processes that are responsible for I/O. MPI's thread-safety will help in providing nonblocking (often called asynchronous) I/O operations. Choosing the appropriate extensions to MPI (including new datatypes and datatype constructors) as well as handling the nonuniformity in access to the external devices is a challenging research area.

10.5 Will There Be an MPI-2?

The MPI Forum deliberately limited the scope of its decisions to the message-passing model, partly in order to complete the MPI specification quickly and partly because there was so much experience with the message-passing model. In this chapter we have touched on several topics that go beyond message passing, but that are becoming more and more significant as users gain experience with them. It may very well be that such programming paradigms as interrupt-driven receives, threads, active messages, remote copies, and parallel I/O will become so widely employed that users will require a standard so that they can write *portable* programs that use such concepts. At such a time it may be appropriate to convene a new incarnation of the MPI Forum both to absorb the changes that wide experience with MPI will have suggested and to expand the scope of MPI to encompass a wider set of parallel programming constructs.

10.6 Final Words

In this book we have attempted to illustrate the use of MPI in a wide variety of parallel programs from elementary examples to libraries and complex applications. Along the way we have touched on some of the subtler aspects of the message-passing approach and how MPI deals with these issues. We have introduced parts of a parallel computing environment that enhances programming with MPI. Guidance has been offered both for implementing MPI and for porting existing programs to MPI.

MPI offers the potential of a spurt in the growth of parallel software, long identified as the principal obstacle to the widespread use of parallel computing technology. The combination of efficiency, portability and functionality offered by MPI on both parallel supercomputers and workstation networks will form the basis of parallel computing for years to come.

Glossary of Selected Terms

The following is a glossary of the most commonly used terms in this book. It is far from complete, but is intended to provide a number of useful definitions in one place.

Active Messages An active message is normally a short message that causes remote execution on the receiving process of a specified section of code, while delivering to that code the active-message "payload." Analogous to remote procedure calls used in most Unix systems, the active-message paradigm is a means both for implementing higher-level protocols like MPI and for direct programming in certain situations. Active messages are an extension to the message-passing model envisaged by MPI.

Application Topology Application topologies are the natural process interconnection implied by the algorithm, in parallel. MPI supports the mapping of application topologies onto virtual topologies, and virtual topologies onto physical hardware topologies.

Attributes Attributes in MPI are integers (in Fortran) or pointers (in C) that can be attached, by key value, to a communicator.

Asynchronous Communication Asynchrous communication often means the same as nonblocking communication. This is generally communication in which the sender and receiver place no constraints on each other in terms of completion, and which may also overlap as much as possible with computation. The term asynchronous communication is not used in MPI.

Bandwidth The bandwidth of a message transmission is the reciprocal of the time needed to transfer a byte (the incremental per-byte cost).

Blocking Communication Blocking communication refers to communication in which the call does not complete until the buffer is available for reuse (in the case of the send) or use (in the case of a receive). See *Blocking Send* and *Blocking Receive*.

Blocking Receive A receive that blocks until the data buffer contains the selected message. See *Nonblocking Receive*.

Blocking Send A send that blocks until the data buffer is available for reuse. This may or may not require recipient to begin the process of receiving the message. The details of the blocking depend on the implementation, and the amount of buffering that the system may choose to do or be able to do.

Buffered Communication Communication in which the send operation (which may be blocking or nonblocking) may make use of a user-provided buffer, in order to ensure that the send does not block while waiting for space to store the user's message. This is primarily of use with blocking sends, where it removes the possibility that the matching receive may need to start before the blocking, buffered send call can return. Buffering may involve additional copying of data and can impact performance.

Buffering Buffering refers to the amount or act of copying (or the amount of memory) that the system uses as part of its transmission protocols. Generally, buffering helps avoid deadlocks, making programming easier for specific cases but less portable and predictable.

Caching of Attributes The process of attaching attributes in MPI to a communicator. See *Attributes*.

Cartesian Topology Cartesian topology is the type of virtual topology that supports regular mapping of processes into an N-dimensional name space. Examples include two- and three-dimensional logical process topologies used for linear algebra and PDE computations.

Collective Communication Collective communication involves operations such as "broadcast" (*cf* MPI_Bcast) and "all reduce" (*cf*, MPI_Allreduce) that involve the entire group of a communicator, rather than just two members, as in point-to-point communication.

Communication Modes MPI provides buffered, ready, standard, and synchronous communication modes for point-to-point communication.

Communication Processor A communication processor is generally the hardware component that provides the local access of a processor to the parallel computer network. Such processors are also called "router chips" and "mesh-routing chips" or MRCs on some systems. As time passes, the communication processor and its "glue chips" are becoming capable of more than simple transfers to and from CPUs, and may be capable of "gather/scatter"-type operations and other high-speed memory accesses without direct CPU intervention.

Communicator A communicator is a group of processes plus the notion of safe communication context. There are two types of communicators in MPI: intracommunicators (the default), and intercommunicators. Communicators guarantee that communication is isolated from other communication in the system and also that collective communication is isolated from point-to-point communication.

Context In MPI, the context is not a user-visible quantity, but it is the internal mechanism by which a communicator endows a group with safe communication space, separating such communication from all others in the system and also separating point-to-point and collective communication of a communicator's group.

Contiguous Data The simplest message buffers consist of data that is not dispersed in memory, but rather is contiguous. MPI deals with this case, and also with more general noncontiguous data, through datatypes.

Datatypes The MPI objects that support general gather and scatter of complicated data specifications are called datatypes. The simple ones are built in, and user-defined data types are called derived datatypes.

Deadlock The state of execution where the computation cannot proceed because an impasse is reached where two or more processes depend directly or indirectly on each other for a result before continuing. A good example is two processes trying to receive from each other, then send to each other, in a blocking communication mode.

Event The unit of logging for program instrumentation. Events are considered to have no duration.

Graph Topology Graph topology is the type of virtual topology that allows general relationships between processes, where processes are represented by nodes of a graph.

Group A group (or process group) is an ordered collection of processes. Each process has a rank in the group. The rank runs from 0 to one less than the number of processes.

Group Safety Group safety is the type of insulation from message-passing provided by contexts of communication in MPI. Each communicator has a group, and that group communicates in a specific context, independent of all other communication for that group (with different communicators) and all other groups.

Heterogeneous Computing An environment that has distinct data formats, and/or distinct computational capabilities is considered heterogeneous.

InterCommunicator Intercommunicators support both a "local" and "remote" group view of the world, and can be used in client-server-oriented point-to-point computation.

Interconnection Network The hardware that connects processors to form a parallel computer.

IntraCommunicator Intracommunicators (conventionally, communicators), are less general than intercommunicators, in that they have only a "local" view of processes, but support both point-to-point and collective communication.

Key Value The MPI-defined integer that is used to name a particular attribute to be cached is called the key value. The names are process local, so that all communicators on a process can easily share similar attributes.

Latency Latency in the sense of a message-passing system refers to the cost to set up a message transmission. It is the "startup cost" before any bytes of data can be sent. High latency means that messages are costly up front, and may be cheap in the limit of large messages only if the per-byte rate is small (respectively, the bandwidth is high).

MPE MPE is the MultiProcessing Environment add-on software provided with this book to enhance message-passing programming with MPI, including graphics and profiling capabilities.

Message Passing Interface Forum (MPIF) The MPI Forum convened to create a "de facto" standard for message passing, independent of standards bodies. The group consisted of representatives from vendors, universities, and natial laboratories. Researchers from both the United States and Europe were represented.

Multicomputer A term sometimes used to describe a parallel computer where processors with their own private memories are networked.

Node "Node" is used in two senses in this book. In one sense, it is synonymous with processor; in the other it refers to the nodes of a graph, which is a standard computer science data structure.

NonBlocking Communication In a nonblocking communication, the call does not wait for the communication to be completed. See NonBlocking Receive and NonBlocking Send.

Nonblocking Receive A receive operation that may return before the data buffer contains an incoming message. This is often used to provide the location and layout of the data buffer to the lower-level message passing hardware to provide better performance.

Nonblocking Send The send may return before the data buffer is available for re-use. The intent is that the send returns almost immediately. A nonblocking send must not require a matching receive to start before returning.

Object-Based Library Libraries (as defined in Chapter 6) are object-based when they take advantage of hierarchical data structures, uniform calling sequences, and information hiding but do not use inheritance to build complex codes from simpler codes. The resulting programs are similar to functional decompositions. Though the use of data objects is a great help to organization and understanding, there is not the full potential for optimizations nor for code reuse.

Object-Oriented Library Object-oriented libraries (as mentioned in Chapter 6) go beyond object-based libraries in their use of inheritance. Inheritance is used to build up complex relationships from simpler relationships. Simpler class structures are used to build more complex ones, leading to code reuse and, more important, to sources of optimization for the kinds of libraries considered in this book.

Pairwise Ordering The "pairwise ordering" property of message-passing systems is essential to the message-passing programming paradigm of MPI and its ancestor systems. This property guarantees that two messages sent between a pair of processes arrives in the order they were sent. With the introduction of "contexts," this requirement is weakened to require that two messages sent between a pair of processes using the same communicator arrive in the same order they were sent. MPI does weaken this further by changing the order of messages of different tags between the same processor pair.

Parallel Library A library is an "encapsulation" of an algorithm in a way that is meant to be convenient for multiple uses in a single application and/or reuse in multiple applications. Library writers for parallel computers can build robust libraries because MPI specifically provides features to help libraries to isolate their communication from that of users, and other libraries.

Libraries are a mainstay of scientific programming in a number of technical computing environments, but their additional complexity in the parallel computing world has limited their wide use thus far. MPI will help promote a significant body of library codes, since it provides a convenient, and portable basis for robust libraries.

Persistent Requests Persistent requests are used when multiple communications are to be started, tested, or completed, in order to reduce costs and provide the user with access to higher performance.

Physical Topology Physical topology is the topology of the parallel computer interconnection network, such as a mesh or hypercube.

Point-to-Point Communication Point-to-point communication is between two members of a communicator; (generically, a send-receive type call).

Portability Portability is the concept of f moving a program from one environment to another. The degree of portability indicates the amount of work needed to get the program to run again. High-quality portability (also called performance portability, or transportability) implies that reasonable performance is retained as a product of that porting process. MPI is designed to help ensure that high performance is possible across a number of different parallel platforms.

Process A process is the smallest addressable unit of computation in the MPI model. A process resides on a processor (or node). MPI does not discuss how processes are born, die, or are otherwise managed.

Processor A processor is (loosely) the CPU, memory, and I/O capabilities of a subset of a parallel machine (or a workstation in a workstation cluster). A processor supports the execution of one or more processes in the MPI model, but MPI makes only limited connection between processes and processors in environmental inquiry routines and in two topology-related mapping routines.

Quiesence The quiesence property requires that programmers guarantee that no outside communication will impinge on a group of processes during a specific period of execution, in order for a given operation to execute correctly. Quiescence demands that no pending point-to-point communication is in place and that no other processes will send any messages between two points of synchronization for a group of processes. This strategy is not required for most of MPI; the notable exception is during the creation of intercommunicators, where a quiescence guarantee is required of two "leader" processes in the "peer communicator."

Race Condition A race condition is the situation in which two or more processes or threads strive for a resource and obtain it in an unpredictable fashion. Race conditions often mean that a program sometimes works and sometimes breaks.

Ready Communication Mode Also known as *Ready send*. In a ready communication mode, the system is allowed to assume that the receiver has already posted the receive prior to the sender posting the send. If the receive has not been issued when the send occurs, the send is erroneous and the behavior is undefined (error detection is encourage but not required by MPI). The ready send may also be either blocking or nonblocking, as defined above.

Reduce An operation that reduces many data items by combining them together to form a result.

Request Object A request object is returned by MPI in response to an operation that will have a subsequent "wait" before it is completed. A good example is `MPI_Irecv`. The request object is used with `MPI_Wait` and similar calls to find out whether the original operation is complete.

Safe Programs In this book, and in the MPI standard, reference is made to "safe" and "unsafe" programs, independent of the concept of thread safety. A safe program is a program that does not rely on any buffering for its correct execution.

Standard Mode The standard communication mode of MPI corresponds most closely to current common practice.

Status Object The status object is the MPI means for returning information about an operation, notably a receive. For thread safety, this object is returned at the time the receive completes; for efficiency, the format of the receive object is an array for Fortran and a structure for C.

Subgroup MPI works on communicators that have groups. Other communicators based on subgroups of the "world group" are also possible. Subgroups are just as flexible as groups from which they are defined, and no distinction is necessary, except that it is convenient to call certain groups "subgroups" and certain communicators "subcommunicators" when describing algorithms.

Synchronization A synchronization is an operation that forces a group of processes all to pass through a critical section of code before any can continue. Many MPI collective operations are potentially synchronizations, but not all are required to be implemented with this property (except `MPI_Barrier`, which is specifically designed to be a synchronization). See also *Synchronous Communication Mode*.

Synchronous Communication Mode The sender in the synchronous communication mode may not return until the matching receive has been issued on the destination process. Synchronous sends may be either blocking or nonblocking, depending on whether the data buffer provided to the send is available for reuse when the send call returns.

Thread A thread is the atomic notion of execution within an MPI process. Each MPI process has a main thread and may have additional threads, provided a thread-safe programming environment and threads package are available. MPI mandates thread safety, but does not tie MPI specifically to any thread paradigm or standard.

Thread Safety Thread safety is the quality of software semantics that guarantees that independently executing threads will not interfere with each other by accessing data intended for a different thread. Implementing thread safety requires eliminating most global state and explicitly managing use of any global state that can not be eliminated. MPI is designed to be thread safe.

Topology See *Virtual Topology*.

Type Map A type map is the sequence of pairs of basic MPI datatypes and displacements that make up, in part, a derived datatype.

Type Signature The type signature is the MPI concept that extracts just the sequence of datatypes from a type map.

User-Defined Topology If MPI's virtual topologies are insufficient, then users can easily build their own topologies. Such topologies are often application-oriented.

Virtual Shared Memory Virtual shared memory is a software and/or hardware model in which the system provides the user with the impression that there is a single address space for the purpose of programming the system.

Virtual Topology Virtual topologies are a naming of processes in a communicator other than the rank naming. Graphs, Cartesian grids, and user-defined arrangements are all possible. Virtual topologies link applications more closely to communicators because the names of processes reflect the communication pattern needed for it. See also *Application Topology*.

A Summary of MPI Routines and Their Arguments

A.1 C Routines

This section describes the C routines from [24].

```
int MPI_Abort(MPI_Comm comm, int errorcode)
```
Terminates MPI execution environment

```
int MPI_Address(void* location, MPI_Aint *address)
```
Gets the address of a location in memory

```
int MPI_Allgatherv(void* sendbuf, int sendcount, MPI_Datatype
        sendtype, void* recvbuf, int *recvcounts, int *displs,
        MPI_Datatype recvtype, MPI_Comm comm)
```
Gathers data from all tasks and deliver it to all

```
int MPI_Allgather(void* sendbuf, int sendcount, MPI_Datatype
        sendtype, void* recvbuf, int recvcount, MPI_Datatype
        recvtype, MPI_Comm comm)
```
Gathers data from all tasks and distribute it to all

```
int MPI_Allreduce(void* sendbuf, void* recvbuf, int count,
        MPI_Datatype datatype, MPI_Op op, MPI_Comm comm)
```
Combines values from all processes and distribute the result back to all processes

```
int MPI_Alltoallv(void* sendbuf, int *sendcounts, int *sdispls,
        MPI_Datatype sendtype, void* recvbuf, int *recvcounts, int
        *rdispls, MPI_Datatype recvtype, MPI_Comm comm)
```
Sends data from all to all processes, with a displacement

```
int MPI_Alltoall(void* sendbuf, int sendcount, MPI_Datatype
        sendtype, void* recvbuf, int recvcount, MPI_Datatype
        recvtype, MPI_Comm comm)
```
Sends data from all to all processes

```
int MPI_Attr_delete(MPI_Comm comm, int keyval)
```
Deletes attribute value associated with a key

```
int MPI_Attr_get(MPI_Comm comm, int keyval, void **attribute_val,
        int *flag)
```
Retrieves attribute value by key

```
int MPI_Attr_put(MPI_Comm comm, int keyval, void* attribute_val)
```
Stores attribute value associated with a key

`int MPI_Barrier ( MPI_Comm comm )` *Blocks until all process have reached this routine.*

`int MPI_Bcast(void* buffer, int count, MPI_Datatype datatype, int`
`        root, MPI_Comm comm )`
Broadcasts a message from the process with rank "root" to all other processes of the
group.

`int MPI_Bsend_init(void* buf, int count, MPI_Datatype datatype, int`
`          dest, int tag, MPI_Comm comm, MPI_Request *request)`
Builds a handle for a buffered send

`int MPI_Bsend(void* buf, int count, MPI_Datatype datatype, int dest,`
`          int tag, MPI_Comm comm)`
Basic send with user-specified buffering

`int MPI_Buffer_attach( void* buffer, int size)` *Attaches a user-defined buffer for sending*
`int MPI_Buffer_detach( void** buffer, int* size)` *Removes an existing buffer (for use in MPI_Bsend, etc.)*
`int MPI_Cancel( MPI_Request *request )` *Cancels a communication request*

`int MPI_Cart_coords(MPI_Comm comm, int rank, int maxdims, int`
`          *coords)`
Determines process coords in Cartesian topology given rank in group

`MPI_Comm_compare(MPI_Comm comm1, MPI_Comm comm2, int *result)` *Compares two communicators*

`int MPI_Cart_create(MPI_Comm comm_old, int ndims, int *dims, int`
`          *periods, int reorder, MPI_Comm *comm_cart)`
Makes a new communicator to which topology information has been attached

`int MPI_Cart_get(MPI_Comm comm, int maxdims, int *dims, int`
`          *periods, int *coords)`
Retrieve Cartesian topology information associated with a communicator

`int MPI_Cart_map(MPI_Comm comm, int ndims, int *dims, int *periods,`
`          int *newrank)`
Maps process to Cartesian topology information

`int MPI_Cart_rank(MPI_Comm comm, int *coords, int *rank)` *Determines process rank in communicator given Cartesian location*

```
int MPI_Cart_shift(MPI_Comm comm, int direction, int disp, int
          *rank_source, int *rank_dest)
```
Returns the shifted source and destination ranks given a shift direction and amount

```
int MPI_Cart_sub(MPI_Comm comm, int *remain_dims, MPI_Comm *newcomm)
```
Partitions a communicator into subgroups that form lower-dimensional cartesian subgrids

```
int MPI_Cartdim_get(MPI_Comm comm, int *ndims)
```
Retrieves Cartesian topology information associated with a communicator

```
int MPI_Comm_create(MPI_Comm comm, MPI_Group group, MPI_Comm
          *newcomm)
```
Creates a new communicator

```
int MPI_Comm_dup(MPI_Comm comm, MPI_Comm *newcomm)
```
Duplicates an existing communicator with all its cached information

```
int MPI_Comm_free(MPI_Comm *comm)
```
Marks the communicator object for deallocation

```
int MPI_Comm_group(MPI_Comm comm, MPI_Group *group)
```
Accesses the group associated with given communicator

```
int MPI_Comm_rank(MPI_Comm comm, int *rank)
```
Determines the rank of the calling process in the communicator

```
int MPI_Comm_size(MPI_Comm comm, int *size)
```
Determines the size of the group associated with a communictor

```
int MPI_Comm_split(MPI_Comm comm, int color, int key, MPI_Comm
          *newcomm)
```
Creates new communicators based on colors and keys

```
int MPI_Comm_test_inter(MPI_Comm comm, int *flag)
```
Tests to see whether a communicator is an intercommunicator

```
int MPI_Dims_create(int nnodes, int ndims, int *dims)
```
Creates a division of processes in a Cartesian grid

```
int MPI_Errhandler_create(MPI_Handler_function *function,
          MPI_Errhandler *errhandler)
```
Creates an MPI-style error handler

```
int MPI_Errhandler_free(MPI_Errhandler *errhandler)
```
Frees an MPI-style error handler

```
int MPI_Errhandler_get(MPI_Comm comm, MPI_Errhandler *errhandler)
```
Gets the error handler for a communicator

int MPI_Errhandler_set(MPI_Comm comm, MPI_Errhandler errhandler) *Sets the error handler for a communicator*
int MPI_Error_class(int errorcode, int *errorclass) *Converts an error code into an error class*
int MPI_Error_string(int errorcode, char *string, int *resultlen) *Returns a string for a given error code*
int MPI_Finalize(void) *Terminates MPI execution environment*

int MPI_Gatherv(void* sendbuf, int sendcount, MPI_Datatype sendtype,
          void* recvbuf, int *recvcounts, int *displs, MPI_Datatype
          recvtype, int root, MPI_Comm comm)
Gathers into specified locations from all tasks in a group

int MPI_Gather(void* sendbuf, int sendcount, MPI_Datatype sendtype,
          void* recvbuf, int recvcount, MPI_Datatype recvtype, int
          root, MPI_Comm comm)
Gathers together values from a group of tasks

int MPI_Get_count(MPI_Status *status, MPI_Datatype datatype, int   *count) *Gets the number of "top-level" elements*
int MPI_Get_elements (MPI_Status *status, MPI_Datatype datatype,   int *elements) *Returns the number of basic elements in a datatype*
int MPI_Get_processor_name(char *name, int *resultlen) *Gets the name of the processor*
int MPI_Graph_create(MPI_Comm comm_old, int nnodes, int *index, int   *edges, int reorder, MPI_Comm *comm_graph) *Makes a new communicator to which topology information has been attached*
int MPI_Graph_get(MPI_Comm comm, int maxindex, int maxedges, int   *index, int *edges) *Retrieves graph topology information associated with a communicator*
int MPI_Graph_map(MPI_Comm comm, int nnodes, int *index, int *edges,   int *newrank) *Maps process to graph topology information*
int MPI_Graph_neighbors_count(MPI_Comm comm, int rank, int   *nneighbors) *Returns the number of neighbors of a node associated with a graph topology*

```
int MPI_Graph_neighbors(MPI_Comm comm, int rank, int *maxneighbors,
        int *neighbors)
```
Returns the neighbors of a node associated with a graph topology

```
int MPI_Graphdims_Get(MPI_Comm comm, int *nnodes, int *nedges)
```
Retrieves graph topology information associated with a communicator

```
int MPI_Group_difference(MPI_Group group1, MPI_Group group2,
        MPI_Group *newgroup)
```
Makes a group from the difference of two groups

```
int MPI_Group_excl(MPI_Group group, int n, int *ranks, MPI_Group
        *newgroup)
```
Produces a group by reordering an existing group and taking only unlisted members

```
int MPI_Group_free(MPI_Group *group)
```
Frees a group

```
int MPI_Group_incl(MPI_Group group, int n, int *ranks, MPI_Group
        *newgroup)
```
Produces a group by reordering an existing group and taking only listed members

```
int MPI_Group_intersection(MPI_Group group1, MPI_Group group2,
        MPI_Group *newgroup)
```
Produces a group as the intersection of two existing groups.

```
int MPI_Group_range_excl(MPI_Group group, int n, int ranges[][3],
        MPI_Group *newgroup)
```
Produces a group by excluding ranges of processes from an existing group

```
int MPI_Group_range_incl(MPI_Group group, int n, int ranges[][3],
        MPI_Group *newgroup)
```
Creates a new group from ranges of ranks in an existing group

```
int MPI_Group_rank(MPI_Group group, int *rank)
```
Returns the rank of this process in the given group

```
int MPI_Group_size(MPI_Group group, int *size)
```
Returns the size of a group

```
int MPI_Group_translate_ranks (MPI_Group group1, int n, int *ranks1,
        MPI_Group group2, int *ranks2)
```
Translates the ranks of processes in one group to those in another group

```
int MPI_Group_union(MPI_Group group1, MPI_Group group2, MPI_Group
        *newgroup)
```
Produces a group by combining two groups

`int MPI_Ibsend(void* buf, int count, MPI_Datatype datatype, int`
`        dest, int tag, MPI_Comm comm, MPI_Request *request)`
Starts a nonblocking buffered send

`int MPI_Initialized(int *flag)` *Indicates whether MPI_Init has been called.*
`int MPI_Init(int *argc, char ***argv)` *Initializes the MPI execution environment*

`int MPI_Iprobe(int source, int tag, MPI_Comm comm, int *flag,`
`        MPI_Status *status)`
Nonblocking test for a message

`int MPI_Irecv(void* buf, int count, MPI_Datatype datatype, int`
`        source, int tag, MPI_Comm comm, MPI_Request *request)`
Begins a nonblocking receive

`int MPI_Irsend(void* buf, int count, MPI_Datatype datatype, int`
`        dest, int tag, MPI_Comm comm, MPI_Request *request)`
Starts a nonblocking ready send

`int MPI_Isend(void* buf, int count, MPI_Datatype datatype, int dest,`
`        int tag, MPI_Comm comm, MPI_Request *request)`
Starts a nonblocking send

`int MPI_Issend(void* buf, int count, MPI_Datatype datatype, int`
`        dest, int tag, MPI_Comm comm, MPI_Request *request)`
Starts a nonblocking synchronous send

`int MPI_Keyval_create(MPI_Copy_function *copy_fn,`
`        MPI_Delete_function *delete_fn, int *keyval, void*`
`        extra_state)`
Generates a new attribute key

`int MPI_Keyval_free(int *keyval)` *Frees attribute key for communicator cache attribute*
`int MPI_Op_create(MPI_Uop function, int commute, MPI_Op *op)` *Creates a user-defined combination function handle*
`int MPI_Op_free( MPI_Op *op)` *Frees a user-defined combination function handle*
`int MPI_Pcontrol(const int level, ...)` *Controls profiling*

```
int MPI_Probe(int source, int tag, MPI_Comm comm, MPI_Status
         *status)
```
Blocking test for a message

```
int MPI_Recv_init(void* buf, int count, MPI_Datatype datatype, int
         source, int tag, MPI_Comm comm, MPI_Request *request)
```
Creates a handle for a receive

```
int MPI_Recv(void* buf, int count, MPI_Datatype datatype, int
         source, int tag, MPI_Comm comm, MPI_Status *status)
```
Basic receive

```
int MPI_Reduce_scatter(void* sendbuf, void* recvbuf, int
         *recvcounts, MPI_Datatype datatype, MPI_Op op, MPI_Comm
         comm)
```
Combines values and scatters the results

```
int MPI_Reduce(void* sendbuf, void* recvbuf, int count, MPI_Datatype
         datatype, MPI_Op op, int root, MPI_Comm comm)
```
Reduces values on all processes to a single value

```
int MPI_Request_free(MPI_Request *request)
```
Frees a communication request object

```
int MPI_Rsend_init(void* buf, int count, MPI_Datatype datatype, int
         dest, int tag, MPI_Comm comm, MPI_Request *request)
```
Builds a handle for a ready send

```
int MPI_Rsend(void* buf, int count, MPI_Datatype datatype, int dest,
         int tag, MPI_Comm comm)
```
Basic ready send

```
int MPI_Scan(void* sendbuf, void* recvbuf, int count, MPI_Datatype
         datatype, MPI_Op op, MPI_Comm comm )
```
Computes the scan (partial reductions) of data on a collection of processes

```
int MPI_Scatterv(void* sendbuf, int *sendcounts, int *displs,
         MPI_Datatype sendtype, void* recvbuf, int recvcount,
         MPI_Datatype recvtype, int root, MPI_Comm comm)
```
Scatters a buffer in parts to all tasks in a group

```
int MPI_Scatter(void* sendbuf, int sendcount, MPI_Datatype sendtype,
         void* recvbuf, int recvcount, MPI_Datatype recvtype, int
         root, MPI_Comm comm)
```
Sends data from one task to all other tasks in a group

`int MPI_Send_init(void* buf, int count, MPI_Datatype datatype, int`
`        dest, int tag, MPI_Comm comm, MPI_Request *request)`
Builds a handle for a standard send

`int MPI_Sendrecv_replace(void* buf, int count, MPI_Datatype`
`        datatype, int dest, int sendtag, int source, int recvtag,`
`        MPI_Comm comm, MPI_Status *status)`
Sends and receives using a single buffer

`int MPI_Sendrecv(void *sendbuf, int sendcount, MPI_Datatype`
`        sendtype, int dest, int sendtag, void *recvbuf, int`
`        recvcount, MPI_Datatype recvtype, int source, int recvtag,`
`        MPI_Comm comm, MPI_Status *status)`
Sends and receives a message

`int MPI_Send(void* buf, int count, MPI_Datatype datatype, int dest,`
`        int tag, MPI_Comm comm)`
Basic send

`int MPI_Ssend_init(void* buf, int count, MPI_Datatype datatype, int`
`        dest, int tag, MPI_Comm comm, MPI_Request *request)`
Builds a handle for a synchronous send

`int MPI_Ssend(void* buf, int count, MPI_Datatype datatype, int dest,`
`        int tag, MPI_Comm comm)`
Basic synchronous send

`int MPI_Startall(int count, MPI_Request *array_of_requests)` *Starts a collection of requests*
`int MPI_Start(MPI_Request *request)` *Initiates a communication with a persistent request handle*
`int MPI_Test(MPI_Request *request, int *flag, MPI_Status *status)` *Tests for the completion of a send or receive*
`int MPI_Test_cancelled(MPI_Status *status, int *flag)` *Tests to see whether a request was cancelled*

`int MPI_Testall(int count, MPI_Request *array_of_requests, int`
`        *flag, MPI_Status *array_of_statuses)`
Tests for the completion of all previously initiated communications

`int MPI_Testany(int count, MPI_Request *array_of_requests, int`
`        *index, int *flag, MPI_Status *status)`
Tests for completion of any previously initiated communication

int MPI_Testsome(int incount, MPI_Request *array_of_requests, int *outcount, int *array_of_indices, MPI_Status *array_of_statuses)
Tests for some given communications to complete
int MPI_Topo_test(MPI_Comm comm, int *top_type)
Determines the type of topology (if any) associated with a communicator
int MPI_Type_contiguous(int count, MPI_Datatype oldtype, MPI_Datatype *newtype)
Creates a contiguous datatype
int MPI_Type_extent(MPI_Datatype datatype, MPI_Aint *extent)
Returns the size of datatype
int MPI_Type_hindexed(int count, int *array_of_blocklengths, MPI_Aint *array_of_displacements, MPI_Datatype oldtype, MPI_Datatype *newtype)
Creates an indexed datatype with offsets in bytes
int MPI_Type_hvector(int count, int blocklength, MPI_Aint stride, MPI_Datatype oldtype, MPI_Datatype *newtype)
Creates a vector (strided) datatype with offset in bytes
int MPI_Type_indexed(int count, int *array_of_blocklengths, int *array_of_displacements, MPI_Datatype oldtype, MPI_Datatype *newtype)
Creates an indexed datatype
int MPI_Type_lb (MPI_Datatype datatype, MPI_Aint *displacement)
Returns the lower-bound of a datatype
int MPI_Type_struct(int count, int *array_of_blocklengths, MPI_Aint *array_of_displacements, MPI_Datatype *array_of_types, MPI_Datatype *newtype)
Creates a struct datatype
int MPI_Type_ub (MPI_Datatype datatype, MPI_Aint *displacement)
Returns the upper bound of a datatype
int MPI_Type_vector(int count, int blocklength, int stride, MPI_Datatype oldtype, MPI_Datatype *newtype)
Creates a vector (strided) datatype
int MPI_Wait(MPI_Request *request, MPI_Status *status)
Waits for an MPI send or receive to complete

```
int MPI_Waitall(int count, MPI_Request *array_of_requests,
          MPI_Status *array_of_statuses)
```
Waits for all given communications to complete

```
int MPI_Waitany(int count, MPI_Request *array_of_requests, int
          *index, MPI_Status *status)
```
Waits for any specified send or receive to complete

```
int MPI_Waitsome(int incount, MPI_Request *array_of_requests, int
          *outcount, int *array_of_indices, MPI_Status
          *array_of_statuses)
```
Waits for some given communications to complete

```
double MPI_Wtick(void)
```
Returns the resolution of MPI_Wtime

```
double MPI_Wtime(void)
```
Returns an elapsed time on the calling processor

A.2   Fortran Routines

This section describes the Fortran routines from [24].

```
MPI_Abort(comm, errorcode, ierror)
integer comm, errorcode, ierror
```
Terminates MPI execution environment

```
MPI_Address(location, address, ierror)
<type> location
integer address, ierror
```
Gets the address of a location in memory

```
MPI_Allgatherv(sendbuf, sendcount, sendtype, recvbuf, recvcounts,
          displs, recvtype, comm, ierror)
<type> sendbuf(*), recvbuf(*)
integer sendcount, sendtype, recvcounts(*), displs(*), recvtype,
comm, ierror
```
Gathers data from all tasks and deliver it to all

```
MPI_Allgather(sendbuf, sendcount, sendtype, recvbuf, recvcount,
          recvtype, comm, ierror)
<type> sendbuf(*), recvbuf(*)
integer sendcount, sendtype, recvcount, recvtype, comm, ierror
```
Gathers data from all tasks and distribute it to all

MPI_Allreduce(sendbuf, recvbuf, count, datatype, op, comm, ierror)
<type> sendbuf(*), recvbuf(*)
integer count, datatype, op, comm, ierror
Combines values from all processes and distribute the result back to all processes

---

MPI_Alltoallv(sendbuf, sendcounts, sdispls, sendtype, recvbuf,
          recvcounts, rdispls, recvtype, comm, ierror)
<type> sendbuf(*), recvbuf(*)
integer sendcounts(*), sdispls(*), sendtype, recvcounts(*),
rdispls(*), recvtype, comm, ierror
Sends data from all to all processes, with a displacement

MPI_Alltoall(sendbuf, sendcount, sendtype, recvbuf, recvcount,
          recvtype, comm, ierror)
<type> sendbuf(*), recvbuf(*)
integer sendcount, sendtype, recvcount, recvtype, comm, ierror
Sends data from all to all processes

MPI_Attr_delete(comm, keyval, ierror)
integer comm, keyval, ierror
Deletes attribute value associated with a key

MPI_Attr_get(comm, keyval, attribute_val, flag, ierror)
integer comm, keyval, attribute_val, ierror
logical flag
Retrieves attribute value by key

MPI_Attr_put(comm, keyval, attribute_val, ierror)
integer comm, keyval, attribute_val, ierror
Stores attribute value associated with a key

MPI_Barrier (comm, ierror)
integer comm, ierror
Blocks until all process have reached this routine.

MPI_Bcast(buffer, count, datatype, root, comm, ierror)
<type> buffer(*)
integer count, datatype, root, comm, ierror
Broadcasts a message from the process with rank "root" to all other processes of the group

```
MPI_Bsend_init(buf, count, datatype, dest, tag, comm, request,
          ierror)
<type> buf(*)
integer count, datatype, dest, tag, comm, request, ierror
```
Builds a handle for a buffered send

```
MPI_Bsend(buf, count, datatype, dest, tag, comm, ierror)
<type> buf(*)
integer count, datatype, dest, tag, comm, ierror
```
Basic send with user-specified buffering

```
MPI_Buffer_attach( buffer, size, ierror)
<type> buffer(*)
integer size, ierror
```
Attaches a user-defined buffer for sending

```
MPI_Buffer_detach( buffer, size, ierror)
<type> buffer(*)
integer size, ierror
```
Removes an existing buffer (for use in MPI_Bsend, etc.)

```
MPI_Cancel( request, ierror)
integer request, ierror
```
Cancels a communication request

```
MPI_Cart_coords(comm, rank, maxdims, coords, ierror)
integer comm, rank, maxdims, coords(*), ierror
```
Determines process coords in Cartesian topology, given rank in group

```
MPI_Cart_create(comm_old, ndims, dims, periods, reorder, comm_cart,
          ierror)
integer comm_old, ndims, dims(*), comm_cart, ierror
logical periods(*), reorder
```
Makes a new communicator to which topology information has been attached

```
MPI_Cart_get(comm, maxdims, dims, periods, coords, ierror)
integer comm, maxdims, dims(*), coords(*), ierror
logical periods(*)
```
Retrieves Cartesian topology information associated with a communicator

```
MPI_Cart_map(comm, ndims, dims, periods, newrank, ierror)
integer comm, ndims, dims(*), newrank, ierror
logical periods(*)
```
Maps process to Cartesian topology information

`MPI_Cart_rank(comm, coords, rank, ierror)`
`integer comm, coords(*), rank, ierror`
Determines process rank in communicator, given Cartesian location

`MPI_Cart_shift(comm, direction, disp, rank_source, rank_dest,`
`          ierror)`
`integer comm, direction, disp, rank_source, rank_dest, ierror`
Returns the shifted source and destination ranks given a shift direction and amount

`MPI_Cart_sub(comm, remain_dims, newcomm, ierror)`
`integer comm, newcomm, ierror`
`logical remain_dims(*)`
Partitions a communicator into subgroups that form lower-dimensional Cartesian subgrids

`MPI_Cartdim_get(comm, ndims, ierror)`
`integer comm, ndims, ierror`
Retrieves Cartesian topology information associated with a communicator

`MPI_Comm_compare(comm1, comm2, result, ierror)`
`integer comm, group, newcomm, ierror`
Compares two communicators

`MPI_Comm_create(comm, group, newcomm, ierror)`
`integer comm, group, newcomm, ierror`
Creates a new communicator

`MPI_Comm_dup(comm, newcomm, ierror)`
`integer comm, newcomm, ierror`
Duplicates an existing communicator with all its cached information

`MPI_Comm_free(comm, ierror)`
`integer comm, ierror`
Marks the communicator object for deallocation

`MPI_Comm_group(comm, group, ierror)`
`integer comm, group, ierror`
Accesses the group associated with given communicator

`MPI_Comm_rank(comm, rank, ierror)`
`integer comm, rank, ierror`
Determines the rank of the calling process in the communicator

`MPI_Comm_size(comm, size, ierror)`
`integer comm, size, ierror`
Determines the size of the group associated with a communictor

`MPI_Comm_split(comm, color, key, newcomm, ierror)`
`integer comm, color, key, newcomm, ierror`
Creates new communicators based on colors and keys

`MPI_Comm_test_inter(comm, flag, ierror)`
`integer comm, ierror`
`logical flag`
Tests to see whether a communicator is an intercommunicator

`MPI_Dims_create(nnodes, ndims, dims, ierror)`
`integer nnodes, ndims, dims(*), ierror`
Creates a division of processes in a Cartesian grid

`MPI_Errhandler_create(function, errhandler, ierror)`
`external function`
`integer errhandler, ierror`
Creates an MPI-style error handler

`MPI_Errhandler_free(errhandler, ierror)`
`integer errhandler, ierror`
Frees an MPI-style error handler

`MPI_Errhandler_get(comm, errhandler, ierror)`
`integer comm, errhandler, ierror`
Gets the error handler for a communicator

`MPI_Errhandler_set(comm, errhandler, ierror)`
`integer comm, errhandler, ierror`
Sets the error handler for a communicator

`MPI_Error_class(errorcode, errorclass, ierror)`
`integer errorcode, errorclass, ierror`
Converts an error code into an error class

`MPI_Error_string(errorcode, string, resultlen, ierror)`
`integer errorcode, resultlen, ierror`
`character*MPI_MAX_ERROR_STRING string`
Returns a string for a given error code

`MPI_Finalize(ierror)`
`integer ierror`
Terminates MPI execution environment

MPI_Gatherv(sendbuf, sendcount, sendtype, recvbuf, recvcounts, displs, recvtype, root, comm, ierror) <type>sendbuf(*), recvbuf(*) integer sendcount, sendtype, recvcounts(*), displs(*), recvtype, root, comm, ierror *Gathers into specified locations from all tasks in a group*
MPI_Gather(sendbuf, sendcount, sendtype, recvbuf, recvcount, recvtype, root, comm, ierror) <type> sendbuf(*), recvbuf(*) integer sendcount, sendtype, recvcount, recvtype, root, comm, ierror *Gathers together values from a group of tasks*
MPI_Get_count(status, datatype, count, ierror) integer status(*), datatype, count, ierror *Gets the number of "top level" elements*
MPI_Get_elements (status, datatype, elements, ierror) integer status(*), datatype, elements, ierror *Returns the number of basic elements in a datatype*
MPI_Get_processor_name(name, resultlen, ierror) character*MPI_MAX_PROCESSOR_NAME name integer resultlen, ierror *Gets the name of the processor*
MPI_Graph_create(comm_old, nnodes, index, edges, reorder, comm_graph, ierror) integer comm_old, nnodes, index(*), edges(*), comm_graph, ierror logical reorder *Makes a new communicator to which topology information has been attached*
MPI_Graph_get(comm, maxindex, maxedges, index, edges, ierror) integer comm, maxindex, maxedges, index(*), edges(*), ierror *Retrieves graph topology information associated with a communicator*
MPI_Graph_map(comm, nnodes, index, edges, newrank, ierror) integer comm, nnodes, index(*), edges(*), newrank, ierror *Maps process to graph topology information*
MPI_Graph_neighbors_count(comm, rank, nneighbors, ierror) integer comm, rank, nneighbors, ierror *Returns the number of neighbors of a node associated with a graph topology*

`MPI_Graph_neighbors(comm, rank, maxneighbors, neighbors, ierror)`
`integer comm, rank, maxneighbors, neighbors(*), ierror`
Returns the neighbors of a node associated with a graph topology

---

`MPI_Graphdims_Get(comm, nnodes, nedges, ierror)`
`integer comm, nnodes, nedges, ierror`
Retrieves graph topology information associated with a communicator

---

`MPI_Group_difference(group1, group2, newgroup, ierror)`
`integer group1, group2, newgroup, ierror`
Makes a group from the difference of two groups

`MPI_Group_excl(group, n, ranks, newgroup, ierror)`
`integer group, n, ranks(*), newgroup, ierror`
Produces a group by reordering an existing group and taking only unlisted members

---

`MPI_Group_free(group, ierror)`
`integer group, ierror`
Frees a group

`MPI_Group_incl(group, n, ranks, newgroup, ierror)`
`integer group, n, ranks(*), newgroup, ierror`
Produces a group by reordering an existing group and taking only listed members

---

`MPI_Group_intersection(group1, group2, newgroup, ierror)`
`integer group1, group2, newgroup, ierror`
Produces a group as the intersection of two existing groups.

`MPI_Group_range_excl(group, n, ranges, newgroup, ierror)`
`integer group, n, ranges(3,*), newgroup, ierror`
Produces a group by excluding ranges of processes from an existing group

---

`MPI_Group_range_incl(group, n, ranges, newgroup, ierror)`
`integer group, n, ranges(3,*), newgroup, ierror`
Creates a new group from ranges of ranks in an existing group

---

`MPI_Group_rank(group, rank, ierror)`
`integer group, rank, ierror`
Returns the rank of this process in the given group

`MPI_Group_size(group, size, ierror)`
`integer group, size, ierror`
Returns the size of a group

MPI_Group_translate_ranks (group1, n, ranks1, group2, ranks2,
        ierror)
integer group1, n, ranks1(*), group2, ranks2(*), ierror
Translates the ranks of processes in one group to those in another group

---

MPI_Group_union(group1, group2, newgroup, ierror)
integer group1, group2, newgroup, ierror
Produces a group by combining two groups

MPI_Ibsend(buf, count, datatype, dest, tag, comm, request, ierror)
<type> buf(*)
integer count, datatype, dest, tag, comm, request, ierror
Starts a nonblocking buffered send

MPI_Initialized(flag, ierror)
logical flag
integer ierror
Indicates whether MPI_Init has been called

MPI_Init(ierror)
integer ierror
Initializes the MPI execution environment

MPI_Iprobe(source, tag, comm, flag, status, ierror)
integer source, tag, comm, status(*), ierror
logical flag
Nonblocking test for a message

MPI_Irecv(buf, count, datatype, source, tag, comm, request, ierror)
<type> buf(*)
integer count, datatype, source, tag, comm, request, ierror
Begins a nonblocking receive

MPI_Irsend(buf, count, datatype, dest, tag, comm, request, ierror)
<type> buf(*)
integer count, datatype, dest, tag, comm, request, ierror
Starts a nonblocking ready send

MPI_Isend(buf, count, datatype, dest, tag, comm, request, ierror)
<type> buf(*)
integer count, datatype, dest, tag, comm, request, ierror
Starts a nonblocking send

```
MPI_Issend(buf, count, datatype, dest, tag, comm, request, ierror)
<type> buf(*)
integer count, datatype, dest, tag, comm, request, ierror
```
Starts a nonblocking synchronous send

```
MPI_Keyval_create(copy_fn, delete_fn, keyval, extra_state, ierror)
external copy_fn, delete_fn
integer keyval, extra_state, ierror
```
Generates a new attribute key

```
MPI_Keyval_free(keyval, ierror)
integer keyval, ierror
```
Frees attribute key for communicator cache attribute

```
MPI_Op_create(function, commute, op, ierror)
external function
logical commute
integer op, ierror
```
Creates a user-defined combination function handle

```
MPI_Op_free( op, ierror)
integer op, ierror
```
Frees a user-defined combination function handle

```
MPI_Pcontrol(level )
integer level
```
Controls profiling (no ierror *argument; see A.14 in [23])*

```
MPI_Probe(source, tag, comm, status, ierror)
integer source, tag, comm, status(*), ierror
```
Blocking test for a message

```
MPI_Recv_init(buf, count, datatype, source, tag, comm, request,
          ierror)
<type> buf(*)
integer count, datatype, source, tag, comm, request, ierror
```
Creates a handle for a receive

```
MPI_Recv(buf, count, datatype, source, tag, comm, status, ierror)
<type> buf(*)
integer count, datatype, source, tag, comm, status, ierror
```
Basic receive

MPI_Reduce_scatter(sendbuf, recvbuf, recvcounts, datatype, op, comm,
          ierror)
<type> sendbuf(*), recvbuf(*)
integer recvcounts(*), datatype, op, comm, ierror
Combines values and scatters the results

MPI_Reduce(sendbuf, recvbuf, count, datatype, op, root, comm,
          ierror)
<type> sendbuf(*), recvbuf(*)
integer count, datatype, op, root, comm, ierror
Reduces values on all processes to a single value

MPI_Request_free(request, ierror)
integer request, ierror
Frees a communication request object

MPI_Rsend_init(buf, count, datatype, dest, tag, comm, request,
          ierror)
<type> buf(*)
integer count, datatype, dest, tag, comm, request, ierror
Builds a handle for a ready send

MPI_Rsend(buf, count, datatype, dest, tag, comm, ierror)
<type> buf(*)
integer count, datatype, dest, tag, comm, ierror
Basic ready send

MPI_Scan(sendbuf, recvbuf, count, datatype, op, comm, ierror)
<type> sendbuf(*), recvbuf(*)
integer count, datatype, op, comm, ierror
Computes the scan (partial reductions) of data on a collection of processes

MPI_Scatterv(sendbuf, sendcounts, displs, sendtype, recvbuf,
          recvcount, recvtype, root, comm, ierror)
<type> sendbuf(*), recvbuf(*)
integer sendcounts(*), displs(*), sendtype, recvcount, recvtype,
root, comm, ierror
Scatters a buffer in parts to all tasks in a group

```
MPI_Scatter(sendbuf, sendcount, sendtype, recvbuf, recvcount,
            recvtype, root, comm, ierror)
<type> sendbuf(*), recvbuf(*)
integer sendcount, sendtype, recvcount, recvtype, root, comm, ierror
```
Sends data from one task to all other tasks in a group

```
MPI_Send_init(buf, count, datatype, dest, tag, comm, request,
            ierror)
<type> buf(*)
integer count, datatype, dest, tag, comm, request, ierror
```
Builds a handle for a standard send

```
MPI_Sendrecv_replace(buf, count, datatype, dest, sendtag, source,
            recvtag, comm, status, ierror)
<type> buf(*)
integer count, datatype, dest, sendtag, source, recvtag, comm,
status(*), ierror
```
Sends and receives using a single buffer

```
MPI_Sendrecv(sendbuf, sendcount, sendtype, dest, sendtag, recvbuf,
            recvcount, recvtype, source, recvtag, comm, status, ierror)
<type>sendbuf(*), recvbuf(*)
integer sendcount, sendtype, dest, sendtag, recvcount, recvtype,
source, recvtag, comm, status(*), ierror
```
Sends and receives

```
MPI_Send(buf, count, datatype, dest, tag, comm, ierror)
<type> buf(*)
integer count, datatype, dest, tag, comm, ierror
```
Basic send

```
MPI_Ssend_init(buf, count, datatype, dest, tag, comm, request,
            ierror)
<type> buf(*)
integer count, datatype, dest, tag, comm, request, ierror
```
Builds a handle for a synchronous send

```
MPI_Ssend(buf, count, datatype, dest, tag, comm, ierror)
<type> buf(*)
integer count, datatype, dest, tag, comm, ierror
```
Basic synchronous send

```
MPI_Startall(count, array_of_requests, ierror)
integer count, array_of_requests(*), ierror
```
Starts a collection of requests

```
MPI_Start(request, ierror)
integer request, ierror
```
Initiates a communication with a persistent request handle

```
MPI_Test(request, flag, status, ierror)
integer request, status(*), ierror
logical flag
```
Tests for the completion of a send or receive

```
MPI_Test_cancelled(status, flag, ierror)
integer status(*), ierror
logical flag
```
Tests to see whether a request was canceled

```
MPI_Testall(count, array_of_requests, flag, array_of_statuses,
            ierror)
integer count, array_of_requests(*),
array_of_statuses(MPI_STATUS_SIZE,*), ierror
logical flag
```
Tests for the completion of all previously initiated communications

```
MPI_Testany(count, array_of_requests, index, flag, status, ierror)
integer count, array_of_requests(*), index, status(*), ierror
logical flag
```
Tests for completion of any previously initiated communication

```
MPI_Testsome(incount, array_of_requests, outcount, array_of_indices,
            array_of_statuses, ierror)
integer incount, array_of_requests(*), outcount,
array_of_indices(*), array_of_statuses(MPI_STATUS_SIZE,*), ierror
```
Tests for some given communications to complete

```
MPI_Topo_test(comm, top_type, ierror)
integer comm, top_type, ierror
```
Determines the type of topology (if any) associated with a communicator

```
MPI_Type_contiguous(count, oldtype, newtype, ierror)
integer count, oldtype, newtype, ierror
```
Creates a contiguous datatype

MPI_Type_extent(datatype, extent, ierror) integer datatype, extent, ierror *Returns the size of datatype*
MPI_Type_hindexed(count, array_of_blocklengths,   array_of_displacements, oldtype, newtype, ierror) integer count, array_of_blocklengths(*), array_of_displacements(*), oldtype, newtype, ierror *Creates an indexed datatype with offsets in bytes*
MPI_Type_hvector(count, blocklength, stride, oldtype, newtype,   ierror) integer count, blocklength, stride, oldtype, newtype, ierror *Creates a vector (strided) datatype with offset in bytes*
MPI_Type_indexed(count, array_of_blocklengths,   array_of_displacements, oldtype, newtype, ierror) integer count, array_of_blocklengths(*), array_of_displacements(*), oldtype, newtype, ierror *Creates an indexed datatype*
MPI_Type_struct(count, array_of_blocklengths,   array_of_displacements, array_of_types, newtype, ierror) integer count, array_of_blocklengths(*), array_of_displacements(*), array_of_types(*), newtype, ierror *Creates a structure datatype*
MPI_Type_vector(count, blocklength, stride, oldtype, newtype,   ierror) integer count, blocklength, stride, oldtype, newtype, ierror *Creates a vector (strided) datatype*
MPI_Wait(request, status, ierror) integer request, status(*), ierror *Waits for an MPI send or receive to complete*
MPI_Waitall(count, array_of_requests, array_of_statuses, ierror) integer count, array_of_requests(*), array_of_statuses(MPI_STATUS_SIZE,*), ierror *Waits for all given communications to complete*
MPI_Waitany(count, array_of_requests, index, status, ierror) integer count, array_of_requests(*), index, status(*), ierror *Waits for any specified send or receive to complete*

```
MPI_Waitsome(incount, array_of_requests, outcount, array_of_indices,
          array_of_statuses, ierror)
integer incount, array_of_requests(*), outcount,
array_of_indices(*), array_of_statuses(MPI_STATUS_SIZE,*), ierror
```
Waits for some given communications to complete

```
double precision MPI_Wtick()
```
Returns the resolution of MPI_Wtime

```
double precision MPI_Wtime()
```
Returns an elapsed time on the calling processor

B The Model MPI Implementation

In Chapter 8 we described an approach to implementing a system like MPI based on the idea of an abstract device interface. Here we describe the concrete implementation of MPI that has resulted from building on that interface, together with other aspects of a convenient parallel programming environment.

B.1 Features of the Model Implementation

Although the MPI Standard specifies what user programs will look like, actual implementations of the MPI library will differ in various ways. In this section we describe some of the characteristic features of the particular implementation from Argonne National Laboratory and Mississippi State University.

B.1.1 User Features

The model implementation is a complete implementation of the MPI Standard and is freely available from `info.mcs.anl.gov` in the directory `pub/mpi`. The implementation was done by members of the MPI Forum and has tracked the standard as it has evolved. The model implementation includes all source code. ANSI C prototypes are provided, so that the MPI library can be called from C++. Man pages in standard format for all MPI functions are included, suitable for viewing with any man page viewer such as `man`, `xman`, `tkman`, or `emacs`.

The model implementation is portable to a wide variety of parallel computers and workstation networks. It supports heterogeneous computation while exacting no overhead when in a homogeneous environment. The implementation includes all the tools described in this book, including the MPE library, `upshot`, and the tools for creating profiling libraries.

Configuration is carried out with the aid of the GNU `config` program, which allows great flexibility in installation. Precise installation instructions are supplied with the distribution.

B.1.2 Portability

The model implementation is built on the concept of the abstract device interface described in Chapter 8. Thus, most of the code is completely portable. The portability of the MPI implementation is provided by multiple implementations of the abstract device interface, including a portable one. As this is being written, there are two vendor-specific implementations of the device interface provided: one for Intel NX, which supplies an implementation of MPI on the Intel iPSC/860, Delta, and Paragon, and also one for nCUBE machines. The portable device implementation is written using Chameleon, an extremely thin layer of macros and subroutines that provides support for the Thinking Machines CM-5 via CMMD, and the IBM SP1 and SP2 via EUI-H and MPL. For workstation networks, it uses either p4 or PVM. Thus this implementation can run in almost any parallel environment. Use of the abstract device interface simplifies ports to new communication environments, such as fiber channel or ATM networks.

B.1.3   Efficiency

The portable, public implementation must, of course, yield a slight performance edge to a proprietary one, since it cannot access proprietary low-level system primitives. However, we have been able to achieve quite respectable performance. Figure B.1 shows the bandwidth achieved by our implementation on the IBM SP1, compared with two other message-passing libraries on the SP1. They are EUI-H, a research version of IBM's standard EUI interface, and MPI-F, a prototype MPI implementation from IBM [27]. Note that for medium-sized messages, this portable implementation is achieving 98% of the bandwidth of the high-performance, proprietary vendor implementation. We offer this as evidence that the use of structure in an implementation (abstract device, Chameleon) need not exact a significant penalty in performance.

B.1.4   Auxiliary Tools

The distribution comes with a number of useful tools, many of which have been introduced in this book. The MPE library, including event logging and a simple parallel graphics interface, is included; see Appendix C. The upshot logfile examination tool described below is also included. As demonstrations of what can be done with the MPI profiling interface, three different profiling libraries are included, for simple counting and time accumulation, for upshot logging, and for real-time graphical display of message traffic. Finally, the "wrapper generator" program for creating profiling libraries with a minimum of effort is included in this MPI distribution.

B.2   Installing and Running the Model Implementation

Installation of MPI consists of one call to configure to create the makefiles appropriate for an installation, followed by a call to make. Details are given in the installation instructions that come with the distribution.

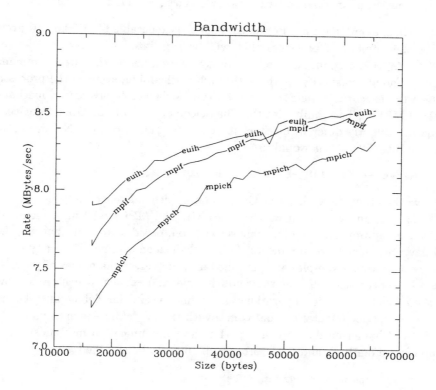

Figure B.1
Bandwidth comparisons on the SP1

MPI does not specify a standard way of starting MPI programs, partly because of the diversity of mechanisms currently used. Our implementation tries to hide these differences as much as possible, although it is not possible to hide them all, since the implementation may be installed in a variety of ways. The basic way of invoking an MPI program is intended to be as similar as possible to invoking an ordinary sequential program. Just as one invokes sequential programs in a Unix environment with

    a.out <command-line arguments>

one can start MPI programs (for this implementation) with

```
a.out -np <number of processes> <command-line arguments>
```

(Of course, `a.out` need not be the name of the executable file.) The new argument gives the number of processes that will be associated with the `MPI_COMM_WORLD` communicator. In many environments, the cited command line will be enough to specify (perhaps through a scheduling system) the processors on which the executable file `a.out` will be run. This simple invocation mechanism is used if MPI has been built with the Chameleon device option. Other "devices" may require a slightly different mechanism. For example, to run the NX device version on the Intel Delta, one would use

```
mexec -t"(10,1)" -f "a.out -np 10"
```

On workstation networks, the Chameleon device references a 'hosts' file, an example of which comes with the MPI model implementation. It selects an appropriate set of machines to run on, based on data in that file, the time of day, and memory requirements. Other Chameleon command-line arguments can be used as well. Examples are `-listnodes`, which gives the names of the machines that have been selected from the "'hosts'" file, and `-trace`, which gives a low-level trace of communication operations, sometimes useful for debugging. Details are given in the documentation that comes with the model implementation.

If the Chameleon device is using p4 as its communication mechanism, then the `-np` can be omitted, and s p4 "procgroup" file can be specified with

```
a.out -p4pg <procgroup file>
```

This approach allows individual machines and separate executables to be directly specified.

C The MPE Multiprocessing Environment Functions

Here we describe the MPE library that has been used in the examples throughout this book. It consists of functions that are

- consistent in style with MPI,
- not in MPI,
- freely available, and
- in the long run will work with any MPI implementation.

These tools are extremely rudimentary and lack many desirable features. Nonetheless, we have found them useful even in their present state. They are continuing to evolve.

The files 'mpe.h' and 'mpef.h' should be include for C and Fortran programs respectively.

C.1 MPE Logging

The logging routines in MPE are used to create logfiles of events that occur during the execution of a parallel program. These files can then be studied after the program has ended. These routines were introduced and discussed in Chapter 3, Section 3.6.3. The format of the log file is roughly that described in [49]. The C bindings are given in Table C.1 and the Fortran bindings in Table C.2.

---

int **MPE_Init_log**(void)

int **MPE_Start_log**(void)

int **MPE_Stop_log**(void)

int **MPE_Finish_log**(char *logfilename)

int **MPE_Describe_state**(int start, int end, char *name, char *color)

int **MPE_Describe_event**(int event, char *name)

int **MPE_Log_event**(int event, int intdata char *chardata)

Table C.1
C bindings for MPE logging routines

These routines allow the user to log events that are meaningful for specific applications, rather than relying on automatic logging of MPI library calls. The basic

MPE_INIT_LOG()

MPE_FINISH_LOG(logfilename)
        character*(*) logfilename

MPE_START_LOG()

MPE_STOP_LOG()

MPE_DESCRIBE_STATE(start, end, name, color)
        integer start, end
        character*(*) name, color

MPE_DESCRIBE_EVENT(event, name)
        integer event
        character*(*) name

MPE_LOG_EVENT(event, intdata, chardata)
        integer event, intdata
        character*(*) chardata

Table C.2
Fortran bindings for MPE logging

routines are `MPE_Init_log`, `MPE_Log_event`, and `MPE_Finish_log`.

`MPE_Init_log` must be called (by all processes) to initialize MPE logging data structures. `MPE_Finish_log` collects the log data from all the processes, merges it, and aligns the timestamps with respect to the times at which `MPE_Init_log` and `MPE_Finish_log` were called. Then, the process with rank 0 in `MPI_COMM_WORLD` writes the log into the file whose name is given as an argument. A single event is logged with the `MPE_Log_event` routine, which specifies an event type (completely up to the user), and one integer and one character string for user data. In order to place in the logfile data that might be useful for a logfile analysis or visualization program (like `upshot`), the routines `MPE_Describe_event` and `MPE_Describe_state` allow one to add event and state descriptions and to define states by specifying a starting and ending event for each state. One can also suggest a state color to be used by the logfile visualizations program. In the case of `upshot`, the color can be of the form `"red:vlines"` in order to specify simultaneously a color for a color display and a bitmap for black-and-white displays (such as books).

Finally, `MPE_Stop_log` and `MPE_Start_log` can be used to dynamically turn logging on and off. By default, it is on after `MPE_Init_log` is called.

These routines are used in one of the profiling libraries supplied with the distribution for automatic event logging for MPI library calls.

C.2   MPE Graphics

Many application programmers would like to enhance the output of their programs with some simple graphics, but find learning the X11 programming model too much of a burden. To make it easier, we have defined a small set of simple graphics primitives that can be used in MPI programs. An introduction to this library is given in Chapter 3, Section 3.7. The C bindings for these routines are given in Table C.3. (We note that some MPI implementations may not be compatible with X11; our implementation assumes that X11 routines can be called directly from programs that are also using MPI.)

---

int **MPE_Open_graphics**(MPE_XGraph *handle, MPI_comm comm, char *display,
        int x, int y, int is_collective)

int **MPE_Draw_point**(MPE_XGraph handle, int x, int y, MPE_Color color)

int **MPE_Draw_line**(MPE_XGraph handle, int x1, int y1, int x2, int y2,
        MPE_Color color)

int **MPE_Draw_circle**(MPE_XGraph handle, int centerx, int centery, int radius,
        MPE_Color color)

int **MPE_Fill_rectangle**(MPE_XGraph handle, int x, int y, int w, int h,
        MPE_Color color)

int **MPE_Update**(MPE_XGraph handle)

int **MPE_Num_colors**(MPE_XGraph handle, int *nc)

int **MPE_Make_color_array**(MPE_XGraph handle, int ncolors, MPE_Color array[])

int **MPE_Close_graphics**(MPE_XGraph *handle)

Table C.3
C bindings for MPE graphics routines

```
MPE_OPEN_GRAPHICS(handle, comm, display, x, y, is_collective, ierror)
            integer handle, comm, x, y, ierror
            character*(*) display
            logical is_collective

MPE_DRAW_POINT(handle, x, y, color, ierror)
            integer handle, x, y, color, ierror

MPE_DRAW_LINE(handle, x1, y1, x2, y2, color, ierror)
            integer handle, x1, y1, x2, y2, color, ierror

MPE_DRAW_CIRCLE(handle, centerx, centery, radius, color, ierror)
            integer handle, centerx, centery, radius, color, ierror

MPE_FILL_RECTANGLE(handle, x, y, w, h, color, ierror)
            integer handle, x, y, w, h, color, ierror

MPE_UPDATE(handle, ierror)
            integer handle, ierror

MPE_NUM_COLORS(handle, nc, ierror)
            integer handle, nc, ierror

MPE_MAKE_COLOR_ARRAY(handle, ncolors, array, ierror)
            integer handle, ncolors, array(*), ierror

MPE_CLOSE_GRAPHICS(handle, ierror)
            integer handle, ierror
```

Table C.4
Fortran bindings for MPE graphics routines

C.3   MPE Helpers

In addition to the logging and graphics code, the MPE library contains a number of routines to aid programmers in producing parallel applications. The routine shown in Tables C.5 and C.6, MPE_Decomp1d, was used in Chapter 4 to compute decompositions of an array. Additional routines will be added to the MPE library as we use it.

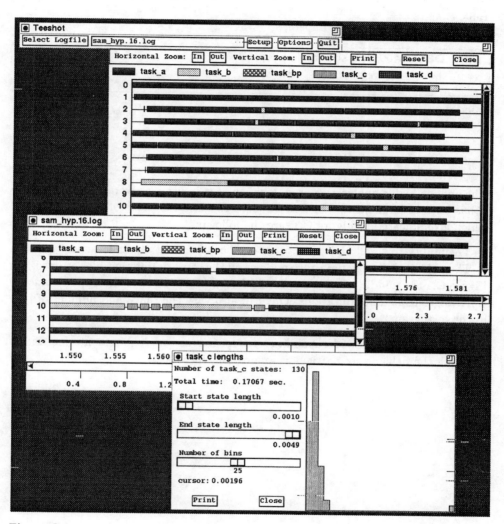

Figure C.1
A screendump of upshot

```
int MPE_Decomp1d(int n, int size, int rank, int *s, int *e)
```

Table C.5
C bindings for Miscellaneous MPE routines

```
MPE_DECOMP1D(n, size, rank, s, e)
              integer n, size, rank, s, e
```

Table C.6
Fortran bindings for Miscellaneous MPE routines

C.4   The Upshot Program Visualization System

The **upshot** logfile analysis program [49] has been in use for several years. Recently it has been re-implemented in Tcl/Tk [60, 61]. Useful features of **upshot**, some of which are indicated in Figure C.1, are the following:

- The ability to scroll and zoom in an out both horizontally and vertically
- The ability to display multiple windows on the same or different files at once. (In Figure C.1 the middle window is a detailed view of a portion of the upper window.)
- Histograms of state durations. One can also vary the range and number of bins in the histogram.

We are continuing to add capabilities to **upshot** as our requirements for understanding the behavior of particular applications increase.

D MPI Resources on the Information Superhighway

Here we describe how to get access to MPI-related material on the Internet.

Examples of MPI programs. All of the examples used in this book are available by anonymous `ftp` from `info.mcs.anl.gov` in directory `pub/mpi/using/examples`. This directory is organized by book chapter. The file 'README' lists the files by chapter. A Unix 'tar' file (compressed) containing all of the examples is available in 'examples.tar.Z'. Instructions for unpacking this file are in the 'README' file.

The model implementation includes a set of example and test programs as well.

The model implementation. The model implementation is available by anonymous ftp from `info.mcs.anl.gov`. The 'README' file in directory 'pub/mpi' describes how to fetch and install the most recent version of the model implementation. Argonne National Laboratory expects to distribute the model implementation and the example programs on CD-ROM as well.

The MPI Standard. To obtain a copy of the MPI Standard itself [24], send a message containing

```
send mpi-report.ps from mpi
```

to `netlib@ornl.gov`. You will receive a compressed postscript file. It is also available by anonymous ftp from 'pub/mpi/mpi-report.ps.Z' at `info.mcs.anl.gov`. (Netlib is also a good source of programs for numerical analysis; in addition, both PVM and p4 are available here.)

Discussion on MPI. There is a newsgroup, `comp.parallel.mpi`, devoted to the discussion of all aspects of MPI. Discussion of MPI-related issues also sometimes occurs in the more general group, `comp.parallel`, devoted to parallel computers and computation.

World Wide Web. The World Wide Web (WWW) can be thought of as a planet-wide hypertext document. Using a WWW reader, such as `xmosaic` or `tkwww`, you can read documents, fetch files, and follow links to related information all over the planet.

Information on MPI is available at

```
http://www.mcs.anl.gov/mpi/index.html
```

New information on MPI resources will be made available here.

A version of the MPI standard is available on the WWW at

http://www.mcs.anl.gov/mpi/mpi-report/mpi-report.html

A "frequently asked questions" (FAQ) page is available at

http://www.cs.msstate.edu/mpi/mpi-faq.html

There is a great deal of information on parallel programming projects and tools on the WWW. We encourage you to investigate other sites on the Web for other resources on MPI and parallel computing.

E Language Details

In this appendix we briefly discuss some details of C and Fortran that interact with MPI.

E.1 Arrays in C and Fortran

This section discusses the layout of Fortran arrays in memory and talks very briefly about how implicit "reshapes" of arrays are handled in Fortran 77. All arrays are stored in memory according to some rule, defined by the language, that says how to map the indices of an array reference such as a(i,j,k,l) into a computer's memory. Understanding and exploiting this rule is important in creating efficient representations of data.

E.1.1 Column and Row Major Ordering

Many discussions of the differences between Fortran and C arrays refer to "column" and "row" major ordering. These terms come from looking at a two-dimensional array as representing a matrix. To understand this, consider the $m \times n$ matrix

$$
\begin{pmatrix}
a_{11} & a_{12} & a_{13} & \cdots & a_{1n} \\
a_{21} & a_{22} & a_{23} & \cdots & a_{2n} \\
\vdots & \vdots & \vdots & \vdots & \vdots \\
a_{m1} & a_{m2} & a_{m3} & \cdots & a_{mn}
\end{pmatrix}
$$

If we use the Fortran declaration

```
real a(m,n)
```

and represent the matrix element a_{ij} with a(i,j), then *column major ordering*, used in the Fortran language, means that the elements are stored by columns; that is, they are stored in the order a(1,1), a(2,1), ..., a(m,1), a(1,2), ..., a(m,n). *Row major ordering*, used in the C language, means that the elements are stored by rows; that is, a[0][0], a[0][1], ..., a[0][n-1], a[1][0], ..., a[m-1][n-1]. We have used Fortran and C array notation here to emphasize how each is stored in memory.

E.1.2 Meshes vs. Matrices

While a matrix-based view of arrays is very common and often helpful, there are many applications where a different view of arrays is natural. For instance, the 2-d Poisson example in Chapter 4. The solution to the problem had a natural representation as a function $u(x, y)$. We solved this on a discrete mesh of points (x_i, y_j) and used the Fortran element u(i,j) to represent $u(x_i, y_j)$. While this approach seems entirely natural, consider how this appears:

$$
\begin{array}{cccc}
\texttt{u(1,m)} & \texttt{u(2,m)} & \cdots & \texttt{u(n,m)} \\
\texttt{u(1,m-1)} & \texttt{u(2,m-1)} & \cdots & \texttt{u(n,m-1)} \\
\vdots & \vdots & \vdots & \vdots \\
\texttt{u(1,1)} & \texttt{u(2,1)} & \cdots & \texttt{u(n,1)}
\end{array}
$$

Viewed this way, the *rows* are stored together! What is going on?

The real story is that Fortran arrays are (always) stored so that, when we look at how the elements are placed in memory, we see that the first index varies most rapidly. In fact, the rule for mapping a Fortran array into memory is quite simple: If the array is declared as A(N1,N2,...), then A(I1,I2,...) is the (I1-1) + N1*((I2-1) + N2*(...))th element (starting from zero).

The rule for C is the opposite; the *last* index varies most rapidly. When considering the special case of two dimensions, and looking at the arrays as representing matrices, we see how these lead to the row- and column-major interpretations.

E.1.3 Higher Dimensional Arrays

Once we know how arrays are laid out in the computer's memory, we can use that information to design ways to access sections of multidimensional arrays, planes with one coordinate constant, for example. If we wish to send a plane of data out of a 3-d array, we can form three different datatypes, one for each coordinate direction.

For concreteness, consider a Fortran array dimensioned as

```
double precision a(nx,ny,nz)
```

If we want to send or receive the elements a(sx:ex,sy:ez,k) for some value of k, we can define a vector datatype newz:

```
    call MPI_Type_vector( ey-sy+1, ex-sx+1, nx,
                          MPI_DOUBLE_PRECISION, newz, ierror )
    call MPI_Type_commit( newz, ierror )
    call MPI_Send( a(sx,sy,k), 1, newz, dest, tag, comm, ierror )
```

To understand this, we need only look at the discussion of arrays above. For the elements a(sx:ex,sy:ey,k), we see that the data consists of ey-sy+1 groups ("columns") of ex-sx+1 elements ("rows"); the rows are contiguous in memory.

The stride from one group to another (i.e., from a(sx,j,k) to a(sx,j+1,k)) is just nx double precision values. Note that this is an example of a vector type with a block count that is different from one.

Similarly, to send or receive the elements a(sx:ex,j,sz:ez) we can use

```
call MPI_Type_vector( ez-sz+1, ex-sx+1, nx*ny,
                      MPI_DOUBLE_PRECISION, newy, ierror )
call MPI_Type_commit( newy, ierror )
```

The explanation for this is the same as for a(sx:ex,sy:ez,k) except that the stride between elements is nx*ny double precision values.

The final case, to send or receive the elements a(i,sy:ey,sz:ez) requires a little more work because we can not use the blocklength argument in MPI_Type_vector. In this case, we take advantage of MPI's ability to form a datatype from an MPI datatype. First, we for a datatype for the elements a(i,sy:ey,k):

```
call MPI_Type_vector( ey-sy+1, 1, nx,
                      MPI_DOUBLE_PRECISION, newx1, ierror )
call MPI_Type_commit( newx1, ierror )
```

Next, we form a vector of these types. Since the stride between these elements is probably not an integral multiple of ey-sy+1, we use MPI_Type_hvector; this routine measures the stride in bytes.

```
call MPI_Type_extent( MPI_DOUBLE_PRECISION, sizeof, ierror )
call MPI_Type_hvector( ez-sz+1, 1, nx*ny*sizeof,
                       newx1, newx, ierror )
call MPI_Type_commit( newx, ierror )
```

An approach similar to that in Section 5.4 can be used to generate more general datatypes.

E.2   Aliasing

MPI routines such as MPI_Allreduce have both input and output buffers. It might seem natural to use code like this:

```
sum = ...
call MPI_Allreduce( sum, sum, 1, MPI_INT, MPI_SUM,
                    MPI_COMM_WORLD, ierr )
```

This code is incorrect; we mentioned in Section 3.1 that the input and output buffers had to be distinct (nonoverlapping). This is a requirement of Fortran that some programmers are not aware of. The ANSI Fortran 77 standard, in Section 15.9.3.6, states that if an actual argument is repeated, then the routine may not assign a value to it. Repeating an argument is called *aliasing*. This prohibits the form of use of the `MPI_Allreduce` call given above, because the second use of the repeated argument `sum` has a value assigned to it by the routine. For consistency, the C versions of the MPI routines share this restriction (even though the C language does not prohibit aliasing).

Bibliography

[1] Srinivas Aluru, G. M. Prabju, and John Gustafson. A random-number generator for parallel computers. *Parallel Computing*, 18:839–847, 1992.

[2] Andrew W. Appel. An efficient program for many-body simulation. *SIAM Journal of Sci. and Stat. Comp.*, 6, January 1985.

[3] B. S. Baldwin and H. Lomax. Thin-layer approximation and algebraic model for separated turbulent flows. January 1978. AIAA-78-257.

[4] Joshua E. Barnes and Piet Hut. A hierarchical O(N log N) force calculation algorithm. *Nature*, 324(4), December 1986.

[5] A. Beguelin, J. Dongarra, G. A. Geist, R. Manchek, and V. Sunderam. A user's guide to PVM: Parallel virtual machine. Technical Report TM-11826, Oak Ridge National Laboratory, 1991.

[6] A. Beguelin, G. A. Geist, W. Jiang, R. Manchek, K. Moore, and V. Sunderam. The PVM project. Technical report, Oak Ridge National Laboratory, February 1993.

[7] L. Bomans, D. Roose, and R. Hempel. The Argonne/GMD macros in FORTRAN for portable parallel programming and their implementation on the Intel iPSC/2. *Parallel Computing*, 15:119–132, 1990.

[8] James Boyle, Ralph Butler, Terrence Disz, Barnett Glickfeld, Ewing Lusk, Ross Overbeek, James Patterson, and Rick Stevens. *Portable Programs for Parallel Processors*. Holt, Rinehart, and Winston, 1987.

[9] T. A. Brody. Random-number generation for parallel processors. *Computer Physics Communications*, 56:147–153, 1989.

[10] Ralph Butler, William Gropp, and Ewing Lusk. Developing applications for a heterogeneous computing environment. In Mary Eshaghian and Vaidy Sunderam, editors, *Workshop on Heterogeneous Processing*, pages 77–83. IEEE Computer Society Press, April 1993.

[11] Ralph Butler and Ewing Lusk. User's guide to the p4 parallel programming system. Technical Report ANL-92/17, Argonne National Laboratory, October 1992.

[12] Ralph Butler and Ewing Lusk. Monitors, messages, and clusters: The p4 parallel programming system. *Parallel Computing*, 20:547–564, April 1994. (Also Argonne National Laboratory Mathematics and Computer Science Division preprint P362-0493).

[13] Robert Calkin, Rolf Hempel, Hans-Christian Hoppe, and Peter Wypior. Portable programming with the PARMACS message-passing library. *Parallel Computing*, 20, April 1994.

[14] N. Carriero and D. Gelernter. How to write parallel programs. *ACM Computing Surveys*, 21(3):323–356, September 1989.

[15] Fei-Chen Cheng. Unifying the MPI and PVM 3 systems. Technical report, Mississippi State University — Dept. of Computer Science, May 1994. Master's Report. (Available by anonymous ftp: *cs.msstate.edu*, pub/reports/feicheng.ps).

[16] Parasoft Corporation. Express version 1.0: A communication environment for parallel computers, 1988.

[17] ParaSoft Corporation. *Express C User's Guide, Version 3.0*, 1990.

[18] T. Crockett. File concepts for parallel I/O. In *Proceedings of Supercomputing'89*, pages 574–579, 1989.

[19] J. M. del Rosario and A. Choudhary. High performance I/O for parallel computers: Problems and prospects. *IEEE Computer*, March 1994.

[20] J. J. Dongarra, J. DuCroz, I. Duff, and R. Hanson. A set of Level 3 basic linear algebra subprograms. ACM Trans. on Math. Soft., 5, December 1989.

[21] J. J. Dongarra, J. DuCroz, S. Hammarling, and R. Hanson. An extended set of Fortran basic linear algebra subprograms. ACM Trans. on Math. Soft., 5, 1988.

[22] Nathan Doss, William Gropp, Ewing Lusk, and Anthony Skjellum. A model implementation of MPI. Technical report, Argonne National Laboratory, 1993.

[23] Message Passing Interface Forum. Document for a standard message-passing interface. Technical Report Technical Report No. CS-93-214 (revised), University of Tennessee, April 1994. Available on **netlib**.

[24] Message Passing Interface Forum. MPI: A message-passing interface standard. Computer Science Dept. Technical Report CS-94-230, University of Tennessee, Knoxville, TN, April 1994. (To appear in the International Journal of Supercomputer Applications, Volume 8, Number 3/4, 1994).

[25] I. Foster, W. Gropp, and R. Stevens. The parallel scalability of the spectral transform method. *Monthly Weather Review*, 120(5):835–850, 1992.

[26] Geoffrey C. Fox, Mark A. Johnson, Gregory A. Lyzenga, Steve W. Otto, John K. Salmon, and David W. Walker. *Solving Problems on Concurrent Processors*, volume 1. Prentice Hall, 1988.

[27] Hubertus Franke, Peter Hochschild, Pratap Pattnaik, and Marc Snir. An efficient implementation of MPI. (contact: Hubertus Franke, frankeh@watson.ibm.com), 1993.

[28] N. Galbreath, W. Gropp, D. Gunter, G. Leaf, and D. Levine. Parallel solution of the three-dimensional, time-dependent Ginzburg-Landau equation. In *Proceedings of the SIAM Parallel Processing for Scientific Computing Conference*. SIAM, 1993.

[29] N. Galbreath, W. Gropp, and D. Levine. Applications-driven parallel I/O. pages 462–471, November 1993. Proceedings of Supercomputing 93, Portland, Oregon.

[30] Al Geist, Adam Beguelin, Jack Dongarra, Weicheng Jiang, Bob Manchek, and Vaidy Sunderam. *PVM: Parallel Virtual Machine—A User's Guide and Tutorial for Network Parallel Computing*. MIT Press, 1994.

[31] G. A. Geist, M. T. Heath, B. W. Peyton, and P. H. Worley. PICL: A portable instrumented communications library, C reference manual. Technical Report TM-11130, Oak Ridge National Laboratory, Oak Ridge, TN, July 1990.

[32] G. A. Geist, M. T. Heath, B. W. Peyton, and P. H. Worley. A users' guide to PICL, a portable instrumented communication library. Technical Report ORNL/TM-11616, Oak Ridge National Laboratory, Oak Ridge, TN, October 1990.

[33] John R. Gilbert and Robert Schreiber. Optimal data placement for distributed memory architectures. In *Parallel Processing for Scientific Computing*, pages 462–471. SIAM, March 1991.

[34] Brian K. Grant and Anthony Skjellum. The PVM Systems: An in-depth analysis and documenting study: Concise edition. Technical Report UCRL-JC-112016, Lawrence Livermore National Laboratory, August 1992. (Revised).

[35] Leslie Greengard. *The Rapid Evaluation of Potential Fields in Particle Systems*. ACM Press, 1987.

[36] W. Gropp and E. Smith. Computational fluid dynamics on parallel processors. *Computers and Fluids*, 18:289–304, 1990.

[37] William Gropp and Ewing Lusk. An abstract device definition to support the implementation of a high-level point-to-point message-passing interface. (in progress).

[38] William D. Gropp. Solving PDEs on loosely-coupled parallel processors. *Par. Comput.*, 5:165–173, 1987.

[39] William D. Gropp and I. C. F. Ipsen. Recursive mesh refinement on hypercubes. *BIT*, pages 186–211, 1989.

[40] William D. Gropp and Ewing Lusk. A test implementation of the MPI draft message-passing standard. Technical Report ANL-92/47, Argonne National Laboratory, December 1992.

[41] William D. Gropp and Barry Smith. Chameleon parallel programming tools users manual. Technical Report ANL-93/23, Argonne National Laboratory, March 1993.

[42] William D. Gropp and Barry Smith. Users manual for KSP: Data-structure-neutral codes implementing Krylov space methods. Technical Report ANL-93/30, Argonne National Laboratory, August 1993.

[43] Erik Hagersten, Anders Landin, and Seif Haridi. DDM — a cache-only memory architecture. *IEEE Computer*, pages 44–54, September 1992.

[44] R. J. Harrison. Portable tools and applications for parallel computers. *Intern. J. Quantum Chem.*, 40(847), 1991.

[45] R. J. Harrison and E. A. Stahlberg. Massively parallel full configuration interaction. benchmark electronic structure calculations on the Intel Touchstone Delta, 1993.

[46] M. T. Heath. Recent developments and case studies in performance visualization using ParaGraph. In G. Haring and G. Kotsis, editors, *Performance Measurement and Visualization of Parallel Systems*, pages 175–200, Amsterdam, The Netherlands, 1993. Elsevier Science Publishers.

[47] M. T. Heath and J. A. Etheridge. Visualizing the performance of parallel programs. *IEEE Software*, 8(5):29–39, September 1991.

[48] R. Hempel, H.-C. Hoppe, and A. Supalov. *PARMACS 6.0 Labrary Interface Specification*. German National Research Center for Computer Science, December 1992.

[49] Virginia Herrarte and Ewing Lusk. Studying parallel program behavior with **upshot**. Technical Report ANL–91/15, Argonne National Laboratory, Argonne, IL 60439, 1991.

[50] C.-T. Ho and L. Johnsson. On the embedding of arbitrary meshes in Boolean cubes with expansion two dilation two. In *Proc. 1987 ICPP*, pages 188–191, 1987.

[51] R. W. Hockney and J. W. Eastwood. *Computer simulation using particles*. Adam Hilger, Bristol, UK, 1988.

[52] Institute of Electrical and Electronics Engineers, New York. *Draft Standard for Information Technology–Portable Operating System Interface (POSIX) – Part 1: System Application Program Interface (API) – Amendment 2: Threads Extension [C Language], Draft 8*, October 1993.

[53] L. Johnsson. Communication efficient basic linear algebra computations on hypercube architectures. *J. Par. Dist. Comp.*, 4:133–172, 1987.

[54] Charles H. Koelbel, David B. Loveman, Robert S. Schreiber, Guy L. Steele Jr., and Mary E. Zosel. *The High Performance Fortran Handbook*. MIT Press, 1993.

[55] Vipin Kumar, Ananth Grama, Anshui Gupta, and George Karypis. *Introduction to Parallel Computing: Design and Analysis of Algorithms*. Benjamin/Cummings, 1994.

[56] Leon Lapidus and George F. Pinder. *Numerical Solution of Partial Differential Equations in Science and Engineering*. Wiley-Interscience, 1982.

[57] C. Lawson, R. Hanson, D. Kincaid, and F. Krogh. Basic linear algebra subprograms for Fortran usage. ACM Trans. on Math. Soft., 14:308–325, 1989.

[58] Benoit B. Mandelbrot. *The Fractal Geometry of Nature*. W. H. Freeman and Company, 1983.

[59] Piyush Mehrotra, Joel Saltz, and Robert Voigt, editors. *Unstructured Scientific Computation on Scalable Multiprocessors*. MIT Press, 1992.

[60] John Osterhout. Tcl: An embeddable command language. In *Proceedings of the Winter 1990 USENIX Conference*, pages 133–146. USENIX Association, January 1990.

[61] John Osterhout. An X11 toolkit based on the Tcl language. In *Proceedings of the Winter 1991 USENIX Conference*, pages 105–115. USENIX Association, January 1991.

[62] John Ousterhout and Fred Douglis. Beating the I/O bottleneck: A case for log-structured file systems. *ACM Operating Systems Review*, 23(1):11–28, January 1989.

[63] Ramesh Pankajakshan and W. Roger Briley. Parallel solution of unsteady incompressible viscous flows. (in preparation).

[64] H.-O. Peitgen and D. Saupe. *The Beauty of Fractals*. Springer-Verlag, 1988.

[65] S. C. Pieper, R. B. Wiringa, and V. R. Pandharipande. Variational calculation of the ground state of ^{16}o. *Physical Review C*, 46:1741–1756, 1992.

[66] Charles L. Seitz et al. The C programmer's abbreviated guide to Multicomputer programming. Technical Report Caltech-CS-TR-88-1, California Institute of Technology, January 1988.

[67] Charles L. Seitz, Sven Mattisson, William C. Athas, Charles M. Flaig, Alain J. Martin, Jakov Seizovic, Craig M. Steele, and Wen-King Su. The architecture and programming of the Ametek series 2010 multicomputer. In *Proceedings of the Third Conference on Hypercube Concurrent Computers and Applications (HCCA3)*, pages 33–36. ACM Press, January 1988. (Symult s2010 Machine).

[68] Anthony Skjellum and Chuck H. Baldwin. *The Multicomputer Toolbox:* Scalable parallel libraries for large-scale concurrent applications. Technical Report UCRL-JC-109251, Lawrence Livermore National Laboratory, December 1991.

[69] Anthony Skjellum, Nathan E. Doss, and Kishore Viswanathan. Inter-communicator extensions to MPI in the MPIX (MPI eXtension) Library. Technical report, Mississippi State University — Dept. of Computer Science, April 1994. Draft version.

[70] Anthony Skjellum and Alvin P. Leung. *Zipcode:* A portable multicomputer communication library atop the Reactive Kernel. In *Proceedings of the Fifth Distributed Memory Computing Conference (DMCC5)*, pages 767–776. IEEE Press, April 1990.

[71] Anthony Skjellum, Steven G. Smith, Nathan E. Doss, Alvin P. Leung, and Manfred Morari. The design and evolution of zipcode. *Parallel Computing*, 20, April 1994.

[72] Anthony Skjellum, Steven G. Smith, Charles H. Still, Alvin P. Leung, and Manfred Morari. The Zipcode message-passing system. In Geoffrey C. Fox, editor, *Parallel Computing Works!* Morgan Kaufman, 1994. (book chapter).

[73] Lafe K. Taylor, Judy A. Busby, Min Yee Jiang, Abdollah Arabshahi, Kidambi Sreenivas, and David L. Whitfield. Time accurate incompressible Navier-Stokes simulation of the flapping foil experiment, August 2–5 1993. Presented at the Sixth International Conference on Numerical Ship Hydrodynamics, Iowa City, Iowa.

[74] Lafe K. Taylor and David L. Whitfield. Unsteady three-dimensional incompressible Euler and Navier-Stokes solver for stationary and dynamic grids, June 24–26 1991. AIAA 91-1650. Presented at the AIAA 22nd Fluid Dynamics, Plasma Dynamics and Lasers Conference, Honolulu, Hawaii.

[75] Thorsten von Eicken, David E. Culler, Seth Copen Goldstein, and Klaus Erik Schauser. Active messages: A mechanism for integrated communication and computation. In *Proc. of the 19th Int'l Symposium on Computer Architecture*, Gold Coast, Australia, May 1992. (Also available as Technical Report UCB/CSD 92/675, CS Div., University of California at Berkeley).

[76] David Walker. Standards for message passing in a distributed memory environment. Technical report, Oak Ridge National Laboratory, August 1992.

[77] David L. Whitfield and Lafe K. Taylor. Discretized Newton-relaxation solution of high resolution flux-difference split schemes, June 24–26 1991. AIAA-91-1539. Presented at the AIAA 10th Computational Fluid Dynamics Conference, Honolulu, Hawaii.

[78] R. B. Wiringa. Variational calculations of few-body nuclei. *Physical Review C*, 43:1585–1598, 1991.

[79] P. H. Worley. A new PICL trace file format. Technical Report ORNL/TM-12125, Oak Ridge National Laboratory, Oak Ridge, TN, October 1992.

Subject Index

Function and Term Index